WITHDRAW
UTSA LIBRARII

D0769286

RENEWALS 458-4574

DATE DUE

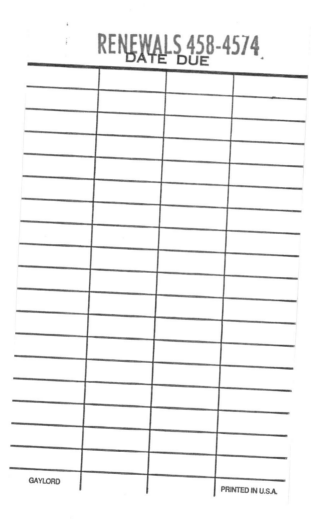

GAYLORD

PRINTED IN U.S.A.

Singing in the Wilderness

Singing in the Wilderness

Music and Ecology in the Twentieth Century

Wilfrid Mellers

University of Illinois Press
Urbana and Chicago

Publication of this book was supported by a grant from
the Henry and Edna Binkele Classical Music Fund

© 2001 by the Board of Trustees of the University of Illinois
All rights reserved
Manufactured in the United States of America
C   5   4   3   2   1
∞ This book is printed on acid-free paper.

Library of Congress Cataloging-in-Publication Data

Mellers, Wilfrid Howard, 1914–
Singing in the wilderness : music and ecology in the twentieth
century / Wilfrid Mellers.
p.   cm.
Includes bibliographical references and index.
ISBN 0-252-02529-6 (cloth : alk. paper)
1. Music—20th century—History and criticism. 2. Nature
in music. I. Mellers, Wilfrid Howard, 1914– . Caliban reborn.
II. Title.
ML197.M268   2001
780'.9'04—dc21   00-011646

Library
University of Texas
at San Antonio

Contents

Preface

In 1967 I published a book entitled *Caliban Reborn: Renewal in Twentieth Century Music*. It began with a familiar theme—"the Decline of the West"— as musically manifested in the late work of Richard Wagner and the early work of Arnold Schoenberg. From that point it sought for green shoots of renewal—new approaches to human experience that proved to be, in many ways, extremely old. *Caliban Reborn* has been out of print for many years. This present book starts from the same point, incorporating in its early chapters material from the original *Caliban Reborn*, substantially rewritten. After this preludial matter, however, *Singing in the Wilderness* takes a different course, less generalized and more specific, for it concentrates on the theme of wilderness not only in sociological and psychological terms but also in an ecological, and even geographical, sense.

The argument of the book starts, in part 1, with the "twilight" of "Europe," as audible in Wagner's late works and Schoenberg's early ones, and in two operatic parables written at the turn of the century: Frederick Delius's *A Village Romeo and Juliet*, a version of Shakespeare's Renaissance story transplanted into nordic forests and mountains, making an elegy for Eden; and Claude Debussy's *Pelléas et Mélisande*, which paradoxically "celebrates" purposelessness and the cult of the Absurd. In both operas humankind is presented as lost within Milton's "blind mazes of this tangled wood": for what happens within the forest of the mind reflects and is reflected by what happens in the world "out there." The fourth chapter in this section, mostly on Leoš Janáček's *Cunning Little Vixen*, indicates that, even in the twentieth century, the old relationship between nature and nurture could still occasionally exist in the real world. Part 2 of the book moves from the Forest Within

to the Forest Without—as evident in France. Charles Koechlin, a contemporary and colleague of Debussy, fused the elegancies of "civilization" with a
forêt féerique as much legendary as archaically French; in an ambitious series of works based on Rudyard Kipling's *Jungle Books*, he embraced real
jungles in the external world, as well as those within the mind. From Koechlin,
Singing in the Wilderness proceeds to his slightly younger contemporary,
Darius Milhaud, also French and highly sophisticated, but Mediterranean,
Provençal, and Jewish, in touch with different realms of experience. In youth,
moreover, Milhaud lived for a while in Brazil, as Paul Claudel's secretary,
where he was influenced by Brazil's culture and by the immense rain forests
that pervade the vast land.

In part 3 the transition is made from "old" Europe to Brazil, a world at once
old and new, as is manifest in the work of Heitor Villa-Lobos, whose largely
empirical training impinged on his studies in Paris, with explosive effect. This,
the longest chapter in the book, is ballasted by a chapter on Villa-Lobos's
Mexican contemporary, Carlos Chávez, which explicitly reveals the connec-
tion between the jungle within the mind and the asphalt jungle of a rapidly
industrialized metropolis. For Chávez was at once a composer of the Mexican forests and deserts and of the skyscrapers of Mexico City and New York,
where he intermittently lived, collaborating with a New Yorker, Aaron
Copland.

Part 4 further explores interrelationships between nature's wildernesses
and human beings' machines. Carl Ruggles was a New Englander who
hymned the American wilderness in music that had much in common with
the expressionism of Schoenberg's free atonal works. Complementarily,
Edgard Varèse was a Parisian-rooted New Yorker who explored affinities
between an "eternal present"—as manifest in Debussy's revolutionary freeing of the chord from antecedence and consequence—and the ongoing noises
and sounds of an industrial city. Harry Partch, living and working in the
California deserts, explicitly opted out of Western civilization to seek the
"genesis" of a new music theater that was in principle ancient. Steve Reich,
of a younger generation, carried the rediscovery of "process" a stage further,
since he translated music, originally acted through in the moment of
per-form-ance, from "primitive" communities into the "savage" city. This rebirth has a parallel in a culturally still newer (and geologically still older)
world, Australia, where Peter Sculthorpe, subject of the final chapter of part
4, is a modern but aboriginal white composer of the Outback.

The fifth and last part of the book concerns the sundering of the barriers
between civilization and wilderness, since it is about two New World (Ameri-

can) composers who fused the ongoing process of folk musics both agrarian and urban with conventions derived both from European-style art music and from technologies promoted by industrialism. Duke Ellington was a black jazz performance artist who became an internationally recognized composer; George Gershwin was a white New Yorker reared on Broadway and in Tin Pan Alley who, at the end of a short life, created a grand opera of which the human themes—including racial relationships in the Deep South—are identical with the technical means whereby the piece compromises between Art and Commerce. Whatever the destiny of art may be in our bewilderingly changing world, Gershwin's *Porgy and Bess* will be a signpost to it. Gershwin and Ellington—both born at the very end of the nineteenth century—are not the "greatest" twentieth-century composers, but in social, philosophical, and ecological terms there are no composers more relevant to our future, assuming that we have one.

PART ONE

The Forest Within

1

Wagner, Schoenberg, and the Twilight of "Europe"

RICHARD WAGNER'S *Tristan und Isolde,* we are often told, was the beginning of modern music. It was also the end of the cycle in human history that began with the European Renaissance, and there is a sense in which Wagner lived through, in both his life and his art, the spiritual revolutions we now associate with Freud, Jung, and Marx. It is significant that Wagner, representing Europe's ultimate climacteric, should have deified the ego in its most fundamental impulse, that of sex. Whereas Beethoven in his last works appeased the anguish of sonata conflict in the oneness of fugue and the continuity of song variation, Wagner started from the most fundamental reality known to him: the surge of harmonic tensions that was his own erotic life. From them he derived in his later work a polyphonic-harmonic texture that became a cosmos. He thought of himself as fulfilling a role in humankind's story parallel to that occupied by Christ and regarded Bayreuth as an inevitable step in the making of modern culture.

In a sense *Tristan und Isolde* was a dramatization of the triangular relationship between Wagner and Otto and Mathilde Wesendonck. More significant, however, is that in this most directly autobiographical of his works Wagner should have recreated the Tristan legend, for of all the great medieval stories, that of Tristan most potently expresses human beings' simultaneous longing for the senses' fulfillment and for their extinction. At the end of the cycle that began with the Renaissance, Wagner imbues this theme of Eros and Agape with five hundred years' burden of consciousness, sensuality, aspiration, frustration, and guilt. The significance of his passion-laden chromatic harmony is indeed latent within the opera's first few bars, since the notorious "Tristan chords" consist of interlocked perfect and imperfect fourths. In the Middle Ages the perfect fourth, and its inversion, the fifth, had been musical synonyms for God, being the absolute consonances according to Pythagorean science; whereas the imperfect fourth and fifth (the tritone) was the Devil: *si contra fa diabolus est*. The genesis of the opera is thus the most fundamental of all dualisms, since the Fall is inherent in sexuality. In this sense the four-and-a-half hours of the opera are a protracted attempt at an orgasm that would relieve the dichotomy between spirit and flesh. The rising sixth and declining chromatic scale with which the Prelude opens is repeated sequentially *time out of mind*. It urges the music forward, since the sequences rise; yet each sequence is also a cessation, a failure, insofar as it falls back to the point it started from, to try again. From the anguish of the rising-falling phrases in their recurrent sequences, and from the drooping appoggiaturas and interlocked dissonances, proliferate most of the themes of the gigantic score, in what Wagner positively, if wistfully, called "endless melody." Only at the very end is frustrated aspiration resolved.

Moreover, the manner of the resolution is significant. From the literary-dramatic point of view Wagner's adaptation of the Tristan story is designed to show in three stages (or acts) how the only fulfillment is that of personal passion; how this cannot be achieved except by separation from the material world of society, culture, and domestic loyalties; and finally how it cannot be attained within time at all. In a sense, as Joseph Kerman has demonstrated,[1] the end is implicit in the beginning. In the first act the lovers believe they have accidentally consumed death in the form of the love potion, and this liberates their passion from conventional restraints. The second act displays their failure to live out their love in the world. The climax—when Melot stabs Tristan or, rather, Tristan impales himself on Melot's sword—is the consequence of conflict generated by mundane compromise. It induces what we would call a nervous breakdown, from which state of paralysis Tristan hears, at the beginning of act 3 (which is rooted in F minor, traditional key of the infernal regions), the monody of a shepherd's pipe. This rustic cantillation, simulated by an orchestral cor anglais, sounds like a forlornly broken vision of Paradise Lost. At the beginning of the end of the harmonic cycle of European humanism, Tristan-Wagner hears, emerging out of the weariest permutation of the Tristan chords, a continuously monophonic, unaccompanied line, which proves to be a linear version of the perfect and imperfect fourths and fifths of the Tristan chords. The melody, having started from a perfect fifth, which is God, crumbles into imperfect fourths and fifths, chromatically meandering in nonmetrical convolutions, seeking but only intermittently refinding the fifth's godly perfection. Both the fluid rhythm and the chromatic melismata recall troubadour monody, its quasi-Asian ancestry melancholically intensified by centuries of European harmonic "consciousness."

Once Tristan hears, however faintly, the shepherd's lament for Eden lost, the process of regeneration may begin, not merely for him, but also for everyone. In the last act of *Tristan* Wagner does what had long been latent in his operatic technique, for the action is traumatic and, with the possible exception of the arrival of King Mark and his entourage, takes place within the hero's mind. Wagner addresses what may be accurately termed Freudian regeneration in that the reminiscence of monodic innocence induces Tristan to yearn, from near-death, for "day." But the resurgence of harmonic passion releases not ecstasy but agony, since what Hardy called "the darts of consciousness" are too great to be borne. So Tristan curses day, which is life, and his blissful anticipation of Isolde's coming subsides in another frustrated cadence. At this point the monodic piping becomes the *empty* sea, the unconscious unknown to which, with not even the most distant glimpse of Isolde's ship, he must surrender. Surrender is effected in Tristan's immense monologue, remotely accompanied by the piping, so that although the process of curse and relapse is repeated, it is changed. Now the pipe lures Tristan away from amnesia toward an acceptance of his and our pain. He relives the events of this past, not only the events of the opera, but also those of his childhood and of the lives and deaths of his father and mother. His long recapitulation of the events of the first act is a resolution at once musical and experiential: so the last curse becomes the purgation of his guilt, a re-cognition that it was *I myself* who brewed the potion. A man is responsible only to himself: an ultimate climax to humanism which is also an admission of humanism's inadequacy, since revelation is also initiation. When Isolde at last arrives, Tristan revives in a state beyond day or curse or yearning; and the shepherd pipes a "new tune," from which chromatic anguish has been purged away, leaving it innocently diatonic, even pentatonic.

Seventeenth-century humanism had thought of sexual orgasm as a dying that seemed to negate time. Now the admission is overt; the only escape from duality is in death itself, and Tristan expires to a merging of the love and death themes, now one. The ultimate beatitude is left to Isolde, as the orchestra painfully resolves the tritonal tension of the Tristan chords into a luminous B major triad, sustained infinitely in the sense that whenever the chord fades to silence must seem too soon. B major, we may note, is the dominant of E major, which in the classical baroque age was the key of light and of heaven because it was the highest, sharpest major key in common use, as F minor—

the flattest minor key in common use—had been affiliated with darkness and hell. Wagner's opting for B major's five sharps characteristically outbids tradition, as he aurally demonstrates that the lovers, no longer separate beings, are the male and female principles within Wagner himself, and within us all. Wagner gives to the female the heavenly gift of intuition; in Isolde's pure anima Tristan's animus is absorbed and absolved—an odd but, on reflection, logical end to a man whose life was male egoism incarnate.

Like Beethoven's last piano sonatas and late string quartets, Wagner's *Tristan* is an end to and an inversion of humanism. The distinction between them lies in the fact that Beethoven entered his paradise in the sublime melodic proliferations of the Arietta in opus 111, whereas Wagner does not quite effect this lyrical consummation. The shepherd's "new tune" is notably inferior to his tremulously chromatic original monody, whereas Beethoven's Arietta may be construed as the fulfillment of a life's work. This may be why Beethoven's last compositions had no direct successors, whereas Wagner's were the beginning of modern music. The greatness of *Tristan* is that although it tells us that perfect love cannot be realized in temporal terms, it reaffirms the nobility of human aspiration, as does, on a vaster scale, the subjective mythology of *The Ring* cycle. By the time we reach *Götterdämmerung* (which is later in date than *Tristan*), the Dark Forest is the artist-hero's mind; and although Brunnhilde is the white dove, the troubadour's eternal beloved to be won or lost, the light and dark forces that fight for her are inextricably mingled, being aspects of a single consciousness. This is why the villainous Hagen has no less uncanny presence than Wotan (Wagner as penitent sinner and scapegoat) and is why Siegfried (Wagner as knight-errant and dragon-slayer) becomes his own betrayer, as did Wagner in his life. To so cataclysmic an upheaval there can be no simple social answer: no canalizing of harmonic tension by jolly fugato or by the time-dominated public conventions of communal dance or dance-directed aria. Such external symbols of the things that make human society workable have vanished: there is no fugato, no aria, no dance, only the surge of the symphonic texture that must work out the motives' musical and experiential destiny not merely, as in *Tristan*, over four hours, but through four huge operas. One may feel claustrophobia in submitting so utterly and for so long to Wagner's ego, yet one has no choice in the matter, since Wagner's ego attains the "terrifying honesty" of the greatest art. Wagner's gods are men and women—as we might be if we could be Wagner. Yet the cycle concludes with a man-god's twilight; a man relinquishes his attempt to be responsible for his destiny and Valhalla perishes in the purgatorial flames. Like the Wagnerian sequence itself, it returns to its source, renewed in the waters of the unconscious, the fire and water being complementary, as they are in Beethoven's opuses 106 and 111.[2]

If *Tristan* and its renunciatory sequel *Parsifal* counteract the dominance of the will, from which the principles of European opera had painfully evolved, they also uncover a path through the dark forest that later composers, were they brave enough, might follow. This is evident in Arnold Schoenberg's evolution from *Verklärte Nacht*, written in 1899, through *Erwartung* (1909) to *Pierrot Lunaire* (1912). Begun as early as 1895, *Verklärte Nacht* was originally a string sextet, but was later transformed into a work for string orchestra. Yet although in either form its medium is purely instrumental, the piece is also a one-act, symphonically subjective opera on a theme intimately related to *Tristan;* it even has a literary text in the form of an unuttered prose-poem by Richard Dehmel, describing the walk of two lovers through a dark forest. The Woman bears within her another man's child, probably that of the husband she doesn't love, and the child is the burden of her and her lover's guilt. Walking through the tenebrous wood, speaking with mounting agitation of their awareness that their love cannot but entail pain, they enter a clearing in the forest that is transfigured (*verklärte*) by moonlight. Here they make love, and in the act the burden of guilt is assuaged, so that the child may be accepted as their own. This is a Freudian regeneration myth, rendered audible in music. To begin with, the texture is even more sumptuously chromatic than that of *Tristan*, while the dialogue between high (female) strings and low (male) strings makes the operatic affiliations palpable. As the texture grows more harmonically agitated, however, so it becomes more freely polyphonic; the Wagnerian sequences flow into a "transfiguring" ecstasy—in which sense *Verklärte Nacht* is a *positive* successor to *Tristan*.

Despite the freedom of its polyphony, *Verklärte Nacht* is not technically innovative. Its conception of tonality is traditional, the D minor in which it opens being associated by Schoenberg (as by Beethoven and Mozart) with the strife that is life's essence, while the D major in which it closes effects resolution. The moment of transfiguration in the moonlit glade prompts an excursion into F sharp major—another notch up the cycle of fifths from the B major in which *Tristan* terminates. Nonetheless, the lyrical momentum of the music tends to override the Wagnerian sequences, and the more airborne the polyphony becomes, the more chromatic is its texture, aspiring toward an unequivocal chromaticism that can release us from the earth-pull of harmonic tension. This release arrives in Schoenberg's "free" atonal period and specifically in *Erwartung*, the literary theme of which is almost identical with that of *Verklärte Nacht*. The earlier work was a "subjective" drama that occurred entirely in instrumental terms. In *Erwartung* the drama is theatrically objectified, but the implications of *Tristan* and *The Ring* are fulfilled, since there is only one character, within whose mind the action takes place.

Significantly, this character is, like Isolde, a woman wandering, this time alone, in Milton's "blind mazes of this tangled wood." She is possessed by a sexual passion of Tristanesque impetuosity. Although waiting to meet her lover in the wood, she knows that he will not come, since he has deserted her for a ghostly, white-armed other woman who is probably, psychologically speaking, his mother. A climax comes when she stumbles over his murdered body. It is not clear who murdered him; she speaks confusedly of the "other woman" and of an indiscriminate "they." But it is unclear because the action does not exist outside her mind. She enters the dark forest of the unconscious, at first in a mingling of memories and inchoate desires. Her discovery of the body is her recognition of loss and complementarily of guilt and renunciation. From here on her unconscious takes over; the text was devised for Schoenberg by Marie Pappenheim, almost in terms of a Freudian clinical casebook, of which Schoenberg's "free" atonality becomes the near-spontaneous expression. Yet the pattern established by *Tristan, Parsifal,* and *Verklärte Nacht* is extended, for submission to the unconscious again brings release. The piece ends with a "transfigured" vision of her lover, wherein passion is absolved, hatred forgotten. The process is subjective; we don't know whether her love ever was or could be fulfilled in the conditions of temporality.

This is why *Erwartung*, even more than *Tristan*, is a symphonic opera wherein the drama happens in the orchestra. The vocal line carries speech-song to an extreme of melodic disintegration, as it follows the vagaries of half-feeling, half-thinking semiconsciousness; yet we have only to consider the first words the Woman sings to see how speech-rhythm counteracts the earth-bound tug of meter and harmony. This fluctuating rhythm is intimately related to the expressivity of the orchestral texture which, in auralizing the dark forest, creates too the life of the psyche, as the Woman murmurs in self-communion. For this reason, the parlando line of the voice is not separate from the orchestral fabric. Although the score contains (since it expresses the disintegration of mind and senses) a minimum of repetition and organization, the most dramatically crucial phrases the Woman sings are those that are most potent in the orchestral parts and that recur, if not in exact repetition, in permutations readily recognizable as such. Early in the piece the Woman hopes that, if she cries forcefully enough, her lover will hear her. This phrase is echoed when she admits that he hasn't and won't come. Alternating seconds and thirds are the core of the passage in which she panics, imagining that she is pursued by wild things of the woods, while the "cry" motif recurs in anguished inversion when she finds, or thinks she finds, her lover dead. This leads to the wonderful passage wherein she relives her past meetings with her lover in the garden that, being cultivated and walled, seems safe compared with the forest's wilderness. Here the luminosity of texture creates affirmation out of negation and something like order out of disorder. The affirmative quality survives, even when she succumbs to jealous nightmare. A climax of absolution comes when she asks, "Hast du sie sehr geliebt?" but can add that he is not to blame. During the course of the opera's "stream of consciousness" she comes to admit that the tree trunk she had stumbled over is identical to the trunk of the murdered lover she discovers, or imagines she discovers, in nightmare. They are her own guilt, and like Tristan she learns it was "I myself" who brewed the potion. With self-knowledge, the guilt may be lifted and, as morning glimmers through the tangled wood, she may experience a vision wherein she sees her lover, "alive and well." The opera ends with her ineffably moving cry of "O, bist du da? Ich suchte," as the sensory life of the orchestral texture dissolves in contrary motion chromatics.

It is difficult to know what to call this if it is not, as well as a moment of vision, an act of faith—attained only by the *relinquishment* of consciousness, of corporeal rhythm, of thematic definition, and of harmonic volition. Significantly, the complicated score of *Erwartung* was completed with extraordinary rapidity, in a matter of two weeks, so it is evident that the abstruse cross-references we have commented on cannot have been a product of intellectual contrivance. At the end the inner drama fades into the "flood" of the unconscious, transforming the dark forest into primeval water. This harks back to the gurgling waters at the end of *The Ring* and looks forward to the waters that will engulf Berg's *Wozzeck*, while his small son plays ball, as innocent of death as of whatever life has in store for him. Although these waters are images of decay, water may also be redemptive, and such a mystical interpretation of the release from consciousness becomes explicit at the end of *Die Jakobsleiter,* the oratorio that was intended to be the consummation of Schoenberg's "free" chromatic phase, though it remained significantly unfinished. The ladder of the title links dying mortality to some putative reincarnation, and the final passage of the score describes a woman (again) on her deathbed, whose disembodied soul floats upward as the declamatory speaking voice is metamorphosed into wordless song, winging over the orchestral texture, distributed throughout the hall on loudspeakers. Like the

visionary moment in *Erwartung,* this transfiguration is not elegiac and proved
to be a beginning as well as an end in modern compositional techniques.

This is clear if one considers *Pierrot Lunaire*—generally admitted to be a key
work in twentieth-century music—as a successor to *Erwartung.* Here we are
a stage further from Wagnerian monomania, for the hero has become a
clown—Pierrot, who is a symbol of alienated modern humanity. The rich
sensory life of symphonic textures has given way to a rare, but dense, cham-
ber-music idiom. The lyricism of the vocal line has almost vanished also, for
Pierrot's song-speech, though freely notated in pitch and duration, is now
closer to speech than to song. Yet at the same time this Pierrot is a reincarnation of Tristan and of *Erwartung*'s anonymous Woman. Though pathetic, he
still yearns for the dream's fulfillment and in nightmare imagines that he has
himself murdered love. Because the voice can no longer sing, the instruments
seek the maximum intensity from the minimum of physical force, so *Pierrot
Lunaire* is a sequel to the Woman's cry of "Ich suchte" and if, in one sense,
this is a piece about loss, it is also an (increasingly forlorn) search for belief.

Since *Pierrot Lunaire* is a further twitch to the death throes of humanism
we aren't surprised that its human expressionism contains elements of magic.
The twenty-one surrealist poems, German translations of the French of
Arthur Giraud, are grouped in three sets of seven, both magic numbers, as
is twenty-one. Colin Sterne has demonstrated how all Schoenberg's music,
even from his early tonal years, was fanatically dedicated to numerological
processes; he even contrived to die on his astrologically appointed day.[3] It is
as though he had to seek some cosmological—extrahuman—certitude to
offset his obsession with the flux, and this magic mythology is discovered,
like *Erwartung*'s moment of vision, *through* submission to the unconscious.
Similarly, the contrapuntal ingenuities that here appear as substitutes for
harmonic and tonal criteria led Schoenberg to the serial principle. Even
Erwartung's amorphous "stream of consciousness" embraces a harbinger of
this, in that Schoenberg associates a recurrent ostinato with the Path the
Woman must take through the blind mazes of that tangled wood. The
ostinato is the WAY, as is the Row, when Schoenberg arrives at his fully fledged
serial principle. A Schoenbergian Row fulfills some of the functions of an
Indian *rag* in that all the melodic and harmonic aspects of a composition are
derived from it. As the composer Fartein Valen put it, "the Row is God's Will,"
a certitude beyond the flux.

The transition from free atonality to serialism may be traced through the
three times seven movements of *Pierrot Lunaire.* If the Woman in *Erwartung*
is Isolde in a state of nervous collapse, Pierrot is the Artist—Schoenberg him-

self—weary with insatiable love-longing. Columbine, the lover and mate, cannot satisfy his yearning, which nonetheless can neither be laughed away in the dandy's frivolity nor religiously sanctified by an appeal to the Madonna. The romanticized love-dream turns into the fin de siècle image of drops of blood on the lips of a consumptive. It is significant that the first cycle of seven numbers—closest to the tonal freedom of *Erwartung*—ends with a song wherein Pierrot is sick unto death with unappeasable love-longing; that this music of a latter-day Tristan should be scored for declaiming voice with flute only; and that the melismatic nature of the flute line should be even more Asian in feeling than is the shepherd's piping in act 3 of *Tristan*, largely because it is further removed from "Western" harmonic implications. This monodic song, in which the "decadent" irony of the text becomes a means of self-effacement, leads into the second cycle of seven poems, wherein Pierrot descends into the dark forest to confront, pitiful though he be, the images of crime, guilt, and punishment that had obsessed Tristan and *Erwartung*'s Woman.

The first movement of the second cycle—the climax of the whole work—is a passacaglia in which the ground bass is the only path that can lead through the mad maze of the tangled wood. But this path, through the sequence of songs, is increasingly difficult to delineate. The wings of giant moths obscure the light of the sun, as Pierrot sees himself as blasphemer, grave robber, and murderer. Although elaborate contrapuntal devices are introduced to maintain some pretense of "conscious" certitudes through "unconscious" lunacy, and although the solo flute monody returns, the work's ultimate climax occurs in the instrumental interlude that links Pierrot's moon-vision to this self-crucifixion in the fourteenth song.

Yet the equations between Pierrot and Artist and Christ and scapegoat are not taken up, for the final group of seven songs eschews religion and transcendentalism in favor of fantasy. Given the crisis of twentieth-century humanism, there were two possible ways forward: to transcend "reality" in mysticism or to relinquish consciousness as completely as is humanly possible, accepting the arbitrary lunacy of life as the only truth we may embrace. In *Pierrot Lunaire* Schoenberg adopts the second alternative. In the last cycle of seven songs, nostalgic reminiscences of the zany Italian Comedy, dadaistic nonsense, and dreams of a fairy-tale world in which guilt is inoperative momentarily take over—"Moonspot" being only an ambiguous exception to this, since its canonic ingenuities are on the verge of parody: the dirty spot (of guilt) that Pierrot frenziedly attempts to rub off his night-black jacket proves to be literally moonshine.

In the latter part of his life Schoenberg, like Freud, sought for a *new* integration of the splintered personality that could only be, at this stage of Europe's checkered history, in some sense religious. Both men were Jewish, born about the same time in the same melting pot of a city; both started from the primary urge of sexuality; both faced up to the hiatus in human creativity that a dedication to selfhood had led to. Freud sought to reintegrate the dislocated facets of the personality; Schoenberg sought a linear and polyphonic (later serial) reintegration of the chromatically splintered musical cosmos. But whether the path Schoenberg followed through the Dark Forest led to religious transcendence—as it did potentially in *Verklärte Nacht* and *Erwartung* and in the (significantly unfinished) masterwork of his maturity, the opera *Moses und Aron*—or whether it led—as it did in *Pierrot Lunaire*— to the irrationally absurd, it offered alternatives to the Faustian dominance of ego and will that had shaped, over the centuries, the Western world. At the turn from the nineteenth into the twentieth century, two complementary operatic parables confronted this human predicament—Delius's *A Village Romeo and Juliet* and Debussy's *Pelléas et Mélisande.*

NOTES

1. Joseph Kerman, *Opera as Drama,* rev. ed. (London: Faber and Faber, 1989), 225.

2. See the relevant chapters in Wilfrid Mellers, *Beethoven and the Voice of God* (London: Faber and Faber, 1983).

3. Colin C. Sterne, *Arnold Schoenberg: The Composer as Numerologist* (Lewiston: Edwin Mellen Press, 1993), 1–2.

2

A Village Romeo and Juliet as a Parable of Childhood, Love, and Death

IN ALL FREDERICK DELIUS's most typical music, tension between the chromaticism of the harmony and the pentatonic aspirations of the melody induces a nostalgia that differentiates it from Wagner's late work, its ostensible source; it yearns for a lost Eden, rather than for Wagner's Paradise Regained. Not for nothing is Delius's most perfectly realized work, the choral and orchestral *Sea Drift*, a setting of part of Walt Whitman's poem about a child's first cognition of mortality as he responds, on the verge of the illimitable sea, to a sea bird's cry to its lost, dead mate; and not for nothing do the fluctuating chromatic appoggiaturas of *A Song of the High Hills* dissolve, in the heart-rending wordless choral episode, into lines that are, individually considered, as pentatonically innocent as a folk song. The link with, and difference from, Wagner becomes palpable if we consider Delius's finest opera, *A Village Romeo and Juliet*, as a sequel to *Tristan und Isolde*, with which it shares both poetic theme and technical means to its end.

Both operas address the impossibility of achieving identity between flesh and spirit in the temporal world. The story is the same, though Delius gives it a naturalistic rather than legendary setting. He lighted on the tale in the writings of a mid-nineteenth-century German Swiss author, Gottfried Keller, who relocates the story of Shakespeare's Romeo and Juliet in a modern Swiss village. As treated by Delius, the aura seems more Scandinavian than Swiss, describing the composer's fascination with Norwegian mountains and fjords and a life severely common without being commonplace. Although a long way from the Shakespearean story's aristocratic Renaissance court, Delius's "common" society nurtures seeds of heroism. The Tristan theme still attains grandeur, and Delius scores his opera for an orchestra larger than Wagner's.

But there is one crucial distinction between the star-crossed lovers in the two operas. Delius's lovers are plebeian and young; they are destroyed, like Wagner's more mature lovers, by the world of material possessions and social obligations, but their answer, when buffeted by their parents' squalid squabbles, is not to try, like Tristan and Isolde, to grow up, but to wish they were children again. Indeed, in the libretto Frederick and Delka Delius cobbled together in a medley of English and German, the first scene is a prologue presenting the hero and heroine when they were chronologically still juvenile.

The initial musical theme of the prologue presents, over a C major pedal point, a scale declining from C to G, extending to a godly falling fifth, G to C. Melodically this contains (in the declining scale and interval) a Fall, but also (in the prevailing pentatonics) the innocence of Eden, thereby providing a mythical and psychological backdrop to the story. After a conventional modulation to the dominant, the lines flow freely as the scene presents two fields in a pastoral landscape. Though the hour is burgeoning dawn, by the time the action starts the tonality has sunk to B flat, a tone lower than C. The energy and agony of human strife are latent in an upward-surging chromatic theme, thrusting from the bass. Manz, an affluent farmer, approaches from the near distance, singing as he plows; and if his song touches on nature's fertility, its agitation also reveals how nature's spontaneous growth has been corrupted by human rancor. Whereas the initial nature-and-work music had moved freely around traditionally pastoral F major, F minor intrudes when Manz refers to the Wild Lands that separate his field from that of Marti, who thereby becomes a rival as well as a neighbor. At this early point in Delius's opera F minor's devilish potential is manifest in music that depicts the jealousy that sunders the two friends, for Manz and Marti both covet the wasteland between their properties—land that, but for the obliquities of the law, would have devolved to a gypsy from a (perhaps significantly) martially trumpeting grandfather. But being an outsider and a Dark Stranger, as well as illegitimate, the gypsy could not establish his rights, and legal contrivance lets loose chaos in the stability of village life.

At the very moment when this Fall becomes apparent in the dialogue, the children of the once-friendly enemies appear, bearing their fathers' lunch. Manz's son, Sali, and Marti's daughter, Vreli, are heralded in paradisal E major, the upward-thrusting agitation of their parents' motif being metamorphosed into bliss. But they immediately mimic the fallen world, for they indulge in a game (centered a devilish tritone away from E major on B flat minor) about a fairy-tale Prince, Princess, and Robber Chief. Vreli says she's scared in the wilderness, but Sali vows to protect her from things that go bump in the night and from the most baleful beasts. For the "time being," there is a respite as the fathers greet the children in another illusory moment of E major beatitude, which reinforces the irony that the wildest of wild beasts will be Vreli's father. This dark ambiguity is hinted at as the children wander, while their fathers eat, to the edge of the wood, lured by distant music— the fiddling of the Dark Stranger, who spins a cantilena in swinging 6/4, still in E major. When he appears on the scene, however, we're disturbingly aware of his ambivalence, for although he communes with the wild woods and untamed winds, his main tune emulates, in its dotted 6/8 rhythm, his *limp*— itself a kind of Fall in that he, like Lucifer, had been ousted from Eden. Gradually, his music merges into a dragging, nagging, peg-legged dance rooted on G. Admitting in his song to his illegitimate state and his dispossession, he claims that he has the right to offer the children his Wild Lands as a playground. If this seems a positive gesture, it is also a treacherous labyrinth manifest in the orchestra's deliquescent chromatics. This is the first overt statement of the choice between "Wilderness" and "Civilization," or between Blakean Innocence and Experience: a choice to which there can be no clearcut answer. Although the music momentarily suggests that the rout of nature's wilderness by greedy humanity is a disaster, the effect remains equivocal—here, throughout the evolution of the opera, and perhaps of Delius's music as a totality.

The immediate consequence, however, is a palpable and dreadful Fall, for after the Dark Stranger has limped off, the farmers act out their jealous rage, quarreling over which of them owns which bit of land—by right of authoritarian power, if not of law. The rising chromatic figure in the bass generates fury until the prologue ends with mutual curses. The sins of the fathers are visited on the offspring, for the farmers forbid their respective son and daughter ever to meet again. The end of the scene is abrupt: a savage plagal cadence in infernal F minor.

Between the prologue and the second scene six years have elapsed. The boy and girl have grown from childhood to adolescence, but are still at the dawn of adult consciousness. The opening theme is an intensified version of the prologue's theme, but the key is no longer neutral C major, but C minor, Beethoven's key of strife, only one step up the cycle of fifths from dire F minor. Delius allows the evils consequent on materiality to take place offstage; we discover—from the visually presented scene and from snatches of dialogue—that in the intervening six years the farmers' prosperity has been gobbled up in lawsuits over the disputed territory. The children meet, timidly, outside Marti's house, now literally fallen in a ruin audibly manifest in the music's sighing declensions. Life tentatively resurges as Sali and Vreli admit that they would like to be friends, though they don't yet recognize that they embryonically love one another. They know they need to right old wrongs, for which they were not responsible. Tonality flows more freely, with bird-chirping arabesques on woodwinds, as they affirm that they won't be oppressed by the squalor of the past. When they agree covertly to meet in the Wild Lands (where else?), we hear the first intimation of the famous Paradise Gardens theme—a rising pentatonic arpeggio, rounded off by a declining scale—a musical image for youthful promise and the inevitability of death. Upward pentatonics, wafting through the Fall theme now fully chromaticized, create a vulnerable ec-stasis; but as the basic tonality droops from C to pastoral F, there's a hint of threat in the quiet beat of timpani.

For scene 3 there's a further declension to Lydian B flat minor. If this fall might be expected to enhance will-lessness, it also brings hope, perhaps because its Lydian sharp fourths were traditionally associated with healing, but more because, in a Delian context, any relinquishment of mind and will may be construed as a virtue. The theme, though still derived from the chromaticized Fall theme, is now garlanded with fluttering pentatonics, making an arabesque of birds, winds, and rustling leaves. The Wild Lands, unlike the deserted farm and village, are ablaze with poppies and wild (not cultivated) corn, the orchestral prelude being a paean to created nature and to young love. Sali and Vreli meet, in the Wild Lands, to an Edenic hymn to the sun. Organum in parallel fourths and fifths, played by on-stage horns, evokes magic, to which the Dark Stranger enters to remind the young people of how they had been wont to frolic on his Wild Lands when they were wild kids. Here he seems in no way baleful, but a life force, as his limping 6/8 theme expands into 6/4 cantilena as ripe as the sun-baked corn, while he joyously fiddles in 12/8 quavers, centered around Lydian F *major*.

At this point we may begin to understand how Delius's free tonality functions. His extreme chromaticism, like that of Wagner, represents the flux, identifying experience with the self. *Real* life is what happens within the psyche, and may, like the Dark Stranger, be bliss, terror, or both. Certain absolutes of tonality—the relationships between tonic, dominant, and subdominant, between relative majors and minors—recur in Delius's works as they do in Wagner's, since they are rooted in acoustical and physiological fact. But there is little evidence of socially geared tonal organization, associated with metrically measured time, such as typifies classical baroque, Viennese classical, or even early romantic music. When, later in the opera, Delius calls on social dance forms and unambiguous keys there is usually an ironic undertow, as in the fair scene. This, the music tells us, is how people in social contexts usually behave, but this is not what people are really like. *That* can be discovered only through submission to subjective experience and the flow of chromatic tonality—which tends to atonality and will be achieved in Schoenberg's works. A moment of this transcendent reality occurs when the Dark Stranger leaves the young lovers ecstatically dancing and dueting in the poppy-blazing field. Cavorting through multiple keys, they stress youthful A major, with sharper aspirations toward heavenly E major and B major. When they nostalgically refer, in flatter but benedictory G major, to their "happy childhood," their vocal line is purely pentatonic.

In leaving them, the Dark Stranger promises that they will meet again. Despite the pastoral euphoria, a hint of foreboding is appropriate to the context, for the idyllic scene ends in a violence outstripping that which concludes the prologue. At the height of the frolics in "childhood's happy days," Marti spots his fairy princess daughter disobediently sporting with his enemy's wicked son. The strifeful key of C minor takes over, and the orchestra quivers in augmented fifths that sound like *lacrimae rerum*. The sinister chromatic theme of the earlier fight scene rears in the bass as Marti hysterically assaults his daughter, whom Sali rushes to defend. Fight music of Wagnerian ferocity ensues until Sali, howling through a diminished fourth, fells Marti with a desperate blow. Ambiguity is again manifest; it was "right" that Sali should assist his assaulted beloved, but "wrong" that her father should be attacked, possibly slain.

Whether or not Marti is dead, scene 4 opens with those *lacrimae rerum* whole tones and drooping chromatics wailing throughout the orchestral parts. The ambiguous key is very flat, between E flat minor and B flat minor. When the curtain rises we find Vreli sitting in her deserted home, alone, since her father, though not killed, was rendered insane by Sali's blow and has been taken to an asylum. She croons an exquisite lament about her lonesomeness, in a pentatonicized C minor–E flat major, but chromatically burgeons as she and we realize that Sali stands tentatively in the open doorway. The thrusting figure that "auralizes" the lovers' reunion seems to be distantly related to the fight motif, perhaps because any resistance may be life-assertive. Certainly, this rising motif contains prophetic references to the purgatorial Paradise Gardens theme, and ecstasy mounts, in a flowing 12/8 pulse, as the lovers swear eternal fidelity. Their (quasi-sexual?) climax past, Vreli retrospectively recounts the tale of her father's insanity, pointing out that, deprived of consciousness, he is happy, happy, happy, as never before in his money-as-well-as-earth-grubbing life. We recall Hardy's pain of consciousness and his anguished plea in "Before Life and After": "Ere nescience shall be reaffirmed / How long, how long?" If this seems a dubious positive, we will discover that nescience is the opera's fundamental theme and the ultimate goal of the lovers' *life*-affirming music.

In their time and place Sali and Vreli decide they have no choice but to confront alienation and isolation, wandering together into the Wild Lands that are their true home. We know they have fathers, but do they have "homes"? Their mothers, if they still exist, are never mentioned. In the context of the opera they can find solidarity only in dreams, as becomes evident when, momentarily chanting in G major togetherness, they sink exhausted, to the *lacrimae rerum* appoggiaturas, in one another's arms. A very flat and dreamy G flat major shifts to a baleful F minor as they assert that they will never again part. They sleep by the dying, almost dead, fire.

Sleeping, they *dream* of their mythical-mystical marriage which, like that of Tristan and Isolde, can never occur in the "real" world. Bells toll in a modal B flat minor, recalling the "old," almost forgotten religious life; the orchestra hymns diatonic concords relatable to music current in the village chapel and street. The chorus, representing the people, showers religious-social blessings on the young lovers' heads, though the choral euphony grows progressively more chromatically disturbed. Tonality veers between modal B flat minor and diatonic D flat major, for neither Old World modality nor the then-current *Hymns Ancient and Modern* can be apposite to them, who are no longer social beings, if ever they were. This is why, when they awaken to (chromatic) reality as the morning sun shines through the still-open door, the frantically jangling church bells link the mythical church to the illusory fair. Indeed church becomes fair, since the young people exchange one illusion for another as they wander desultorily, hand-in-hand, into the fairground. The Breughel-like peasants among whom the lovers stray may be dirtily down-to-earth, but they wildly yodel in E major—an ironic heaven indeed. These peasants, animal-like in pretend-happiness, are not far from insane Marti, who became "happy" only in becoming nescient. Though the scene ends in a fade-out in pure E major, its bass has been pervaded by the tipsy rhythms and angularities of the strife motif.

The fifth scene, enacted within the fair, presents the world as circus. Low ländler, polkas, and mazurkas stamp in defined keys and metrical rhythms, emulating the Way of the World which, as in *Tristan*, is itself a deceit. The chorus, now the "common people" thronging the fair, chants slogans of the market economy—"Come buy, try your luck"—to hurdy-gurdy sonorities that are gross if not actively evil. Intermittently, the rowdy social world is penetrated by upsurging pentatonics, reminding us of the lovers' alienated presence, as they try to be blithe as birds, unconscious of being conscious. Even so, consciousness again proves their undoing, for they are *recognized* by a woman of the fair, who gossips about their putative stories, stirring the mire of rancor and jealousy: "He is by far too good for her," and so on. Still oppressed by their fathers' sin, they cannot abide being stared at, weighed, and found wanting. Sali says they must escape to a haven he knows of—in the Paradise Gardens, which are *water* gardens, below or beyond "consciousness." Gradually the low peasant dances of the fair (now centered around the lovers' youthful A major) acquire hints of transcendence. The hurly-burly of the world is metamorphosed into dream or vision in the famous Walk to the Paradise Gardens: a purely orchestral interlude outside time that is, significantly, the opera's ultimate climax. The interlude ends unambiguously in B major, one step up the cycle of fifths from E major and the same key in which *Tristan* ceases rather than concludes.

The sixth scene takes place at the inn—a converted, now decrepit, once grand house—within the Paradise Gardens. Its relation to the "real" fair the lovers have just escaped from is subtle, for the fair is a human contrivance that deliberately purveys (and *sells*) illusion, whereas the inn is a half-magical place where drink may release the unconscious life. The ambivalence of the Vagabonds is here spelled out: they are mysterious, untrammeled, otherworldly or at least unworldly, yet they are directionless because conscienceless, and perhaps beyond consciousness. The Vagabonds' ambiguity thus parallels that of the Dark Stranger who, wild, free, and "natural" as the world is not, encourages the lovers to escape the bonds of temporality and leads them into these water gardens that may or may not be paradise and into the company of the gypsies, creatures of nature who are oblivious of social constraints. Yet the Dark Stranger *is* inscrutably dark and is a fiddler, as was the Devil. Similarly, the Vagabonds, if blessedly free, are also Circe-like beings, minatory in that they won't grow up to acquire moral responsibilities. If "happy," they are so only in the sense in which Vreli's insane father was rendered happy by the arbitrary destiny of Sali's fist. This fist must be why the wordless choral music they chant at the opening of the scene is magically beautiful yet insidiously undermining. It teeters between simple E flat major and an elusively pentatonic C minor, as had Vreli's lonesome lament at the beginning of the second act, and its symmetrical social rhythm is never stabilized. Delius's habitual theme—the relationship between nature and nurture—remains unresolved, as it always must.

This scene is in part retrospective, for the Dark Stranger recounts to the Vagabonds the tale of the Wild Lands and the legal, as well as philosophical, battle between wilderness and civilization. Tonality is free, at first rooted on strifeful C minor, then on darker F minor. The fiddler's long arioso about the Ancient Wound has something in common with Tristan's vaster narration, in which he recalls his childhood and his parents' lives and deaths. But it doesn't involve the redemptive knowledge that it was "I myself" who brewed the potion, for the Dark Stranger merely invites Sali and Vreli to join the fetterless and feckless Vagabonds in the mountains, to rejoice in living, like Debussy's Pan, without before or after, happy as sandboy or girl—or as Vreli's insane father. The weirdly personified Vagabonds—Wild Girl, Slim Girl, Poor Horn Player, and Hunchbacked Bass-Viol Player—exist simultaneously here and now and in a never-never land. They are a lure, but a threat; they welcome, but scorn. Gradually, Sali and Vreli admit that the Vagabonds' life could never be theirs, since they cannot shuffle off consciousness and conscience. That is their plight, and that of modern, post-Renaissance people. Exiled by fate from the world, they have nothing to hope for from "civilization," but neither is nature adequate to their pain. Since they "can't win," they have no choice but love-in-death and death-in-love. Because the Eden of their childhood is irrecoverable, they voluntarily surrender consciousness as they saunter—a word that contains both *sain* and *terre*—from the Paradise Gardens to the Dark River, on which slowly drifting barges are rowed by pilots who, even more than the Vagabonds, are simultaneously real peasants and legendary guardians of the River Styx.

The end of the opera is not, like that of *Tristan,* a dying-into-life and potential rebirth from the unconscious waters. It is a slow dissolution, which is why the orchestral summation, the fulfillment of the Walk to the Paradise Gardens, is potent yet valedictory. The village Romeo and Juliet surrender life because they cannot leave their childhoods behind; Tristan relives his childhood so that Tristan-Isolde may become, in dying, mutually animus and anima. Yet, as we listen to the ecstatic E major climax to Delius's final scene, we may wonder if there is much difference between Wagner's mystical transcendence and Delius's valedictory dream. For Delius too leaves us purged but in ec-stasis. As Sali releases the barge, committing it to the waters, the Vagabonds wail hysterically and laugh maniacally, while the Dark Stranger fiddles as wildly as mad Marti. Slowly the barge, with its human cargo, sinks in an infinite quietude, in Tristan's sharp B major, and to chords chromatically intensified in precisely the same way as are the breaking waves at the end of *Sea Drift.* This is one of the great moments in European music; even so, reeling from it, we should perhaps remind ourselves of the wise words of Lucretius who, in his *De Rerum Natura*, remarked that "as children tremble and fear everything in blinding darkness, so we sometimes dread in the light things that are no whit more to be feared than what children shudder at in the dark, and imagine will come to pass. This terror of the mind then, this darkness, must needs be scattered not by the rays of the sun and the gleaming shafts of day, but by the outer view and the inner law of nature."[1]

NOTE

1. Titus Lucretius Carus, *Titi Lucreti Cari, De Rerum Natura Libri Sex,* trans. and ed. Cyril Bailey (Oxford: Clarendon Press, 1986), book 2, p. 239, lines 55–61.

3

Pelléas et Mélisande as a Parable of Relinquishment

FOR WAGNER THE IDENTIFICATION, in *Tristan,* of love and death amounted to an apotheosis of humanism, for although Tristan, like all of us, has to die, he does so in the belief that his consuming passion is the universe. This is a heroic achievement. More commonly "the twilight of Europe" implied a pessimistic view of human destiny, as is evident in the elegy of Delius's *A Village Romeo and Juliet.* Pessimism might also be the burden of Maurice Maeterlinck's play *Pelléas et Mélisande,* and of Debussy's almost verbatim musicking of it. But although the poetic theme is the same as that of *Tristan,* the treatment of it could hardly be more different. Wagner wrote the libretto of *Tristan* himself, appraising its relevance to his own life, and directing it toward the music that, in its "endless" flow, is his psyche. The music is thus the shaping reality, which achieves its triumph even as it seems to be driven by forces outside the self—by time and by fate (what happens to us).

Debussy, on the other hand, sets the play as a play, allowing the text to shape the music's energy, or lack of it. Technically, his approach returns to Monteverdi's view of opera as a play in music, making allowance for the fact that Monteverdi expected heroic humans to declaim as though they were gods, whereas Maeterlinck's language and Debussy's setting of it, coming at the end of the cycle of European humanism, are as naturalistic in expression as is Delius's declamation in *A Village Romeo and Juliet.* This is a logical extension of Wagner's technique, for his song-speech would have been naturalistic had not he and his creatures been superhuman.

If we compare Debussy with Schoenberg as a successor to Wagner, we may recall that for the Viennese retreat to the unconscious had led to a mystical vision, a renewal of the religious instinct, however thwarted. But for Debussy the state of will-lessness becomes a good in itself. The distinction is evident in the orchestral textures of *Erwartung* and of *Pelléas et Mélisande*. Both start from Wagner's sonorous sensuality; both achieve from it an exquisite refinement that does not cease to be sensual. Yet the expressionist concentration of Schoenberg's harmony stems from a texture increasingly linear and disintegrative. The "air" that he thus lets into the Wagnerian cocoon gives the texture its radiance, and this radiance proves inseparable from the work's approach to a metaphysical vision ("Ich suchte"). If Schoenberg frees Wagnerian leitmotifs into airborne linearity, Debussy does the opposite, insofar as his textures, although more delicate than Schoenberg's, are still more enveloping. It feels like release because the Wagnerian desire egoistically to mold the themes and rhythms has gone; we live and move, insofar as we move at all, within the mists of the unknown that surrounds us. In a sense the sonority is the All: to which, whatever the intensity or even ferocity of our passions, we can only react seismographically.

This is evident in every aspect of musical technique. Thus, whereas Wagner's "endless melody," though repeatedly frustrated, is always sequentially pressing forward, seeking resolution of the Tristan chords' anguish in the shepherd's monodic piping and in the consummation of the Love-Death, Debussy's leitmotifs tend to be isolated from one another and, though they change, they do not grow. Complementarily, his undulating chromatic harmonies differ from Wagner's in that they do not even try to progress. They oscillate around fixed nodal points, so that their sensuality is scarcely related to bodily energy, while the speech-rhythms of the vocal lines (closer to plainchant than to eighteenth- or nineteenth-century operatic recitative) float directionless on the sensuous harmonies. The static nature of this harmony, combined with the often pentatonic arabesques that spring out of it, give Debussy's music an Eastern rather than Western flavor. This derives not, of course, from Debussy's exposure to Javanese gamelan at the Paris Exhibition but from his intuitive need to counteract our Western "pain of consciousness." In Wagner's works the inner life tries to take control, while in Schoenberg's the spirit seeks, if it does not find, a "religious" ecstasy in entering the dark forest of the unconscious. In Debussy's, this retreat to the inner life is content with submission. We are lost, will-less, in the wood's blind mazes, and to accept this as the essential human condition is the only wisdom we can hope for. It doesn't matter that God as creator and preserver is absent or inoperative, for instead of God, there are feelings, sensations, and whatever causes sensations. Accepting the flux, human consciousness becomes existence without duration. There is only the present moment, no causation and no consequence—as is demonstrable in short piano pieces by Debussy that savor a sensory moment, like the prelude "Voiles," wherein a whole-tone chord and a pentatonic arabesque exist for the moment, without before or after. The revolution in Debussy's music lies in that his willlessness no longer induces terror.

Debussy's surrender in *Pelléas* and Delius's in *A Village Romeo and Juliet* differ in that Delius's quasi-Wagnerian harmonic progression still implies desire, however frustrated, and still involves memory of happiness past, whereas Debussy more radically seeks release from both memory (the past) and from desire (the future). This is why Debussy's opera had so disturbing an impact on the human story. Maeterlinck was aware that his play was, as well as a fairy tale, an exploration of the mind's unconscious depths, in accord with the findings of fin de siècle psychology. The Freudian dimensions of his parable are not as explicit as those devised by Schoenberg and Marie Pappenheim for *Erwartung,* but *Pelléas*'s link with *Tristan* and *Erwartung* is nonetheless palpable. The apex of *Tristan* was, we noted, the hero's immense soliloquy—the Delirium wherein he admitted that responsibility for drinking the love potion was his alone, so that he himself is fate, and the recognition is at once his death and his triumph. *Pelléas* reverses this. None of the characters "stands for" Debussy (or Maeterlinck), and Golaud—the only character who attempts to take action about anything—is the villain, albeit a sympathetic one since he is "within" us, as Mark and Melot are within *Tristan.* For Maeterlinck's young lovers the only happiness consists in submission, and since they cannot understand what they are submitting to, submission becomes identified with inanition.

Because Debussy seeks freedom from memory and desire, *Pelléas et Mélisande* takes place in a timeless antiquity that is also an eternal present, and in a *selva oscura* that is also the unconscious mind and the world of dreams. The first sounds we hear in the orchestral prelude are those of a slow, inexorable march, built on a rising fifth, which in the Middle Ages was God, but is here destiny, taking precedence over all. Imposed on it is Golaud's Dorian theme, which might imply action in being a march, the more so because its slightly breathless rhythm is syncopated. Yet Golaud's theme, though a march, is frustrated in that it revolves around itself, unable to break away from its anchor on a pedal D, and peters out over neutral whole-tone chords that are an ellipsis of two Tristanesque tritones, no longer yearning for resolution. Mélisande's theme also floats over a pedal note; whole-tone arpeggios are incapable of growth, while her pentatonically innocent tune drifts, rudderless, on the whole-tone flow.

We encounter Golaud wandering in the blind mazes of an extremely tangled wood. On the way to make an important marriage for reasons of state—an act that might be construed as a betrayal of Venus—he had indulged in the presumptively desultory hunting of a wild boar, which escaped. Golaud's inability to conquer or subdue wildness may point to the inadequacy, or even the misguidedness, of his machismo; even he, the putative man of action, acts to no end. Lost in the Dark Forest through experience he cannot cope with, he lights on Mélisande, who might be a light to him through her innocence, were she not lost herself. As things are, she's weeping by a Holy Well—from which everyone, in this wasteland, is now cut off. At the sight of Golaud she scurries away in jittery pentatonics, threatening to throw herself into the well should he touch her. She would be pure spirit because she fears the contagion of the flesh, by which—she confesses to Golaud, in a quivering of pentatonic thirds—she has been irremediably "hurt." The hurt apparently explains why she has lost the Golden Crown that an anonymous "he" (a prospective mate or even a husband?) had given her, as she is later to lose Golaud's gold ring and any hope of sensual fulfillment. When Golaud, a potential man of action, offers to fish her crown out of the water, she breaks into hysterical protest. Though her music is sensuously erotic in a style appropriate to a fin de siècle, pre-Raphaelite maiden, she doesn't *want* to be whole, hale, or even (in this sense) holy. Her fluttery recitative gives amorphous incarnation to her passivity.

Interestingly, during this introductory scene the vocal lines don't change in character as the exchanges between Golaud and Mélisande grow more agitated. The harmony becomes more shiftily distraught, and the orchestral textures grow anxious in cross-rhythms, yet the music, pervaded by whole-tone sequences, acquires no harmonic momentum, while the speech-inflected murmur of the vocal lines cannot direct the latent flood of passion. Despite the incessant chromatic oscillations, the only real modulation in the scene is the shift to a pentatonic F sharp when Golaud at last tells Mélisande his name, giving identity to a specific human creature. She, faced with that identity, becomes immediately conscious of mortality, pointing out that his hair is graying. Throughout the opera F sharp major is associated with the light that might irradiate the forest's mists. Here, light is no more than a flicker; to his original obsessively syncopated rhythm Golaud crossly tells Mélisande that they can't hang around in the wood forever, his hunting call motif distantly linking him with a remote possibility of action. Although his music mellows slightly into A flat majorish lyricism, she says that she will *do nothing:* but then, once more passive, agrees to go with him if he will promise not to touch her. We might take this as a small victory for Golaud, had he not already proved himself an inefficient man of action in the matter of the wounded boar. His D minor—the key of his original marchlike theme and a traditionally dynamic tonality in Mozart and Beethoven—is perhaps itself "wounded" and "hurt," being closer to the Dorian mode than to a harmonically "functional" tonal center.

The next scene takes place six months later. Mélisande, her innocence presumably submitting to Golaud's experience, has married him; and it is significant that here, as throughout the opera, we become aware of momentary psychological action in an interlude *between* the scenes—just as the most momentous event in *A Village Romeo and Juliet* is the purely instrumental, interludial Walk to the Paradise Gardens. Géneviève, Golaud's mother, is reading a letter that Golaud has written to his half brother, Pelléas, declaiming it in pentatonic incantation to King Arkel, Golaud's immensely old grandfather. The reading sounds like someone telling an old tale: dreamily directionless, though an occasional dissonance (the diminished fourth on the word *sanglot,* for instance) hints at the reality of passion. In his letter Golaud explains how he came upon Mélisande in the forest, when they were both lost, and adds that he knows no more about her now than he did when they first met. He fears that Arkel will disapprove of the marriage and asks Pelléas to light a lantern on the tower that overlooks the sea, should all be well. If, returning with Mélisande, he sees no light, he will sail away and never return—oddly craven behavior for a man of action.

When Géneviève has finished reading the letter, the orchestra sighs a Tristanesque phrase built on a rising fifth and languishing appoggiatura, which takes the place of feelings Arkel cannot bring himself to utter. The phrase appears in many forms, always nondeveloping, while Arkel gives some support to Golaud's dubiety in admitting that he is far from pleased about the marriage, partly because the lovers are ill-matched in age and perhaps in breeding, but more because Golaud has so precipitously abandoned his marriage of convenience, which is the more important since the acting king is sick, probably terminally. Even so, Arkel does not advocate action; what must be, will be, and there may be a pattern in destiny that we cannot perceive. Arkel's theme, rising a fourth and descending by step, is faintly liturgical, without Golaud's whole-tone vacillations, for he is the closest Debussy's world comes to quasi-divine sanctions. Not surprisingly, the theme is related to the fate motif, both in its shape and in the regularity with which it is repeated. Though fateful, it is not sinister but compassionate, even tender.

Arkel, if old and putatively wise, is significantly almost blind: insofar as we can see truly, we cannot see much. Pelléas, who now enters, is the grandson of Arkel and the son of Génevière by the Dying King, whereas Golaud is the son of Génevière by a previous husband, long dead. Pelléas's youthfulness is contrasted with his "gray-haired" half brother, and his music has a simple animation, if not energy. His life-enhancing qualities are manifest in an eager, syncopated rhythm (which subverts momentum less than Golaud's syncopated agitations), and with the sharp key of E major. We may relate it to light that might irradiate the forest's mists, though hardly to the heavenly qualities with which the key was traditionally affiliated. In any case Pelléas's music is obsessed with ostinato figures and oscillations between two tonally neutral chords, so that it "gets nowhere" harmonically. His inadequacy as a harbinger of light is evident when he tells us that he has been summoned to visit a *dying* friend, which may be a premonition of his own death. Arkel persuades him not to leave, since charity begins at home, and his king and father is dying also. The scene ends when, overriding Arkel's doubts, Pelléas submits to destiny in hanging the lantern in the tower, to guide home Golaud with his child bride. In the ensuing interlude the music again becomes the lifeblood of the psyche. The ostinatos and harmonic "nodes" turn into Tristanesque chromatics, energy and yearning being the more desperate for being caged in two-bar periods. The interlude, carrying Golaud and Mélisande over the unknowable sea, also tells us, in anticipating the motives of the next scene, that the love and fate of Pelléas and Mélisande, though they have not yet met, are preordained.

In the next scene—again after an elapse of time—Mélisande is talking to Génevière about the gloom of the castle and the impenetrability of the surrounding forest. They are all in darkness, as blind as ancient Arkel; she wanders to the seashore through an opening in the forest, desperate to glimpse light. The sea itself is shrouded; a tempest is raging far out, and undulating ninth chords combine with a distant chorus of (ghostly?) sailors to suggest the flux of the natural and supernatural worlds. Pelléas comes to look for her, and together they think they see, through the mists, lights that might be a beacon. On the other hand, they may be illusory, as was, perhaps, the lantern that had seemed to welcome Golaud and Mélisande home. Hints of the high, sharp keys of E and F sharp dissolve in tremolando ninths, pierced by echoes of Golaud's boar-hunting motif. The orchestral storm abates when Pelléas rashly tries to take Mélisande's hand to lead her back to the castle. She protests that she cannot touch (even) him, perhaps because she doesn't want to, but also because her arms are full of flowers. The lyrical efflorescence on this phrase gives, in the context of the speech-norm of the recitative, *incar-*

nation to the words, and is the first testimony of their love. But it fades to silence in a mingling of the sea-mist music with the tentative love song. Added sixths glow luminously around an F sharp major triad, F sharp having superseded E major as Debussy's paradisal key.

If Golaud is human will and outworn flesh and Mélisande is spirit that is sensuality and sexuality *in potentia,* Pelléas must be what each needs. The next scene suggests that the fulfillment of sexual love could be the spirit's renewal, for it takes place in a park (comparable with *Erwartung*'s walled garden) by a potentially sacred fountain. To lucent music—based in E major but with minimal harmonic movement—Pelléas tells Mélisande of the fountain's once-miraculous properties. It used to be called Blindman's Well because it cured blindness, but it does so no longer, and Arkel himself is nearly blind. The quasi-religious note is suggested by hymnic diatonic concords, the failure of spirit by undulating chromatics. Tenderly tentative, the young people indulge in love play as Mélisande tries, but fails, to touch the life-giving water with her life-fearing hands—though her long-flowing hair can just reach it. Pelléas riskily reminds her of how Golaud found her by the fountain, just as he has. Reminiscences of Golaud's music provoke agitation in Mélisande, who, idly or nervously playing with Golaud's ring, drops it into the water. She tosses aside the life fulfillment her husband might have offered her. The water noises, as the ripples settle, are will-less and wavery in whole tones. Unsurprisingly, the Golaud theme takes over in the next interlude, which is the longest thus far, and the most Wagnerian in intensity, though it is still intermittently immobilized by pedal notes.

Despite this irresolution, the dark passions disturbed in both Golaud and Mélisande are inimical. In the next scene Golaud recounts to Mélisande how, while out riding, his horse stumbled, on the stroke of twelve, the very moment at which Mélisande dropped the ring into the well. The water-splashing noise of the well scene is darkly transmogrified into the stumble of Golaud's horse, creating a physical sense of oppression, as though the forest were closing in on him. Mélisande sobs in her "hurt" pentatonic minor thirds but denies that her misery has anything to do with the young man; it's just that the castle is so old and dark, and everyone is dying—as, of course, is literally true, though only Arkel and the Dying King are *expecting* death. Mélisande, who had been scared by Golaud's graying hair when they first met, can't accept the simple fact of mortality, and her death fear perhaps has some justification when Golaud, taking her hand ostensibly to comfort her, says he could *crush* it. He has noticed that her ring is missing, and action turns into nightmare as Golaud agitatedly cross-questions her, at first in unaccompanied parlando line, but then accompanied by undirected harmonic patterns and nondeveloping ostinatos from the orchestra. Mélisande pretends, with direly Freudian implications, that she has lost her ring in a cave by the sea. Golaud insists that she go at once to recover it and take Pelléas with her if she's frightened. To sharp harmonic tensions Golaud barks that Pelléas will do anything for her sweet sake, won't he? Mélisande flees, wailing about her unhappiness, to the same cascading thirds as had expressed the first florescence of her love.

So Pelléas and Mélisande descend together to the sea's depths that may be also the womb. The interlude mingles Pelléas's motif of yearning with the fountain's pentatonic babble, but drowns both in undulating chromatics as they enter the sea cave. When they are enshrouded in darkness—in the obscurity of a modal C sharp minor that is the relative of Pelléas's daylit E major—we know that they had no choice but to make their dark pilgrimage, pointless though it seems since they both know that the ring is not, and never was, in the cave. As they creep further in, orchestral sonorities darken and tonality further weakens. Pelléas tells her not to be scared, for they will turn back when they can no longer see any light from the sea. He doesn't attempt to justify the latent (Golaud-like?) sadism of this, even when Mélisande panics as a sudden shaft of moonlight reveals three (probably Freudian) white-haired paupers, starving victims of famine in the wasteland. For the legendary world of the opera has a social context, even though it is seldom admitted to. The whining, quasi-medieval parallel fifths in this pauper music are a striking sound image for the withering of life both within the psyche and in the external world. How closely the inner and outer worlds are connected is indicated by the reappearance of Golaud's motive of aborted action. Mélisande's love becomes nightmare because it cannot be corporeally realized, whether with Golaud or Pelléas, while the world "out there" starves because there is no love to nurture it. One might almost say that the opera is "about" the sundering of the flesh and the word and the consequent death of both.

So the lovers' descent into the waters of the unconscious and the cavern of the womb only appears to lead to love's consummation. They know they have to make the tenebrous descent and that the reason is not the footling one Pelléas offers—the necessity for Mélisande to be able to describe the cave to Golaud. Yet they explore the cavern like children, as a self-scaring game of dares. Mélisande is terrified of the beggars revealed by the transfiguring moon because she can't tolerate the light, even though she and Pelléas, fulfilled together, might bring light to the gloomy forest and cobwebby castle, so similar to that in which Tristan waited, in paralysis or nervous breakdown, for Isolde's approach across the empty sea. But if Mélisande can't stand the light, neither can she accept darkness in lieu of it. She welcomes Pelléas's suggestion that he take her back before light from the sea has totally vanished. Maybe "nous reviendrons un autre jour," he adds, referring to the child's habitual "tomorrow."

With the sundering of flesh from spirit and the decay of volition, the love scene that opens the third act, though parallel to the third act love nocturne of *Tristan,* is a consummation only in dream. The image of Mélisande isolated in her tower emphasizes this, the more so because towers are supposed to be phallic. She croons to herself an incantation about her hair (gold like her lost crown and ring), the lyrical line growing from her "hurt" motif, accompanied by orchestral night noises. The ballad-like simplicity of the lyricism makes her seem a little girl, or a fairy princess, rather than a married woman. Her chant is in Dorian E minor, complementing Pelléas's E major, and its monodic innocence makes a rare reference to Christian sanctions. This further emphasizes the division between spirit and flesh, for when Pelléas tells her—at this crucially amorous moment—that he must leave tomorrow, Mélisande doesn't seem to know whether she is pleased or sorry. She whimpers, "Non, non"; yet although she leans riskily toward him from her tower, she can make no bodily contact with hands or fingers, let alone lips. This harks back to the well scene in the first act, when she dabbled her long hair in the sacred water that her hands couldn't reach. Similarly, from her tower she can envelop him only in the whirl of her hair, which may induce a delirium of rapture, but hardly aids clear vision, and may be illusory. When she is startled by an object glimmering in the dark, she wonders if it is a rose (of sexual fulfillment?). Pelléas doubts whether it is a rose at all, and so do we.

During this scene Pelléas's music grows increasingly sustained in lyricism, and it is almost possible to speak of a climax when he modulates from his E major to F sharp, the key of heightened consciousness, here notated as G flat. The flatness makes a difference, for the lyricism, however tender, hardly marries spirit and flesh. The music representing Mélisande's cascading hair is significantly related to her hurt minor thirds, and at the climax of his passion she utters a shriek, complaining that he is inflicting pain. We'll see later how deeply sadism and masochism are intertwined in this psychological opera; for the moment Pelléas's lust, if that's what it is, has been mollified, and the love theme coos tenuously as doves flitter around the lovers in the gloaming. The modal C sharp minor—which may be reality in comparison to the bliss of its E major relative—is interrupted by footsteps as, to his expectantly syncopated rhythm, Golaud enters. As his hunting horn sounds distantly he self-protectively calls the lovers silly children and leads Pelléas away. The interlude weaves Golaud's theme into Pelléas's and is left suspended, unresolved, if around the transfiguring key of F sharp.

Now it is Golaud's and Pelléas's turn to descend to the depths, and we begin to see how the opera charts a life failure in all the central protagonists. Because Mélisande's innocence could not accept Golaud's experience, she cannot, notwithstanding her music's latent eroticism, be renewed by Pelléas's love; she cannot find the rose for the thorn. But if Mélisande's spirit finds no adequate embodiment, Golaud's corporeality has lost touch with spirit, so that he has no answer to his crisis of jealousy—whether or not it is justified—except madness and despair. He descends with Pelléas into the vault of the castle, where the water isn't living like the sea or the magic well or the fountain, but is stagnant with the stench of death. He plays a sadistic game, echoing the more oblique sadism of Pelléas with Mélisande in their descent into the sea cavern. Golaud's grimmer game seems to be a consequence of his separating love from will, for he deliberately scares Pelléas by flickering his lantern, threatening to push him into the abyss. This must be why his descent, like that of Mélisande, only *seems* to be a prelude to a moment of illumination and forgiveness.

Momentarily, as they return to the light, the cascading whole-tone arpeggios on harp become, freed from antecedence and consequence, "air from the sea"; the breezes mingle with the fragrance of freshly watered roses and with the tolling of bells in (of course) a pentatonic F sharp. Children are splashing in the sea, and there too is childlike Mélisande, with Géneviève, her mother by marriage. Musically, this is a miraculous moment; dramatically, however, it is tragic irony, for after Golaud has confessed that he knows "all about" Pelléas and Mélisande but recognizes that their relationship is "child's play," he exploits the child motif to sinister purpose. He cross-questions Yniold, his little son by his first marriage: Is Pelléas often with Mélisande? What do they talk of? What do they do? Golaud's vocal line is speech-inflected, with no song left; Yniold's answers are in the simplest pentatonicism, like a nursery ditty. Significantly, Golaud's interrogations are accompanied by the whole-tone vaults motives; until that revelation of horror beneath the suave surface of the civilized mind turns into a febrile version of Mélisande's hurt pentatonic thirds, as Golaud painfully crushes Yniold's arm, as he lusted to crush Mélisande's small hand. Experience seems unable to cope with peril, despite the derivation of the word *experience* from the Latin *ex periculo;* and Golaud breaks down, confessing that he, no less than

ancient Arkel, is a *blind man,* stumbling crablike across the seabed, search-
ing for his lost gold (his ring, Mélisande's hair). The contrast between
Yniold's Moussorgskian pentatonics and Golaud's frenzy grows more acute
as his questions nag on. Climactically, he sets the child to spy on the lovers
through a little window. Yniold says they are doing nothing, just standing,
looking; he must get down or he'll scream. Golaud's anguish is manifest in
short, self-revolving phrases in whole tones, as he again inflicts pain on Yniold
by tugging him from the window. The act ends abruptly with unisonal tutti
on the hurt motif inverted—in a Phrygian E minor (Bach's key of cruci-
fixion), as opposed to Pelléas's E major pretend-paradise.

Tragic irony extends into the fourth act, when Pelléas, back in his static E
major, arranges to meet Mélisande, before he leaves, by Blindman's Well. It
is not clear—nothing in this opera ever is—why he is going away: whether
in fear of Golaud's threats or to succor his dying friend or from an incapac-
ity to face the consequence of passion or from a mixture of all these motives.
The water ripples of the fountain in this scene temper their healing properties with agitation, since love seems of its nature inseparable from pain:
Pelléas hurts Mélisande in loving her; Mélisande hurts Golaud in not loving
him; Golaud hurts Mélisande for not loving him and finally hurts innocent
Yniold as scapegoat. The inescapability of pain and death is recognized in
the crucial scene wherein Arkel, in the heightened sharpness of B major—
though not the transcendent sharpness of F sharp major, let alone the ultimate transcendence of C sharp major in which the opera will end—pays
homage to Mélisande for the new life her youth and beauty have brought to
the castle. This may, however, be no more than wish fulfillment, for
Mélisande's therapy has hardly been evident in her effects on the central
characters, nor have we any evidence, apart from Arkel's report, that the dying
king is on the mend. Since we hear no more about his fate, we may suspect
that Arkel is not so much hinting at a rebirth as saying that only through
apprehension of beauty can we bear the fact of decay and death. So his pas-
sively fateful, quasi-religious theme is intertwined with the love theme, high
up in E major, and the fatefulness is stronger than the love. His song of
affirmation, anchored by pedal notes, has no real movement, and movement
is life. Gradually the love theme is metamorphosed into the jealousy theme
of Golaud, who appears with blood on his brow.

As the love theme disperses, Golaud barks testily to Mélisande about the
careless way in which peasants have been dying around the castle, but then
turns to the death within himself, taunting her about her big, innocent eyes.
His declamation grows progressively more hysterical in obsessive repeated

tones and lost, whole-tone scurryings, and now it is he who says that Mélisande must on no account touch him, for he cannot bear the contagion of flesh. He, too, cannot take her hand, but only her long, gold hair, which he seizes savagely, hauling her up and down, forcing her to her knees, the lid being indeed off the libido. When Arkel returns, Golaud tries to regain control, but we are left with Mélisande whimpering, "Je ne suis pas heureuse," and with sighing appoggiaturas that accompany Arkel's statement that, were he God, he would have pity on human suffering. As a mere human, albeit once a king, he can feel for human beings, but can right no wrong. He is more fortunate than Golaud, Mélisande, and Pelléas only because he is very old, habituated to suffering, and inevitably close to its end.

This scene reveals how agonizingly this quasi–fairy tale is rooted in the realities of the human psyche; the next scene is introduced simply to demonstrate their inexorability. The man is father to the child, the child is father to the man; and the little Yniold, representative of the next generation, is trying to shift an enormous stone, behind which he has lost his golden ball, as Golaud had lost his golden ring and Mélisande her golden crown. But his little arm isn't long enough to contact the ball, just as Mélisande's arm couldn't reach the holy water and Pelléas couldn't embrace Mélisande's golden hair as she leaned from her tower. A flock of sheep pad by, baaing pitifully. Their unseen shepherd, when Yniold inquires where they are going and why they're crying, says that they're not going home to their barn, that's for certain. He and they disappear into the mist. Musically, this little scene is, in its rhythmic continuity and simple lyricism, the most self-contained in the opera, and is so because it lives outside the action in the preconscious world of childhood, unable to grow beyond incantatory repetition, "for ever and ever," like an old tale. As we grow up, we lose even this limited self-sufficiency. We disintegrate into fragments, like the flock of sheep, at once one and many. The scene trickles out in a figure of drooping half notes, an inversion of the original nursery rhyme motif.

Pelléas enters to admit that he has been playing "comme un enfant," knowing no more than the sheep what he was doing or where he was going. He must go away, like a *blind man* leaving a house on fire, not because he would not love if he could, but because he cannot distinguish between reality and illusion; he confesses that he cannot remember what Mélisande looks like. When she arrives for their farewell assignation, they attain a moment of tranced speechlessness that is the closest they come to fulfillment. But the slow lyrical expansion of the music, after the castle gates have shut them out, entangles the love theme, the water motif, and Golaud's hunting call with the hollow fifths of fate. From the heightened stillness of F sharp major the music attains a near-Wagnerian climax, though in very brief, panting phrases. This is the lovers' only physical contact, apart from Pelléas's toying with the net of Mélisande's hair; his ultimate confession of love is also a Parsifal-like renunciation. He says he must go away *because* he loves her, which, if true at all, is not the whole truth. For all his and her dubiety, they touch F sharp major once more, if momentarily, before Golaud, an avenging fury, slays Pelléas with his sharp sword, and Mélisande scuttles off into the darkness, quavering, "Je n'ai pas de courage." The end of the scene is as abrupt as the guillotine—in traditionally infernal F minor, in sharpest contrast to the F sharp major climax.

So Mélisande has failed to grow from her potentially life-enhancing innocence to experience and to give her spirit bodily consummation; Golaud has failed to renew his experience in her innocence, so that his flesh turns sadistically destructive; and Pelléas, the half brother and lover who might have restored all to love and life, is slain by their failures, which are inseparable from his own. We don't know what happened outside the castle gates before Golaud's frantic approach, but if the young lovers' passion is consummated in their last moment of F sharp major illumination, when Pelléas says he hears Mélisande's voice floating over the sea, in spring, the consummation can hardly be accounted a triumph. More probably their love is not consummated, and the moment of revelation is a dream of what might have been. In any case the death of Pelléas is a crude murder by a jealous enemy, not a self-immolation that, like Tristan's death, leads to a mystical union with the beloved. Mélisande too, wounded in the affray wherein Pelléas is slaughtered, dies, perhaps not of her wounds but because the pulse of life, with the failure of love, slows to inanition.

The last act opens by her deathbed, with a tremulous, chromatically altered version of the Mélisande theme that, floating around E, chimes through the act like a knell. Interestingly enough this theme—with whole-tone ambiguities and persistent false relations wherein A flats sometimes "stand for" G sharps—is remarkably similar to the ostinato theme that pervades the eerie wasteland Epilogue to Vaughan Williams's Sixth Symphony, composed almost half a century later. Both the chromatic alterations and the almost pulseless repetitions imbue the music with a non-Western passivity—as distinct from a passion that, having been consistently destructive in Pelléas, is spent. Golaud, apparently penitent, seems to admit that the young were innocent, he guilty, as fragments of his theme wander disconsolately in the bass, while the whole-tone fountain quivers on top. Mélisande, accompanied by diatonic concords, asks for the window to be opened, so that she may watch the sun setting on the sea. Arkel asks if Golaud may speak to her and she, assenting, says that there is "nothing to forgive." The knell undulates as everyone except Golaud leaves, in solemn funeral procession. When the orchestra ceases we realize that nothing has been annealed, let alone healed, for Golaud, on the rack, asks her his question: Did she and Pelléas love one another? When she confirms that they did, he retorts that she doesn't understand. He means did they love one another bodily; he has to know, she cannot die on a lie. So, despite his apparent repentance, the horror returns; the obsessive seventh chord once more turns into whole-tone hysteria. It seems we can never undo the consequences of our errors. She whispers "la vérité" . . . and relapses into a coma. So he, and we, never know "la vérité," and this is the essence of the human condition. There is no physical consummation, no metaphysical consolation, only an intense capacity to feel and an Eastern acceptance of the unknowable mysteries of birth, suffering, and death.

To speak of failure, in this twilight of humanism, is hardly relevant. We are all, like Mélisande, deluded by our innocence and, like Golaud, corrupted by our experience, and so, like Pelléas, we never fully realize our love, because we cannot recognize it or distinguish truth from falsehood. The end of the opera accepts this as a perennial human destiny. Arkel prevents Golaud from attempting to awaken the unconscious Mélisande, and the servants enter in ritual procession, to pray (to what or whom?) as Mélisande dies, while the knell slows to immobility, repeatedly returning to Pelléas's E, but with an oppressed, flattened, Phrygian feeling, as in the Epilogue to Vaughan Williams's Sixth Symphony. Mélisande tries to hold her newborn baby (presumably Golaud's), but is too weak to do so. Arkel sings an exquisite benediction on suffering humanity and utters the opera's final words: "C'est au tour de la pauvre petite." The babe is born and life will go on; but the next generation will weep the same tears anew. In the last few bars the cycle starts again, for the simplest, most innocently pentatonic version of Mélisande's theme reemerges from the knell, while the sighing appoggiaturas of the fountain scene become *lacrimae rerum*. The moveless tonality is now C sharp major, the final step up the cycle of fifths from the illumination of F sharp major. It is indeed out of *this* world, almost too far away to be credible; nor is it fortuitous that C sharp major is the major form of the minor key that, as the relative of Pelléas's hopefully paradisal E major, had been "reality." The notion is profoundly Eastern; only in the not-self can the reality beyond our earthly passions be apprehensible.

Yet if the revelation is at hand for dead Mélisande—and this is an open question—what *we* are left with is Arkel's quiet fortitude. The tolling bell is a ritual elegy on European humanism, and *Pelléas et Mélisande*, offering the quintessence of Debussyan theme and technique, is a key work of the twentieth century, germinal because its passion and its relinquishment are alike uncompromising. It offers no heroic apotheosis (like *Tristan*), no metaphysical hope (like *Erwartung*), no refuge in nostalgia (like *A Village Romeo and Juliet*), but it does leave us purged, and for that reason ready to go on living. The beauty of the music is its only necessary justification; because its moments of passion are so exquisite and also so painful, we rejoice in, rather than deplore, the fact that its moments of sensation have no before and after of which we can have certain knowledge. This is why *Pelléas et Mélisande,* offering so gloomy a view of human destiny, is not a depressing work. In the paradoxical nature of its affirmation it has something in common with the moments of sensation that impressionist painters discovered in their seismographic response to the visible world. These painters anarchically inverted architectural values, made backgrounds foregrounds, allowed sitters to look beyond the composition's frame, and accepted the disorder of appearances with apparent equanimity. Yet in both the painting of Monet and of Degas (to cite one painter concerned mainly with the natural world and one concerned mainly with people) and in the music of Debussy, the acceptance of nature's disorder becomes a kind of order. Both find light within the mists of uncertainty wherein we, like Maeterlinck's sheep, have gone astray; and both discover something like happiness in their humility before the natural world and in their admission of human limitation. This is why *Pelléas et Mélisande* continues to have more to offer than its innumerable progeny, which include existential drama, the Theater of the Absurd, and much of the music theater of the twentieth-century avant-garde.

4

Tapiola's Search for Oneness and *Cunning Little Vixen* as a Parable of Redemption

IN THE LATE NINETEENTH and early twentieth centuries Western consciousness disintegrated as the overweening human will lost its way in the "blind mazes" of the psyche, as we have explored by way of works by Wagner, Schoenberg, Delius, and Debussy. Even so, not all of Europe was hypercivilized, and a hint of potential redemption appeared in nordic cultures that flourished in places still near wilderness. Two composers in particular were transitional in time and space. Jean Sibelius was born in 1865 in Finland, a country sparsely populated but densely covered with forests and lakes. Although obviously an heir to a cultural tradition, he was at once an aboriginal and a guardian of civilization. He remarked, "Look at the great nations of Europe and what they have endured! No savage could have stood the things that they have gone through. It is their civilization that has given them such moral strength and courage. . . . I do believe in civilization."[1] The musical evidence of this belief lies in that Sibelius's lifework centered on the symphony, the form that, from the Enlightenment onward, embodied the most heroic attempts to create order through the human will, making unity from contradiction.

Sibelius's first two symphonies had roots in the nineteenth century, even in chronological terms. They are broad, heroic, "conflict" symphonies that were often allied to the classical-romantic symphonies of Tchaikovsky, though Sibelius found the comparison unhelpful, maintaining that his true master was Beethoven. Yet even in these early symphonies is evidence that Sibelius's notion of what a symphony was and ought to be was not conformable with traditional precedents. In particular, the first movement of his Second Symphony explores a technique that would have increasing importance in his later work. Whether or not this technique was suggested by the first movement of the E flat symphony of the empirically Russian Borodin, the work starts with fragments of line, rhythmic motives, even the tone color of an instrument that slowly interact and mutate until they coalesce in the main themes at what would, in classical terms, be the recapitulation. The process is similar to that exemplified in Beethoven's sketchbooks, only whereas in Beethoven's case the creation of themes marks the beginning of the working out of their destinies—that is, of the composition—in Sibelius's case the growth of the themes is the structure of the movement.

A similar technique is used, with more aphoristic concision, in the finale of the Third Symphony and the first movement of the Fifth. But if Sibelius investigates the creation of themes from their constituents, he also winnows down conventional structures to their barest bones. Both processes may be used simultaneously; the two movements just referred to may be regarded either as self-generatively engaged in the creation of themes and the establishment of tonal order or as telescopings of the customary sonata allegro and scherzo. The climax to these complementary tendencies toward concision occurs in the Fourth Symphony, written between 1909 and 1911, at a time when Sibelius's health was seriously threatened and disorders were rife in the public world. The symphony might have as an epigraph William Butler Yeats's words from "The Second Coming": "Things fall apart; the centre cannot hold"; and this is indeed what almost—but not quite—occurs in this piece, which is described as a symphony in A minor, though it is really dominated by the tritone and opens with the interval C to F sharp, cavernously reverberating in the bass. The "theme" of the first movement is self-generated from a brief, contorted figure undulating around a tritone, rises to a climax in a fluttering *moto perpetuo* for strings, and subsides to its source. The scherzo reverses this process, beginning with a deceptively simple theme on oboe, in traditionally pastoral F major transmuted into the Lydian mode, so that its fourth is again tritonal. Incrementally, pastoral quietude is shattered by eruptive tritones. Tonality is also threatened; the whimper of a bit of the melody at the end, in a remote key, is yanked back to the tonic only by a barely audible dominant-tonic cadence on timpani. The slow movement is a cross between thematic generation and a sonata structure so skeletonic as to belie its traditional affirmation, while in the last movement classical rondo disintegrates into its components. The initial themes, radiant in "youthful" A major, bejeweled with glockenspiel, "lack all conviction," in Yeats's terms; and if they become "full of passionate intensity," its consequence is increasingly ferocious dissonance, climaxing in one of the most extreme expressions of chaos in all music. The symphony subsides in desolation, all trace of A major banished in favor of the starkest A minor.

The post-Beethovenian symphony was a public statement, or at least it was concerned with potentially heroic humanity's ability to create order that could be manifest in social and even political terms. Sibelius was, or became, a public figure and a hero identified with his nation's struggle for political autonomy. His first two symphonies could be construed as conflict-and-triumph symphonies in nineteenth-century tradition; and the third and fifth, though more "inward" in their self-germination, end with the victory within the psyche of a man who, being a hero, might effect consequences in the world at large. The Sixth Symphony extends and deepens this, for the "pure water" of its modal textures recreates traditional tonality in positive directions rather than in the Fourth's destructive impulses; this process leads to the one-movement structure of the Seventh Symphony, in which the four movements of a classical symphony are encapsulated within a single rising scale and perfect cadence in C major. Every aspect of the work is thematic growth; in no music is it less possible to separate orchestration from form, since tone color is itself structure, a means of imparting appropriate stress to each melodic strand.

So whatever deference Sibelius paid to classical symphonic form—and he maintained that the Mozart symphonic allegro was his structural ideal—it appears that he did not construct his symphonies exclusively, or sometimes at all, on the dualistic principles of sonata. His forms tend toward the monism he finally achieved in his last symphony, and his role as a public composer is inseparable from his search for renewed private identity and "wholeness." The "terrifying honesty" of the Fourth Symphony holds on for grim life, just surviving its tritonal assaults. The expanded modality of the Sixth Symphony—which Sibelius himself related to Palestrina—gives an almost baptismal significance to the "pure water" image; while the one-movement Seventh Symphony turns out to have points in common with *Tristan*, notwithstanding Sibelius's professed aversion to Wagner and veneration for Beethoven. The link is again by way of the devil-in-music, the tritone, and the whole-tone formulas that accrue from it. The notorious "Tristan chords" consist of two interlinked tritones, which in the "Liebestod" become a dying-into-life. It is not therefore surprising that Sibelius's "morphological" forms function more like Wagner's late works than like the sonata dualities of Mozart and Beethoven. *Their* search for a synthesis of the private and the public life was no longer available. Order was still Sibelius's goal, but after the Fourth Symphony, order called for a precarious equilibrium between civilized awareness and a recognition of separateness and even of a Delian desire to relinquish the self in nature. Wind, water, light, space, solitude—all the qualities of the Finnish landscape—fascinated Sibelius not as an assertion of national (and to that degree public) identity but because they defined an experience with which, as the years passed, he became increasingly obsessed.

Although Delius, in *A Song of the High Hills*, strives to lose the burden of the self in recurrent pentatonicism and in the unbroken flow of orchestral textures, he cannot free himself from the (Wagnerian) pull and throb of harmonic tension. Sibelius, as he communes with nature, goes further in self-obliteration, perhaps because his respect for civilization brought a measure of detachment, but perhaps merely because the Finnish solitudes were limitless and irremediable. And he goes furthest of all in his last completed, large-scale work, for the search for oneness could hardly be carried further than in the one-movement, monothematic *Tapiola*, in which the entire structure proliferates from a single seed. *Tapiola* is the *ne plus ultra* of Sibelian technique, and in it human ego seems to be swept away in nature's infinitudes of time and space—auralized in those pervasive, instantly recognizable drones, internal pedals, and whole-tone nonprogressions, as well as in the orchestra's potent Sibelius sound. It is possible to contend that the Fourth, Sixth, and Seventh Symphonies are more central achievements of European civilization, but it is impossible to deny *Tapiola*'s significance as a document of our time, or of our spiritual legacy from the immediate past. The long, spine-chilling *moto perpetuo* before the coda is surely one of the most terrifying moments in European music.

When, after that, we arrive at the tonic major triad with which the work concludes, we realize what moral strength must have been necessary to make such an affirmation, at the end of such a work. Interestingly enough, the triad is one of B major—the same as that on which the internal turmoil of Wagner's *Tristan* belatedly and protractedly resolves. Although Wagner's apotheosis was that of the self writ very large, it was also a public act in that for Wagner self-fulfillment was also a revelation of public destiny. Sibelius would not have put his victory in such subjective terms, but the grandeur of his heroism does not pale in comparison with Wagner's. And when we look back at Sibelius's oeuvre from the chilling heights of *Tapiola*, we observe how harbingers of that *moto perpetuo* occur from the Third Symphony onward. Similarly, the inhuman howls of the long internal pedal points in *Tapiola* prove to be an extension of one of the most pervasive features of Sibelius's scoring. Accepting *Tapiola* as the quintessential Sibelian work, we recognize that it cannot be fortuitous that when all four movements of the Fourth Symphony, having emerged embryonically from their seminal figures, fade into nothingness, their humanity returns to the earth and air—to that which is nonhuman. Perhaps this dissolution into nature, rather than into Wagner's Love-Death, is one of the few means whereby an artist in an areligious and materialistic society may approach religious experience. But his is not the oneness that Beethoven fought for so strenuously and ultimately found. If in Delius's *A Song of the High Hills* ecstasy is more heart-rending than joyous, in Sibelius's *Tapiola* ecstasy cannot be distinguished from a frigid fright.

That Sibelius was aware of this is suggested by an excerpt from a remarkable letter he wrote in 1911, the year of the Fourth Symphony, and also of that overt farewell to "Europe"—Mahler's Ninth (and last completed) Symphony. "Yesterday," wrote Sibelius, "I heard Bruckner's B flat major symphony and it moved me to tears. For a long time afterwards, I was completely enraptured. What a strangely profound spirit, formed by a religious sense. And this profound religiousness we have abolished in our own country as something no longer in harmony with our time."[2] It is significant that Sibelius composed no music after *Tapiola*, written in 1925, though he lived for another thirty years. The amnesia of his alcoholism was probably more effect than cause, for what could come "after" the hell of *Tapiola?* Unafraid, or at least unbowed, he had expressed an impasse in Europe's spiritual history, bringing home to us, with agonizing intensity, a predicament both psychological and social. Maybe we had to "go through" *Tapiola* in order to live again.

It is indicative of Sibelius's transitional position that we're uncertain whether to think of him as a nineteenth- or as a twentieth-century composer; much of his work stems directly from nineteenth-century traditions, yet *Tapiola*, and a few other pieces, plumb to the heart of "modernity." Another composer, born even earlier in the nineteenth century, also in a land dominated by immense forests, has obvious links with nineteenth-century nationalist traditions, yet was also vividly responsive to the desperations of our human story, writing almost all the music we remember him by over the last twenty years of a life stretching from 1854 to 1928. We are apt to forget, since Leoš Janáček's rural Moravia was so remote from the urban technocracy of Europe's center, that his operas were set in places and during times in which he'd grown up. He was not, like Sibelius, a "European," concerned in symphonic abstraction with the resolution of conflicts between the private and the public life. Essentially a theater composer, he was a man living in a specific community, rendering aurally "incarnate" its human values. More powerfully than any exponent of *verismo* opera, Janáček created "slices of life" in which the passions involved are more complex, but no less vehement, than those in the operas of Ponchielli, if not of Puccini. Janáček's musical language is at once topical and local: simply but profoundly a sublimation of the ways people in Moravian village, town, or city spoke and gestured, while the orchestra rendered audible, visible, and even tactile the environment of the physical world. Short, reiterated motives echo the word and body gestures of "basic" human beings. Only Moussorgsky approaches Janáček in this concern with human elementals.

It is to the point that most of Janáček's representative works were composed shortly before, during, or after World War I, which delivered so savage a blow to the concept of "Europe"; and if we think of Janáček as equivocating between "unconscious" nature and the "hyperconscious" modern psyche, we'll understand why *Kát'a Kabanová* is a supreme masterpiece of our century. Its Russian context—based on a novel by nineteenth-century Ostrovsky—enables Janáček to fuse his ritualism and superstition with the Christian sense of guilt under which he labored, even while abominating it. Kát'a is the female principle incarnate: a good woman sapped of energy and direction by the circumstances she lives in. Eager to fulfil her sensual and sexual nature in loving, she is destroyed by Society as personified by her monstrous mother-in-law, Kabanicha, and Kabanicha's lover, Dikoj, significantly a merchant and a fairly bloated capitalist. Between them, they exert absolute autonomy over their moribund middle-class society.

In a poignant monologue early in the opera Kát'a, talking to herself and to nature's chattering swallows, reveals how she yearns to leave the festering bourgeois world in which she finds herself, to seek extramarital fulfillment with her lover—who is no superman, but more of a man than her wretched husband, crushed by the formidable Kabanicha. What prevents her from escaping is her Christian conscience, since her religion means more to her than subservience to the parochial and clerical establishment, while she's too intelligent to be content with the vacuous fecklessness of Vavara and Kudras, young peasant lovers who carol pentatonically, as blithely as those swallows in the eaves. So Kát'a would seem to be related to Janáček's wife, both as a child bride and as the sober provincial housewife she'll become; to his adolescent daughter who had tragically died; to Kamilla Stösslová, the woman thirty-eight years his junior, for whom he nursed a recreative passion during his sixties and seventies; and even to himself, insofar as this belated eroticism—previously stifled by childhood deprivation, by his apprentice years in a monastery, and by his long war with social, ecclesiastical, and academic establishments—caused him agonies of guilt. The personal implications of

Janáček's operatic themes gave his work its acute reality, in a twentieth-century context, ravaged by war.

All Janáček's music—even his late adventures into the "abstract" medium of string quartet—has more to do with spoken language, gestural behavior, and ritual festivity than with art music in a concert hall. Another piece created during the war, between 1916 and 1919, is "chamber" music in that it is scored for tenor solo, with contralto solo, small women's chorus, and piano. Yet this song cycle, usually known in English as *Diary of a Young Man Who Vanished,* is in fact a mini-opera. Moreover, the tale it tells is from everyday life, for Janáček found the verses, purporting to be by a peasant youth, in a local provincial newspaper. Despite suspicions—quite recently confirmed—that the verses may have been written by an editor with literary ambitions, Janáček believed in their authenticity, the more so because after the work's publication and modest celebrity, no poet emerged to claim royalties.

In any case what matters is that the poems enact Janáček's basic tussle between nature and nurture, since the young farmer, lured by a gypsy who is as much animal as human, leaves hearth and home, racked by guilt. Autobiographical undertones are thus even more potent than they are in *Káťa Kabanová.* The gypsy is as liberating an agent for the young farmer as was Kamilla Stösslová for the old composer; indeed, in a letter to her Janáček overtly equates her with his gypsy siren. And the cycle's end, however uncertain the future may be for the gypsy-enthralled youth, is triumphant—as was, in the virility of his music, Janáček's own end. The tenor's high Cs—ringing proudly over resonant triads in "heroic" E flat major—fill us with the same exultation we feel when, after the blood-curdling organ solo that forms the penultimate movement of Janáček's last major work, the Glagolitic Mass, he rounds off that masterpiece with a pentatonically life-celebrating procession, blazing with trumpets and drums. We emerge from the dark church, and from the buffets of personal fate and impersonal destiny, into the sun, the wind, the rain, and the turning earth that is our temporal home. No composer believed in life more unequivocally, however dubious he may have been about human morality, God's goodness, and the iniquities and obliquities of fate.

Contemporary with his work on *Diary of a Young Man* Janáček embarked on a new opera in 1922. Whereas *Káťa Kabanová* and *Diary of a Young Man* were human dramas in the raw, the new opera, usually known in English as *Cunning Little Vixen,* assays a more allegorical approach to his central theme of nature and nurture. Even so, the libretto was in a sense a "slice of life" with immediately contemporary roots, since (like the *Diary of a Young Man*) it was triggered by a local newspaper, to which Janáček himself contributed. A journalist called Rudolf Těsnohlídek had an immense success with a series of animal cartoons, the "characters" of which became topical and local icons, like the Pip, Squeak, and Wilfrid of my English childhood. Těsnohlídek resembled Janáček in veering between manic exuberance and depressive instability, owing his ultimate success to his work's popular appeal and psychological awareness. As a man, he hardly triumphed over his difficulties, as did Janáček, for he had suicidal tendencies and was eventually arraigned for shooting his wife. It is more probable that she attempted to shoot herself, and the circumstances were too obscure for him to be committed; his literary success with his sprightly Vixen postdated his personal crisis. "People just went crazy over Sharp-ears," he remarked. "I began getting hysterical letters, postcards full of rude words, others full of praise."[3] By popular demand the series of newspaper items was published in book form a year later, with illustrations by Lolek. It remained long in print, sometimes in more than one edition simultaneously. Only in 1985 was the book, a minor classic of Czech literature, translated into English, with a vivacity appropriate to the original. Its enduring fame and its appeal to Janáček are attributable to its insights into the human psyche and into the interrelated worlds of birds, beasts, and insects. Whether or not Těsnohlídek murdered his wife, he apparently would have liked to, and while Janáček was in no way a murderous character, he may have seen a parallel in his own situation with his wife and Stösslová. In any case he was "bewitched" by Sharp-Ears no less than he was by his idolized (and idealized) Kamilla—and more justifiably so, since Broushka's medley of grace, wit, impudence, courage, and toughness, which made her a folk heroine with "the people,"was truer than fact, since Stösslová was a somewhat stodgy provincial woman who reciprocated Janáček's passion with intermittent kindness, but no more. Sharp-Ears was, like the gypsy in *Diary of a Young Man,* a fulfillment in dream, but never was dream fuller of earth and sap. It's worth noting that the Czech title of the cartoon book—*The Adventures of Vixen Sharp-Ears*—has no trace of the opprobrious implications of the English word *cunning.*

Janáček concocted his libretto from the newspaper articles and the later book, borrowing much of the vivacity of Těsnohlídek's prose. He omitted some elements unnecessary to the story and stressed rather than sentimentalized the tragic implications inherent in the cycles of nature by having Sharp-Ears accidentally shot by a gamekeeper—as Těsnohlídek may have shot his wife. Even this unpleasant accident is not, however, all loss, for the

Vixen's pelt becomes a muff for the country girl the gamekeeper marries. *Cunning Little Vixen* is the ultimate ecological opera; throughout, fables of birds and beasts coalesce with the sounds and sights of the human world, including its embryonic "civilization."

We open with an orchestral prelude presenting the natural world in what would be Edenic bliss, but for the presence of fallen humanity. The main theme—as usual with Janáček it may more accurately be described as a "gesture"—consists of four repeated eighth notes that then droop chromatically through a haze of buzzing and murmuring insects, magically scored for woodwind. This creates the atmosphere as well as the sounds of a summer afternoon. The key is basically A flat minor, for Janáček a death-haunted key at the ultimate point of tonal "flatness," though here it indicates that death is itself a natural process, for nature is a perpetual dying-into-life. In the course of the opera we are reminded that this applies to us human creatures as well as to the humming and buzzing ephemera, which is why Janáček's music of the natural world is not radically distinct from his gestural music for human beings, springing from spoken words and bodily movements. The notebooks that Janáček compiled, attempting to transcribe "the music of life," do not differentiate in notational terms between human speech rhythms and the cries of birds and beasts in the context of the arbitrary noises of the world.

In *Cunning Little Vixen* two technical features, recurrent in all his music, are even more than normally pervasive. The first is a pentatonicism in the melodic lines, since pentatonic formulas—which predominate in all folk musics and in children's chants and rhymes, whether in rural or in urban contexts—are those that spring most spontaneously from acoustical premises; the second is that both melodic and harmonic formulas are riddled with whole-tone progressions that of their nature do not, owing to their tritonal implications, progress. Pentatonicism and whole-tone obsessions were first exploited by the Russian "nationalists" who, aware of their geographical and cultural status outside "Europe," were proud of being technically instinctive, beyond German hegemony. We have noted the parallels between Janáček's "primitivism" and that of Moussorgsky; and no more than Moussorgsky did Janáček attempt, as did conservatory-trained Tchaikovsky in the dazzling finale to his Little Russian Symphony, to make folk and whole-tone formulas conformable with classical symphonic structure. He did not need to, since his interest in Moussorgsky paralleled that of Debussy, who relished whole-tone scales and harmonies *because* they denied the "functional" implication of classical and romantic harmony. Debussy, cultivating the "moment of sensation" in and for itself, sought nature's music and extravagantly claimed that there was more to be gained by watching the sun rise than by listening to the Pastoral Symphony. Although Janáček knew and admired Debussy's music, there is no question here of conscious imitation; it is merely that in celebrating nature, Janáček was venturing into Debussyan territory and collaterally called on Debussyan techniques. Already in the introduction to the opera we may savor the interfusion of creaturedom and humankind—aural synonyms for the activities of birds, beasts, and insects, and the gestures of human love and longing. Neither "develops," in the manner of "Western" music, but simply *is*. And although tonality is free, there is no conventional modulation, only a juxtaposition of reiterated motives at different pitches—moments which, like life itself, are consecutive without being consequential. Remarkably enough, Janáček's creature imitations, employing, three-quarters of a century back, only conventional instrumental resources, are scarcely less vivid in verisimilitude than are Peter Sculthorpe's in his Australian new world.

In the first scene the creatures specified are dragonfly, grasshopper, cricket, mosquito, and frog, all sung, danced, and mimed by children, whose innocence may have creaturely attributes. A badger's set is visible in the background, and the Badger is a very "set" creature, first seen smoking a human contrivance in the form of a pipe. Significantly, he resembles one of the human characters, the Parson, and both parts are sung by the same adult male, a ponderous bass rather than a heroic tenor. The relationships between the animal and the human members of Janáček's cast are subtle. The central character, the Forester, is the closest we humans can come to a "natural man," for he lives in and cares for the forest and its inhabitants, even though he does so for dubious, because humanly directed, ends. The Forester's Wife is allied to nature in being his wife, but is more dependent than he on the presumed benefits of human civilization; mistrustful of the wild creatures, she accepts only those that, being domesticated, are to a degree corrupted. The Schoolmaster nurtures distinctively human attributes, since he is devoted to education, which is beyond the creatures' capacities. It is doubtful, however, how far his higher interests promote happiness, and his own life is sadly unfulfilled. The Parson hopefully deals in souls, which the beasts aren't aware of having. The illusoriness of his God is more evident than that of the Schoolmaster's God, and it is to the point that he physically resembles the earth-delving Badger. His unflowing music is singularly unspiritual.

The intrusion of the human world on the creatures becomes palpable when the Forester, a natural baritone, enters, bearing his faithful (but lethal) friend, his gun. Out on a search for poachers (human malefactors), he sits down by a lake for a nap in the afternoon sun, while the creatures Edenically frolic around him—and intermittently gobble one another up. A young Vixen, in this preludial scene played by a child, frisks in, and is startled by and tries to catch a frog who, leaping to safety, lands on the Forester's nose. Rudely awakened, he spots the Vixen, the sight of whom releases the beast latent in him, as in all of us. Animal-like, he pounces on her, with the intention of taking her home as a playmate for his children. However appealing to the kiddies, this is a death for the Vixen. The scene ends tersely, in (of course) A flat minor.

Time passes, as it will, and the scene moves to the Forester's lodge, on a sunny afternoon in autumn, or the *Fall*. The Vixen, growing up, is now played by an adult (preferably beautiful) soprano. She is being fed with milk, like a domestic cat, by the Forester's Wife, who, oblivious of the Vixen's beauty, disapproves of her wildness and dirtiness. The Vixen chats with Lapák, a pet dog who is domesticated enough to be played by a man, not a boy. He's amiable but, being humanly despoiled, is also miserable; lonesome and wifeless, he is obliged to seek the consolations of Art. Just like us, he makes up Sad Songs about Love and Life. The Vixen confesses that she is too young to know much about such matters, though she has picked up a few hints from the rascally starlings and crafty cuckoos. She grows exasperated with the complaining yet complacent hound, as with the Forester's children, who tease her, as well as the dog and cat. That creature corruption is not, however, inevitable on human contact is suggested when, as dusk falls, the Vixen visionarily transforms herself into a young girl, who dances and angelically *flies* to ravishing G flat major love music. This is a fifth lower than D flat, Janáček's habitual love key, which may suggest that animals are a gateway to human rebirth, as the gypsy was for the young farmer, as Stösslová was for Janáček, and as in this opera the Vixen will be for the Forester, and possibly even for the Schoolmaster and the Parson.

In the immediate present, however, the visionary humanizing of the Vixen triggers a small crisis, for when she spots a flock of hens grubbing about in the courtyard, her animal blood reasserts itself. No creatures could be more servilely enslaved to human values than these clones who are happy to work hard, lay eggs, cackle, and bear it. Appalled, the Vixen attacks them ("Friends, sisters, abolish the old order! Create a new world where you will get your fair share of joy and happiness"), thereby enraging the Forester's Wife who, swearing at the Vixen, chases her off with a yell of "You BEAST!" In the commotion, the Vixen snaps her tether, knocks over the Forester, and escapes into the wild woods. The act ends with beastly and avian squawks and skirmishes and with flickering whole-tone scales, interspersed with the Vixen's cries and gestures—compound both of her need for nature's freedom and of her latent aspirations toward "consciousness." The end is abrupt, like the ends of Bruckner's large-scale symphonic allegros that often present humans in the context of nature. The key is E flat major, the major dominant of Janáček's deathly A flat minor; death, with the Vixen's escape, has been momentarily defeated. It's a happy coincidence that E flat major was Beethoven's key of heroism.

If in the first act we've observed the gypsy-Vixen's impact on the human world, in the second act she appears to have learned something from humanity, even in our fallen state. The act begins outside the Badger's set, in the late afternoon. The music is animal-like in its ostinato rhythm and in its teetering whole-tone motif that involves the traditionally devilish tritone; but it also hints at the Badger's humanly old-fogeyish temperament, as distinct from the Vixen's vivacity. Her conversation with the Badger is enlivened with her motif of freedom (pentatonic, with prancing sixth). She sees the Badger as nature's compromise with human establishmentarianism; hating it, she teases him and drives him out of his set. He lollops off, morally outraged, as though he *were* a human being; she, emulating the deception of the cuckoo, takes over his house. Perhaps her cunning is post-lapsarian, for the scene ends in deathly A flat minor.

Moreover, an orchestral interlude transports us into the human world: an inn, where the Forester is chatting to the Parson (who looks and sounds like the Badger) and to the Schoolmaster. They're talking of old times, when they were lads in love, or at least in love with love. They all feel they have been betrayed by their women or dreams of women, but are reluctant to admit that they may have contributed to their betrayals. Mysteriously the Vixen—who had seemed antihuman in the scene outside the Badger's set—now becomes an incarnation of human dreams and sexual fantasies. The human music is at first in folky peasant style, in short fourth-founded phrases insistently reiterated, going nowhere. The harmony, undermined by whole tones, is also directionless. The Parson and Schoolmaster have failed as "conscious" human beings, while being unable to accept nature's blessed unconsciousness. Their motif of regret—rather than of yearning—is in a cross between A flat minor and D flat major: Janáček's keys of death and of love.

Leaving the inn, they trudge off through the night, drearily drunk. The forest they enter is, both within and without the mind, dark indeed, though it is intermittently irradiated with moonlight, as are the dark forests in *Verklärte Nacht* and *Erwartung*. The Schoolmaster, a quavery tenor, *moons* over memories or dreams of love lost, and in his fuddled state mistakes a moon-drenched sunflower for his dearly departed and long-lamented beloved. But the dream girl is really the Vixen, hiding behind a sunflower, and momentarily her presence becomes real as the music suddenly flowers, of course in "loving" D flat major. Meanwhile the bass-voiced Parson-Badger blunders on *his* night walk, his tipsy meditations contorted in rhythm and gruff in timbre, as compared with the Schoolmaster's bleating tenor. His empty fifths and jittery dotted rhythms search for a love lost not merely yesteryear, but long, long ago, in his student days. His lost beloved becomes incarnate in the Vixen who, like the young farmer's gypsy, flashes dazzling eyes from the bushes—and from the sunflower that, like William Blake's, aspires from the grave to "that sweet golden clime / Where the traveller's journey is done." The Forester, younger and more in command of his liquor, spots the Vixen and yells aloud, so that she vanishes in a twinkling. The Schoolmaster and Parson, robbed of their vision and returned to their hazy senses, totter morosely home.

From the disillusioned humans we move back to the animal kingdom and the Vixen's nonhuman fulfillment—glorious as compared with the humans. For the second scene is in tandem with the first, while being also its opposite. Originally, Janáček had intended to make it a separate act, but changed his mind, presumably because he wanted to point out a relation of opposites. Nature cries reverberate around the Vixen's burrow (stolen from the compromisingly human Badger), outside which she lies at ease, muzzle on paws. The nature cries, pentatonic with open fourths, are in A flat *major,* complement of deadly A flat minor, but veer to D flat major, the love key. The wordless cantillation shifts between pentatonicism and the Lydian mode, which embraces the duplicitous tritone, and was traditionally associated with healing— perhaps *because* it's unafraid of the Devil. What is hopefully being healed is the breach between humanity and nature, and at first the healing seems to be on beastly terms. For in this scene the Vixen is courted, and won, by the Lion Fox, who, stepping from the moonlit bushes, handsome and debonair, engages in polite conversation about the weather, far more "civilized" than Parson or Schoolmaster or most of us. His part is sung by a soprano, perhaps because Janáček associates the beasts with instinct and intuition and females; only humanly corrupted animals like dogs and (somewhat surprisingly) badgers are personified by males in this work. The Vixen explains to the fox that she is a hybrid, having been educated "on human lines," in the Forester's house. But she justifiably boasts of her courage in freeing herself: "He struck me . . . and I ran away. I've been an animal since. The forest was darker than night, but I felt free." She has no need of the illusory moonlight, by which the inebriated humans were deceived.

This is the beginning of the animal love scene, the high point of the opera. Characteristically, Janáček studied the mating habits of foxes, as well as their "language" and body movements. Their antics are precisely auralized in the music, and as the foxy lovers burgeon from ritual ceremony into passion there is a (literally?) ravishing fusion of creature music with human love music almost Pucciniesque in ardor. Inevitably, this is centered on D flat major, but with fiery intrusions of the tonic minor and with ecstatic cross-rhythms of twos against threes against fives. The repeated patterns carry the lovers and us orgiastically outside time, with the climax arriving in animal yells falling in whole-tone arpeggios from high B flat to A, then A flat, G, and G flat. The act ends with a paean of created nature, as the wordless chorus takes up the mating chant, interwoven with the pentatonic and Lydian incantation of the act's prelude.

So far humanity and nature have been presented in their presumptive interdependence, but have also revealed differences and contradictions. The third act deals with the tragedy inherent in this disparity, but demonstrates that it is really no tragedy at all, or at least that a choice between tragedy and triumph is available. The orchestral introduction is a superb example of Janáček's gestural music, for it grips us by the scruff of the neck in the venom with which it makes hunting and stalking aurally incarnate. The rhythm and orchestration are ferocious (beastly); tonality mingles whole tones and chromatics in D flat major-minor, veering wildly to the mediant E (standing for F flat) and to the subdominant A flat minor. The stalking hunter turns out to be a poacher, Harašta, who—representing humanity as predator—sings a quasi-folk song in C sharp (equivalent to D flat) minor, about a mythical girl lover who wears an ecologically green skirt. He goes to pick up a dead hare, killed by the Vixen, now a mother, to feed her cubs. The Forester confronts Harašta, with whom, indeed, he is identified, if we recall how the gamekeeper had pounced on the adolescent Vixen when he first saw her. Poacher and gamekeeper, at once enemies and friends, chat about the escaped Vixen: a conversation that prompts Harašta to tell the Forester that he is about to marry the beautiful Terynka, momentarily identified with several lost loves and, by inference, with the Vixen. The traditional equation between sex and death, love and war, is a perennial process reenacted in the next scene, beginning with the entry of the adult fox lovers with their cubs, who dance and sing a merry funeral ceremony around the dead hare.

Fox and Vixen indulge in another love scene, now tenderly mellow, as they try to remember how many children they've had and to speculate on how many they may yet have. Harašta's song about *his* love sounds distantly but raucously, the Vixen remarking that it's a dreadful racket, as it audibly is, compared with the Fox's lovely, openly arpeggiated D flat major melody. Harašta's metrically rigid ditty recalls the savage foreboding of the orchestral prelude to the act and leads to a confrontation—balancing that between Forester and Vixen in act 1—between the human poacher (who may be construed as a Fallen Forester) and the beasts. A frantic skirmish ensues, during which Harašta, confused, angry, embittered, aims his gun at random, this gun being an engine of destruction, no "faithful friend." Acting as arbitrarily as nature, he shoots the Vixen, an act more heinous than nature's, since he, being at least *in potentia* conscious, might have known better. He leaves the Vixen dying, to amorphously floating fourths and fifths, still over a pedal D flat.

The final scene of the action is appropriately betwixt and between humanity and nature, for it takes place in a *garden* behind the inn, converted by artifact-making humans into a spruce bowling green: green as God's grass, but regimented as human architecture. The orchestral prelude is irresolute, dissipating in whole tones and figurations at once physical yet vague, as befits baffled and insecure mortals. Human formalization begins to impose itself as the Forester tells his wife that the Vixen's burrow has been deserted, in music registering anguished consciousness of loss, as well as the desolation of the burrow. The Schoolmaster broods on the parallel between the death of the Vixen and the loss of the lovely Terynka to the dastardly Harašta. The Forester laments the aging of everyone, including his humanized, graying hound. We all chase shadows, as did the Parson and the Schoolmaster when they pursued the Vixen amid the moony sunflowers. The motif of regret sighs in love's D flat major, frail consolation for us creatures who are unique in *knowing* that, in Ben Jonson's words, "you grow old while I tell you this."

For the epilogic scene we return to the gully wherein the opera had opened. The sun peeps out as the Forester walks *uphill*, meditating on his youth when he and his girl (his wife or the legendary lost love or Terynka or the Vixen) were a sleek spruce and a young fir tree, as sparky as the foxy lovers. Exhausted, he nonetheless relishes the beauty of the forest and the humming and buzzing of the creatures. Casting aside *his* "faithful friend," his gun, he sits among the flowers, to quotations from the first bars of the opera. Snoozing, he dreams of the girl who is also the Vixen. Starting into wakefulness, he imagines the Vixen is in front of him, though it is really one of her cubs, resembling her mother, at least to human eyes. A frog jumps on his nose and explains that he's not the frog who hazardously leapt at the beginning of the opera; that was his grandfather. Nature's fecundity is indestructible; the Vixen's death, albeit arbitrary, is no occasion for sentiment, let alone sentimentality. The last section begins with the motif of regret, an emotion of which only we humans are capable. Even so, if we can live in communion with nature and find renewal in its recurrences, regret need not overwhelm us. So the opera ends with another paean to nature, again in D flat major and only a shade less triumphant than the paean of the mated beasts at the end of act 2. Again it is cut off abruptly—as by a Forester's axe or gun—again, we think of Bruckner, though Janáček's nature worship has no need of Bruckner's Christian burden.

It suffices that the forest *endures.* At least it did for Janáček, though whether it can for us is an open question, since industrial pollution and human rapacity threaten the Moravian forests hardly less disastrously than they threaten the rain forests of South America. Janáček's parable of humankind and nature was deeply meaningful when it was created just after World War I. With the passage of time it has become no less meaningful and more desperate. Listening to the blaze of these final pages we pay tribute to a victory of human courage, while recognizing that there can never be another Janáček. It is not a pious reflection, but sober truth, that we shall not look upon his like again.

NOTES

1. Jean Sibelius quoted in Bengt de Törne, *Sibelius: A Close-Up* (Boston: Houghton Mifflin, 1938), 84.

2. Karl Ekman, *Jean Sibelius,* trans. Edward Birse (Helsingfors: Holger Schildts Förlag, 1935), 207–8.

3. Rudolf Těšnohlídek, *Cunning Little Vixen,* trans. Tatiana Firkusny, Maritza Morgan, and Robert T. Jones (New York: Farrar, Straus, and Giroux, 1985), 179.

PART TWO

The Forest Without

5

Charles Koechlin and *le Forêt Féerique*

DEBUSSY WAS AT ONCE a flower of French civilization and a suavely subversive revolutionary whose crucial significance was soon apparent. Charles Koechlin, born in 1867 and thus only five years Debussy's junior, was no less a flower of French civilization and possibly no less revolutionary. Yet he remained a peripheral figure little known to concertgoers, even though he worked at the heart of French musical academia and in an enclave of musicians that included Debussy, Erik Satie, Gabriel Fauré, and Maurice Ravel. Alsatian by heritage, he was in French culture both an insider and an outsider. He "belonged" in that he was heir to French civilization from the Middle Ages to the High Baroque—with Berlioz as an iconoclastic appendage—and also in that he saw no contradiction in being simultaneously a theorist and an "advanced" composer. His first teacher was Massenet, an academician who also purveyed the delights of French opera tragic, sentimental, comic, and farcical; his main mentor was Fauré, who combined exquisite harmonic sensibility with craft and counterpoint, revering Bach just this side of idolatry.

Fauré, though neither religiously nor mystically inclined, paid lip service to French Catholicism; Debussy identified religious sensibility with his fin de siècle sense of beauty; Koechlin made do with an awareness of aesthetic tradition. During his early years Koechlin, coming from an affluent family, was able to indulge his aestheticism, creating prolifically. But his fortune dissipated during World War I, and, with a family to support, Koechlin needed to bolster his pecuniary resources. He did this by producing textbooks on counterpoint, fugue, orchestration, and the craft of composition. These often massive tomes are not citations of preordained rules but deductions from the practice of composers: quintessentially Bach, but also Renaissance polyphonists and living composers, including himself. The books are still valuable, which is not surprising, since Koechlin's numerous minor works, such as the sonatinas and smaller suites for piano, reveal the affinity between his pedagogy and his awareness of inherited but still vital traditions. The modal themes, the dovetailed counterpoint, the luminous diatonic sonorities in these works, written during or soon after the war years, offer the refreshment of a *premier matin du monde*. Satiean in being childlike but not infantile, the tunes are purely modal, and regular barring is dispensed with, the rhythms being free though never congested. The limpidity of the themes depends on a prevalence of conjunct motion mingled with open fourths and fifths. Piled up fourths and fifths give radiance to the harmony, while the modulations favor the basic tonal props of dominant and subdominant; momentarily, they may become recondite without losing clarity, since they are defined by the fluid polyphony. None of the movements cultivates sonata-style architecture; either they are brief binary dances or ternary airs or they are contrapuntal and in particular canonic—derivatives of children's round games. This music is traditional in refashioning the luminosity of French Renaissance music as exemplified in the *chansons* of composers such as Claudin de Sermisy or Guillaume de Costeley. Koechlin's keyboard idiom translates this vocal style into instrumental terms; the diatonic tunes, the flowing rhythms, the consonant harmony create an aural equivalent to sunlit distance: a never-never land that is ever-ever because it lives within the heart.

It is surely relevant to Koechlin's equivocal position between reality and dream, and between the city and the jungle, that so many of the French tunes he emulates or occasionally quotes are hybrids between "unconscious" folk traditions and the domesticated "nursery rhyme" or urbanized pop song that owes its celebrity in part to social and political, sometimes overtly military, events. "Frère Jacques," "Au clair de la lune," "Sur le pont d'Avignon," and "Marlbrouk s'en va-t-en guerre" are merely the best-known instances in which musical and mimetic behavior is hardly separable from the historical and mythological occurrences that made figures like Frère Jacques and Marlborough folk heroes. In "Marlbrouk," for instance, the catchy tune and processional movement combined with military history to win a place for the song in Beaumarchais's fabulously successful quasi-political play, while at the same time it appealed to the romantics' obsession with the humanity of popular song. The Duke of Marlborough became a childhood hero, and ultimately a household name, in many lands. We might even hazard that this motif links Koechlin's awareness of the embryonic consciousness (and mystery) of childhood to his concern with radical social-political causes, though this is not evident in the earliest of his works to attain maturity.

These are "early" because he lived so long and wrote so much, though he was in his forties when he produced the piano suite *Paysages et marines:* pieces that created havens of quiet during the years of World War I. Here the canonic clarities of the piano *sonatines* function on several planes polytonally, clouding a child's wonder with transient shadows. The diatonicism of the *sonatines* is modified by greater plasticity of line: conjunct motion and fourths and fifths still predominate, but modality becomes increasingly ambiguous, since the lines may have more than one tonal center. Counterpoint is sparse; often the parts are doubled in fourths or fifths or tripled in ninths, as in medieval organum; parallel triads may produce clashes between chords fundamentally concordant. In "Soir d'été," for instance, the flexible vocal-style themes, their modal and rhythmic flexibility, and the hollowness of the textures temper the smiling quietude of the childlike pieces; lyricism becomes more rarefied, as it grows into a more adult experience. Yet although the polyharmonies are sometimes abstruse and even chromatic—as in "Paysages d'octobre"—the effect of consonance is not relinquished, since one hears the components of the chords on several planes simultaneously. Even the exceptional appearance of a diminished seventh early in this piece or the static Debussyan ninths in "Poème Virgilien" or the ravishing closing section of "Chanson des pommiers" acquire a gleaming precision; in effect, if not in technical fact, the harmony remains closer to the linear idiom of the fifteenth or sixteenth century than to the chromaticism of the nineteenth. "Chant de pêcheur," one of the typical *ronde français* melodies, contains passages of parallel fourths and, ultimately, seconds.

It is difficult to think of any music—with the possible exception of the sea cavern scenes in Debussy's *Pelléas et Mélisande*—more unearthly, more surreal, in effect. It's worth noting too that the visionary, quasi-surrealistic elements in Koechlin's music seem to be connected with the vernality of childhood, as is suggested by another suite of piano pieces. According to Koechlin himself, the pieces comprising *L'Ancienne maison de campagne,* put together between 1923 and 1933, are aural reminiscences of days spent in childhood on his grandfather's estate near Lake Zurich, as far back as 1882. The polymodal, polyphonic, and polyharmonic techniques are simpler, more "childish," than those of *Paysages et marines,* but are similar in principle; and that the boy Koechlin in one piece identifies the little wood where he and his playmates frolicked with a savage jungle bears on his later obsession with the *nouvelles aventures* of the *Jungle Books* of Kipling.

The title, *Paysages et marines,* accurately identifies the sources of Koechlin's inspiration, which is in elemental instinct. This is why the daylight of his French musical influences tends to merge into the unchartable forest and illimitable ocean, as happens in most of the works of his middle years, many of which are called sonatas, though none is in sonata form. Mostly written between 1915 and 1925, these works are for a melody instrument—because the heart of Koechlin's music is unaccompanied song—and piano (because this polyphonic-harmonic instrument may be treated as an orchestral concourse of lines without ceasing to be pianistic). Of these sonatas, the one for horn and piano, begun in 1918 but not finished until 1925, is perhaps the most basic: unsurprisingly, since the horn in its beautiful "natural" form (for which Koechlin often composed) is a melody instrument that makes its own pitches as does a human voice. In no single work is Koechlin's delicate yet dangerous equilibrium between civilization and the dark forest more palpable.

The first movement evokes the forest that surrounds Debussy's lost human creatures in *Pelléas et Mélisande.* In Koechlin's sonata, however, the forest brings balm to ravaged spirits: the opening theme of the slow introduction, both melodically and harmonically pervaded by open fourths and fifths, is purely modal and ineffably calm—a light inherent in, if never known on, land or sea. The irrational aspects of the forest emerge, however, as the introduction's natural harmonics on horn float into what the composer calls a "gallop"—hunting music fraught with the perils of the chase, yet preserving the regality of the genre. Golaud's ill-fated boar hunt comes to mind, though the slow movement that succeeds the gallop is more redolent of the civilized parlor that succored Koechlin's teacher, Fauré. Even so, the forest bides within our social proprieties, as it does within the daylit innocence of children: so both Fauré's and Koechlin's domestic musics are tinged with enharmonic mysteries and rhythmic obliquities. From the finale of Koechlin's horn sonata any hint of a Parisian salon is banished, for the piece is both wild and heroic, exuberant in open textures and triple-rhythmed body movement. Koechlin said it evokes the sea, which surely bears on the simultaneous blessing and curse the sea brings to *Pelléas's* forest-enshrouded castle. But if the sea in Koechlin's horn sonata is at once life-enhancing and inimical, it is ultimately positive in effect since it leads into a coda recreating the tranced tranquility of the introduction.

The flute, traditionally associated with nature and the pagan god Pan, is hardly less magical than the horn, as is testified by that crucial monody for solo flute composed by Debussy in 1913, just before the onslaught of World War I. Koechlin's sonata for flute and piano, dating from 1915, "travels in imaginary worlds," evoking nature in Mediterranean sun and starry skies and in the twilight of summer nights. Again the slow movement, a songful *siciliano,* is more "humanized" than the wide-spaced, free-flowing first movement, or even than the triple-rhythmed gallop "en plein air" of the finale, wherein energy is disciplined by counterpoint, with canonic "points" on the interval of a falling fourth. Though the sonata is less *mystérieux* than the horn sonata, its end is magical in being ecstatic.

Of deeper substance is the oboe and piano sonata, composed between 1911 and 1918, but not performed until 1925. Traditionally a pastoral instrument, the oboe has romantic undertones, so we are not surprised when the first movement, having welcomed the great outdoors, ends in twilight and brooding night. The large-scale scherzo presents a faun dancing in the forest, a mercurial harlequinade that, capering through what Koechlin calls "fanciful bitonality," transforms Pan into a whirling dervish. But Koechlin's contrapuntal precision resists chaos, so the slow movement may be another grave *cantilena* for oboe, filigree-embroidered by piano. The finale is more civilized, in what Koechlin called his "familiar" vein. Even so, it flows compulsively, like the sea, embracing polymodal equivocations.

Although most of Koechlin's sonatas are for pastoral wind instruments, he also created, during his vintage decade from 1915 to 1925, a cello sonata, a viola sonata, and a big violin and piano sonata that may be his major achievement in chamber music. None of its four movements is in sonata form; all make from the incongruous mating of lyrical violin with modern concert grand a strange ethereality. The work opens, in sharply radiant B major, with a slow movement on a long, flowing, diatonic theme, typically mingling conjunct motion with open fourths and fifths; the piano part is wide-spaced, with many major ninths and tenths; the directive is "calme, lumineux, et féerique." Evolution is linear, with organum effects in the inner parts, the polymodality of which does not sully the calm. The scherzo is preluded by muted quasi-horn effects "dans un décor de forêt légendaire." But the substance of the movement is a triple-rhythmed rondo underpinned by drones on open fifths, soon expanded to ninths. The surging spaciousness relates the piece to Koechlin's sea music rather than to his forest murmurs; its polymodality and polymeter hint at danger as well as mystery. Against this open-airiness the slow movement is again nocturnal, "grave et féerique." The melody has no defined tonal center; the organum devices—piled up fifths making major ninths—carry the techniques of *Paysages et marines* into even more disembodied exaltation. The coda has a lovely airiness in its violin melody, in its superimposed fifths, and in the cunning placing of the tenths in the piano's left hand.

The finale is on a scale proportionate to the work, being a polyphonic rondo with a main theme reminiscent of a French folk dance, initially accompanied by bare fifths. The first episode, un- or freely barred, has suave polyphonic contours that sound archaic (fifteenth century?), though the modality grows ambiguous as the themes are canonically extended. References to the first rondo tune recur as guidelines through the melée. The polyphonic, polymodal, polyharmonic, and polymetrical piano part is difficult to negotiate, and Koechlin talked of making an orchestral version of it—as he did of other sonatas for melody instrument and piano. He didn't get around to this, perhaps because he came to realize that the piano idiom works beautifully on its own terms, given an empathetic pianist. This becomes impressively evident when, through a coda of tumultuous arpeggiated fifths, the rondo's original tonality of D major is metamorphosed into the shining B major in which the sonata had opened, a further notch up the cycle of fifths from "celestial" E major. The work's peroration is a broad chanting of the main rondo melody over diatonic triads, often with added seconds. Although the resonance is powerful, it remains luminous, since the absolute consonances still dominate the harmony. The music creates an aural equivalent for intensely white light. It is a pity that this majestic and mysterious, if admittedly difficult, sonata is infrequently performed.

In all these piano pieces and chamber works Koechlin creates what he calls "imaginary landscapes" that are basically Old French, while embracing classical antiquity in both its civilizing rationality and in its vestiges of primal irrationality; consider the quasi-monodic Pan-piping in "Le Chevrier" from *Paysages et marines.* If the decor is what Renaissance people called Arcadian, we must remember that the real Arcadia in ancient Greece was not picturesquely civilized but wildly barbaric; its mythical reputation as a paradise on earth derived from its being remote, and therefore unknown. This bears on the link between Koechlin's elegant landscapes and the elements in his music that, dealing in nightmares as well as in daydreams, hint at savagery and peril. Sometimes, as in *Les Heures Persanes,* he makes specific reference to the "magic of the East." But this set of sixteen piano pieces, inspired by the travel writings of Pierre Loti and perhaps by the *Arabian Nights,* is no more Eastern in technique than are *Paysages et marines;* their mystery lies in that they are a *voyage imaginaire* that effaces temporal progression in their slow pulse or pulselessness and in ornament, gyrating around nodal points. Even the few fast pieces disown progression: the one depicting crowds swarming in city streets swirls, as do crowds, without direction, while the climactic movement, "Derviches dans la nuit," whirls, as dervishes are wont, so fast that the dancers become, in T. S. Eliot's words, a "still point of the turning world." To listen to these mostly very slow and very soft pieces in sequence makes for an experience even stranger than that of hearing *Paysages et marines,* since tranquility proves not only narcotic but also hallucinatory, as the pieces trace a succession of two days and nights, irradiated by the sun, soothed by the light of the moon. Cosmological light and dark are a recurrent theme in Koechlin's work; here they are presented *in essentia,* in a piano idiom potently sensuous, yet oddly disembodied. This other-worldly work was created between 1913 and 1918, contemporaneously with World War I.

As happens so often in Koechlin's piano writing, in *Les Heures Persanes* the two hands we are equipped with often seem insufficient, perhaps because Koechlin, like his hero Berlioz, composed from melody "outwards," completing each line as an entity before adding other parts. This is a sophistication of the practice of medieval and early Renaissance polyphonists, about whom Koechlin was well informed, and even in his large symphonic works he seldom cultivates Teutonic sonata style but rather explores dream and myth through polymodal polyphonies similar to those of *Paysages et marines* and *Les Heures Persanes.* Indeed, in 1921 Koechlin made of *Les Heures Persanes* an orchestral version that he believed was one of his most significant works. The difference between the piano and the orchestral version is comparable with that between a black-and-white film and colored images in virtual reality. The piano sonorities glimmer with mysteries; the orchestral textures—with sustained drones on strings, tremulous woodwind arabesques, and reverberations of harp or vibraphone to make the roses of Isphahan glow *au soleil du midi*— create an aural world in which we live, move, and have our being—much as, in listening to Ives's *Central Park in the Dark,* we inhabit that spooky place while the sounds last. Although Koechlin's piano version is effectively marvelous, the orchestral version is extraordinary. Unfortunately it is rarely played, though fine recordings of both versions now make comparisons feasible.

But an orchestral work even bigger than *Les Heures Persanes* became Koechlin's best-known work by reputation, if not through frequency of performance. It may not be fortuitous that this work, or series of works, has a source doubly remote from Koechlin's beloved France; for the *Jungle Books* were written in the last decade of the nineteenth century by an Englishman, Rudyard Kipling: the only major writer to hymn the pride and prejudice of industrialized, imperialized Edwardian Britain and to find in the colonial dream a parable of nature and nurture—of the relationship between the jungle and civilization—that encapsulates the main theme of this book. For Kipling's Indian tales and verses—principally *Plain Tales from the Hills,* the

two *Jungle Books,* and *Kim*—see the East-West experience in terms of an idealized community in which "natural" and humanly contrived values weigh
equally. In the *Jungle Books* Mowgli is a white boy who, mislaid in the jungle,
is reared by beasts who are molded by the Law of the Jungle—pragmatic standards that have rudimentary, but possibly profound, relationships to human
morality and behavior, since the Law, however ill-defined, is (as Angus Wilson has put it) the "absolute and categorical barrier that stands between man
and anarchy, and, more importantly, between man and the probably mean-
ingless death and destruction that await him and all his works."[1] The Mowgli
tales take place in a world that is at once the reality we live in and the Garden of Eden—Kipling's dream of childhood—and if Mowgli is a human
creature who returns to nature, the creatures who nurture him are at once
superb in their instinctual creaturedom and images of human potential. The
hieratic language the creatures speak reveals their simultaneously bestial and
human state, climactically in "The King's Ankus," in which the immemorially ancient white cobra reveals to Mowgli the lust for possessions that (nega-
tively) distinguishes human from beast. Finally, in "The Spring Running,"
the Leopard explains how the jungle Law differs from human laws, in that it
cannot allow for laughter or tears. This is why Mowgli has to leave the jungle
Eden and be transformed into Kim, the hero of Kipling's supreme achievement. For Kim, though not jungle-reared, is still a child of nature who would
pragmatically be a "Friend to All the World." Kim is also a pilgrim companion to a holy lama: the one guilelessly committed to the world as it passes,
the other committed to self-abnegation and a reality beyond the flux.

Given that *Kim* and the *Jungle Books* are simultaneously about the Imperial Dream and the adolescent innocence necessary to sustain it, we may
understand why the books' techniques batten alike on literary and oral traditions, as is still more obvious in the marvelous *Just So Stories* for younger
children which, written in the following year (1902), make use of narrative
techniques, incantatory refrains, and mimetic rhythms such as are common
to fairy tales and orally transmitted sagas. The *Just So* creatures inhabit the
same human-mythical region as do the nurturing beasts in the *Jungle Books,*
and it is not difficult to understand why such beings should invite projection in musical terms. No wonder the *Jungle Books* seduced Koechlin, as they
did a very different composer, the Australian Percy Grainger, when his father
presented him with the books in 1897.[2]

Koechlin embarked on his *Jungle Book* settings at about the same time,
though the two men cannot have known one another's music. Koechlin's
earliest vocal and orchestral jungle pieces, being parasitic on Wagner's works

and on Debussy's early nature musics, are far from being vintage Koechlin. A slow starter, he was in his forties when, in 1911, he produced the first of his four symphonic poems on the *Jungle Books,* wherein the reasons for his obsession with them become triumphantly audible. The pieces form a purely orchestral totality, though they were written over a wide span of years, from 1911 to 1939. In the order in which they are usually performed, these symphonic poems trace a cycle from Blakean innocence to experience, perennially recurring, like a fairy tale, "for ever and ever." Significantly, the movement that stands first, though it was not the first to be composed, is called "La Loi de la jungle" (1934) and defines the Laws of Nature in monodic terms—which we have seen to be the basis of Koechlin's approach to composition. There is a single theme, monodic, monolithic, modal. Melodic lines and percussive rhythm, unharmonized, reverberate like the forest, with no development, only repetition, which, slightly varied, becomes a tortoiselike form of evolution, as unsentimental as nature itself. Occasionally, monody expands into an organum of parallel fourths or fifths, which does not affect the monophonic principle. Such growth as there is thus resembles that of nature, which, having its own laws, is not identified with chaos. The strangeness of the music suggests, however, that nature's laws, if pertinent to us, are not ours.

The acuity of Koechlin's ear in hearing this humanly elusive monody is remarkable; the second movement, "Les Bandar-Log" (1939) is celebrated as one of the marvels of twentieth-century orchestral writing. Its cunning is related to the fact that this is the furthest the jungle gets from nature's primal law, for it is about the animals closest to humans, apes, through whose frantic antics nature aspires to our kind of consciousness. The music begins predictably enough by evoking nature by way of polymodality springing from nature's primeval fourths and fifths. Nature's quietude is soon perturbed by the gibbering simians, whose squawks are scored with dazzling virtuosity. For the apes, like humans, try out one clever trick after another, offering near-parodies of expressionism, impressionism, serialism, perhaps even of electronic music. These parodies are at once grotesque and serious, since they indicate how *imitation* threatens nature's validity. Academic fugue is a negation in this polymodal, polymetrical piece, as it is in Ives's Fourth Symphony, written more than twenty years previously, though it cannot have been known to Koechlin in the thirties. Although Koechlin's polymorphous scherzo is alarmingly pertinent to us, we cannot identify with it. The coda reaffirms nature's fourth- and fifth-founded infinitudes. Timelessly, the jungle survives our apish assaults.

In this ape movement nature veers toward humanity; in "La Méditation de Parun-Baghat" (1936) humanity seeks to identify with nature. The literary source of this piece is not the *Jungle Books* but *Plain Tales of the Hills;* its theme, however, is linked to that of the *Jungle Books* and is very close to *Kim,* since it is about a government official of presence and portent who relinquishes power to commune with God in a mountainous wilderness. Koechlin's musicking of the fine tale begins with a drone, over which murmurs a monody. But whereas the monody of the first movement was both lawful and awe-ful, this monody, being that of a human being rather than of the jungle, is freely expansive, recalling both Christian plainchant and Buddhist incantation. Imperceptibly monody flowers into harmonic polyphony, the open spaces of which remind us of Koechlin's wind-and-mountain music in his quasi-medieval French works. Here, however, the open fourths, fifths, and ninths also suggest the open spaces music of a New World composer, Aaron Copland; and there's a deeper affinity with that American master of the asphalt jungle, Charles Ives, especially with the nature mysticism of the Thoreau movement of the Concord Sonata. Indeed, Koechlin's nature mysticism has much in common with that of the (part-time) hermit of Walden Pond. Opting out, this music evades tension between mortal human passion and the mountains' immortal imperviousness—a tension such as typifies the surging rhythms and wailing appoggiaturas of Delius's *Song of the High Hills.*

The last and most magnificent of the linked symphonic poems was the first to be composed (between 1911 and 1927), though it wasn't performed until 1932. It is inspired by Kipling's epilogic tale from the *Second Jungle Book,* recounting Mowgli's leaving the jungle at the (belated) onset of puberty. Lasting half an hour, the piece is a consummation of Koechlin's music that inspired his friend Darius Milhaud to hazard that it was a seed from which the most forward-looking music of the *next* generation would spring. With no barriers between modality, tonality, and atonality, "La Course du printemps" (Kipling's title was "The Spring Running") evokes the stirring of spring in human and beast, this time with the crucial difference that a man is discovering the dimension in his life that is beyond brute creation. The piece's kaleidoscopic structure emulates that of life itself, from the nature murmurings of the beginning through the chitter of birds and yowls of animals to the thudding of Mowgli's padding feet and pounding heart. The music, driven by burgeoning sexuality, seeks a restored whole; it stops and starts, uncertain of when or where. The scrunchy, sappy sonorities again remind us of Ives (in, for instance, *Three Places in New England*), for they effect a collocation of opposites which—like Ives's whirling leaves and water and his independently parading bands—merge into nature's eternal present. The form is a vast rondo, since after each exuberant "running" the forest returns to near-immobility, only for the next running to take off even more strenuously, ultimately to climax with creaturely commotion in full pelt. Mowgli bounds back from the jungle to *human* life that nonetheless, after this initiation rite, can never be the same. Although the piece closes on an Ivesian Unanswered Question, as the coda reinstates the jungle-in-itself, this proves to be Koechlin's message to humankind, as distinct from the birds, beasts, and reptiles. The energy of the music's loping motor rhythms in 6/8 or 12/8, the surging concatenations of strings, woodwind, brass, and percussion end in a stillness beyond time—outsider music in the profoundest possible sense. The Koechlin of "The Spring Running" and the Ives of the Fourth Symphony are both religious composers, beyond accredited creeds.

In this spring running the jungle is real; in another major work closely related to it, the jungle is inward. *Le Buisson ardent* is a double symphonic poem begun in 1938 while the *Jungle Book* cycle was still in process, but not completed until 1945, at the end of World War II. More personal, even autobiographical, than the *Jungle Book* sequence, it is based on a novel by Koechlin's friend Romain Rolland and concerns a spiritually ailing artist in a materially sick society. The opening drone-based section depicts the meandering labyrinth of dejection into which the artist-hero has sunk, to be reanimated by a vision of Moses's Burning Bush—not here a Christian symbol but Pan or the *Foehn* or the god of spring, who arrives in a whirlwind alarmingly emulated by ondes martenot, moaning through an immense static chord of superimposed fifths. Pitch-obliterating glissandos combine with tonally rootless whole-tone figures to counter the miasma of despair, climaxing in brass fanfares and a more metrically organized melody chanted by full orchestra, but subsiding into silence.

For again this superabundant life exists within a context of empty eternity. In the second part of the symphonic poem, form is stabilized as a wavering, stepwise melody flowers, on ondes martenot, through superimposed fifths. Brass fanfares swirl into a round dance dominated by canonic points that assert an archetypal principle of unity. The simple modality and lilting triple rhythms of the fugued dance song are a sublimation of the *enfantines* in Koechlin's piano sonatinas, appropriately enough, since the Blakean burden of his art is that "Without Contraries is no Progression." The artist-hero—Rolland's Jean-Christophe or Koechlin himself—is thus reawakened, and the joyous dance finds apotheosis in a grand chorale in which ondes martenot, piano, large organ, tam-tam, and bells (not to mention five saxophones) reinforce the normal symphony orchestra. These sonorities anticipate the overtly religious and doctrinally Catholic "transfigurations" in the large-scale works of Messiaen. There is also a parallel with the Australian Percy Grainger, especially with his *The Warriors,* scored for an immense, in part ad hoc, orchestra, in the form of an "imaginary ballet." Written during the very years when Stravinsky was gestating his *Le Sacre du printemps,* Grainger's work envisaged "'a sort of Valhalla gathering of childishly overbearing and arrogant savage men and women of all ages, arm in arm in united show of gay and innocent pride and animal spirits, fierce and exultant.'"[3] Grainger was off the mark in believing that his naive global village fiesta had something in common with Stravinsky's Spring Rite of sacrificial murder and fertility in prehistoric Russia and in war-racked twentieth-century Europe. It may seem odd that uncivilized Grainger and hypercivilized Koechlin should imaginatively overlap, yet the ultimate point of Koechlin's music is the necessity for civilization's recurrent *renewal,* whether in a spring running or through the supernatural agency of the *Foehn. Le Buisson ardent* is a meticulously composed work compared with Grainger's juvenilely prankish *Warriors,* but it is much less meticulous than Stravinsky's barbaric but geometrically organized *Rite.* There is often an element of (goatish) caprice, overriding intellect and will, in Koechlin's junglelike fecundity.

Indeed, since visions are not rationally measurable, there may be a link between Koechlin's visionary qualities and a lack in him—shared with Grainger and Villa-Lobos—of self-criticism. His big works are wondrous when irradiated by vision, but may be prolix when they aren't, as even *Le Buisson ardent,* though not the *Jungle Book* cycle, is intermittently.

Koechlin's dedication to his craft, especially in contrapuntal terms, didn't necessarily entail an awareness of the relationship of parts to whole; nor, despite his melodic approach, did he create, as did Ravel, unforgettable tunes. Similarly, the flexibility of his rhythms fascinates, yet, unless he is inspired, it may not grip us by the lapel, let alone the scruff of the neck. Bearing on this is the fact that though Koechlin was a solitary and nature mystic, he was also open to the world, in its gregarious vulgarity. Since his substitute for religion was a belief in the integrity of art per se, he was not a doctrinal Marxist or a card-carrying Communist; he did emulate his hero Berlioz— also elitist by instinct and populist by sympathy—in composing works for ceremonial occasions, while in private life he espoused liberal causes always with vigor and sometimes with courage. Again, from his Old World he parallels Ives in his New World, for Ives was a New England transcendentalist who was also open to the rawly demotic immediacy of his environment, sundering barriers between high and low, as between art and life.

This may be why Koechlin, a solitary who hated the materialism of modern society and made music about mountain peaks and labyrinthine glades, was also devoted to the popular art of the cinema. He devised and wrote music for film scripts, in one of which he himself hoped to play opposite his idol, Lillian Harvey, for whom he composed well over a hundred pieces. When she ceased to acknowledge his tributes, about which she was not shocked, but bemused, he switched his affections to Clara Bow, then to Ginger Rogers, and then to Jean Harlow, making music for all of them which, although in his "familiar" style, is no less elegant than his pieces in the French tradition. Whatever obscure psychological motives nurtured his obsession, his worship of cinematic sirens relates to the naive elements in his *enfantines* and to his perennial duologue between reality and illusion. It may also bear on his equivocation between sunlit city and hazy forest and between a cosmological sun and moon. To this we may find affinities in the art of his friend and slightly younger colleague, Darius Milhaud.

NOTES

1. Angus Wilson, *The Strange Ride of Rudyard Kipling: His Life and Works* (London: Secker and Warburg, 1977), 123–24.

2. Wilfrid Mellers, *Percy Grainger* (New York: Oxford University Press, 1992), 18.

3. Ibid., 36.

6

Darius Milhaud's *Le Boeuf sur le toit*

KOECHLIN BELONGED to French civilization but his music flourished in legendary landscapes of dream and myth, whether medieval French, classical Greek, Mediterranean, or vicariously (by way of British Kipling) Indian or African. Darius Milhaud parallels this, with the difference that he was Provençal by birth and Jewish by religion. Faithful to both traditions, he relished his Mediterranean culture—sun-baked and sea-salted, flavored with a Hebraicism affiliated with Moorish elements in southern France and Spain. The mixture was further enriched by his spending 1917–18 in Brazil, where he went partly to escape from war-racked Europe (he was unfit for military service) and partly to work, unarduously, in the diplomatic service as secretary to the poet Paul Claudel. His Brazilian adventure linked his native Aix— which embraced classical antiquity within its medieval heritage—to new worlds geographical and spiritual; it also provided a transition to a second life in the New World, to which he was driven, during World War II, by the Nazi occupation of France. California, for all its rootlessness, reminded him geographically of his native Provence, and although he returned to France in his old age, he did not reject his California home-away-from-home.

Milhaud's provincial childhood and his creative energy justified his calling his autobiography *Ma vie heureuse*.[1] His yea-saying is a key to his prodigality and his impermanence. A professional composer to the point of being a force of nature, he exuded music "regardless," hardly asking whether it was good, bad, or indifferent, so long as it was apposite to an occasion. His friend Francis Poulenc, admiring Milhaud's music, nonetheless confessed that he could not "play ducks and drakes with my gift," as did Milhaud.[2] An apocryphal but telling story describes how Milhaud, arriving at Yehudi

Menuhin's American home for a meal and to try out a new violin sonata, discovered that he'd left the score at home. Asking for an hour's grace, he sat down and wrote another sonata: a process less burdensome than returning to recover the original. If much of the vast output of Milhaud, a composer scarcely less fecund than Koechlin, has gone with the wind, what survives is a body of music that, sharing the social aims of folk and pop music, may spill over into concepts of grandeur quite remarkable, albeit seldom remarked on because the works are seldom heard. The problem is inherent in the kind of composer Milhaud was, which is why it is important to understand the world that made him.

In the late 1930s Paul Collaer, a life-long friend of Milhaud, wrote a tribute to the companion of his boyhood, publishing it retrospectively in 1947.[3] After Milhaud's death it was revised and updated with the help of material provided by Milhaud's widow;[4] but its value still lies mostly in the early chapters wherein Collaer evokes Provence in its Mediterranean, Greco-Roman classicism and in its Christian medieval legacy that in turn embraced Hebraic and Moorish traditions. Collaer's poetic prose reveals how cultural history conditioned the composer's musical makeup—the qualities that relate him to Debussy, Emmanuel Chabrier, Ravel, and Satie, while differentiating him from Teutonic traditions, especially Wagner, his *bête noire*. Milhaud's "artistic" heritage accorded with the spirit and the techniques of Provençal song and dance; even his most famous technical innovation—the polytonality he did not invent but practiced more assiduously than did Ravel or Koechlin— is not unconnected with the (democratically?) simultaneous blowing of the same tune in different or not-quite-the-same keys by bands in the Provençal village square. This may bear on the fact that he was conservative and subversive alike—and admired Koechlin so deeply because he was a staunch advocate of French contrapuntal tradition and at the same time a visionary revolutionary.

One of the earliest of Milhaud's works to explore polytonality is the song cycle *Poèmes juifs*, opus 34, written for soprano and piano in 1916, just before he went to Brazil. The work suggests how Milhaud's Provençal-Jewish ancestry enabled him to exploit Brazilian popular musics, for these "Jewish poems" have nothing to do with Hebraic liturgical incantation, but are settings of anonymous poems picked up in a periodical and set to music by a Provençal living in Paris. The verses triggered powerful responses in Milhaud; love, joy, and grief are invigorated by religious conviction and yearning for a Promised Land not altogether distinct from an Eternal Beloved. Each song is based on an ostinato pattern, usually defined by the pianist's left hand.

Against the ostinato, the pianist's right hand traces polytonal filigrees, while the voice insinuates a third line, seductively emotional, sometimes in yet a third key. The effect of the polytonality is not so much harsh as scrunchy in sonority, at once sweet and acid, especially in the two opening songs, which are lullabies. The eight songs of the cycle display, however, considerable variety in mood and manner. "Chant de laboureur" complements the gently sensual "Chant de nourrice" in being a paean of praise to Israel; "Chant d'amour" is a love song in which the voice soars while the piano babbles like birds; "Chant de forgeron" is a bellicose clarion call to the new Messiah, preparing for a grandly epiphanic lament. In these fine songs all the elements of Milhaud's "Brazilian" pieces are embryonic: hypnotic ostinatos, bittersweet polytonal harmony, melismatic linear embroidery. In the light of this, Milhaud's Brazilian adventure may be viewed as a voyage of *self*-discovery. The heart of the songs is in their humanly immediate vocal line, while the pungent sonorities of the piano create the milieu within which the singer lived, sang, and suffered. Each of the songs is dedicated to a Jewish friend or to the memory of one deceased.

When Milhaud adapted these techniques to his Brazilian works he was less personally involved; in Brazil in 1917 and 1918 he was *en vacances,* exploring musical potential rather than his own heart. If he was consistent in using polytonality, he wasn't systematic. Abominating system as inimical to spontaneity, he cultivated polytonality in tribute to nature's polymorphous perversity, hogging all the keys at once—as Charles Ives's pioneering father used to say—in a spirit of democratic fair play and sundering barriers between elitism and populism in the process. Since this may encourage a surrealistic dadaism, it also bears on the relation between his South American adventure and the position he occupied in Parisian music of the twenties. Most of Milhaud's Brazilian pieces were worked on and written out after he had returned to France. The first two, however, were actually produced in Rio in 1918, being closely related works designated as opuses 47 and 48. The former, the Sonata for Flute, Oboe, Clarinet, and Piano, seems to have been preludial to the latter, a ballet prompted by the fortuitous appearance in Rio of Diaghilev's Ballets Russes, with Nijinsky still dancing, if near the end of his tether.

The sonata doesn't sound like abstract chamber music, being atmospheric and latently choreographic. The first movement, marked "tranquille," begins with a level ostinato on piano, over which the wind instruments weave melodic filigrees, undulating primitively around nodal points, occasionally leaping in gestures that could be those of dancers or could be the capers of beasts or the flutterings of birds. The notion lends itself to polytonality, since each line (or creature) goes its own way; but one could hardly call the music savage, for there is a sweet euphony at the heart of the ensemble, as there is in the boy Poulenc's almost exactly contemporary *Rapsodie nègre*. The effect is of a forest dream, rather than of a rite actively indulged in, which is apposite to the young Milhaud in the exotic environment he found himself in. The same may be said of the short scherzo, marked "joyeux," which is sappy in polytonal textures. The third movement, marked "emporté," is wilder, though it lets its hair down in so disreputable a manner that it sounds comic rather than ferocious. So we aren't surprised when the finale, marked "douloureux," returns to the forest-scape of the first movement, with a gentle but remorseless ostinato defined by the piano. Through it, the wind instruments cry even more "animistically" than in the first movement, rounding off a creation that works as pure music, whatever intimations it may offer of a scene and story.

That a scene and story are latent, however, seems probable, since composition of the sonata led immediately to the "ritual ballet" or "poème plastique," *L'Homme et son désir* (opus 48, 1918), based on creation myths of native South Americans. Milhaud wrote, "Isolated from most of the rest of the world, . . . we had time to enjoy the gentle unfolding of the ballet as though it were a kind of beloved plaything. While I wrote my score, Claudel worked out the smallest details of the choreography with our friend Audrey Parr, who designed the décor according to his instructions. She had a delightful home at Petropolis, to which we journeyed on weekends to escape the tropical summer heat. There she constructed a table model of a theater, divided into three horizontal levels representing three levels of dramatic consciousness."[5] On top were the Elementals—the Hours, the Moon, and the Clouds; the middle level presented the main action, turning on the relation of human to forest; the lower level embraced night and dream, memory and love.

The theatrical aspects of the danced myth could hardly be more rudimentary. The action, set in the immensity of the Brazilian rain forests, describes a man's rebirth through the agency of a ghostly woman who seems to be simultaneously Sex and Death—forces traditionally twinned throughout world cultures. There's an obvious parallel with the neo-primitive masterpiece that Diaghilev had recently danced in Paris, Stravinsky's *Le Sacre du printemps*, wherein a sacrificial murder and fertility rite parallel the "death of Europe" and its putative resuscitation. Strictly speaking, Stravinsky's orchestral and mimetic work was a game, for no girl was murdered, and the miming of her death took place in the gilded luxury of a Parisian theater, with the music played by a penguin-suited symphony orchestra that was itself a product of industrial technology. Even so, the game was potent enough to seize people by the scruff of the neck and, unleashing communal guilt, provoke a riot. Milhaud's parallel neo-primitive rite lacked this incandescence, not merely because his genius couldn't rival Stravinsky's electrical charge, but also because his rite wasn't part of his heritage. Although Milhaud's Provençal-Hebraic origins encouraged empathy with the eroticism and exoticism he found in Brazil he didn't "belong" to the rain forest as Stravinsky—however cosmopolitan he became—was heir to the Russian steppes. Compared with *Le Sacre*, Milhaud's *L'Homme et son désir* is accurately described, in the composer's phrase, as a "beloved plaything."[6] That it comes out as startling but comical doesn't alter the fact that surrealistic mirth may be a valid response to death and destruction.

When the piece was produced in Paris in June 1921, it was a *succès de scandale*, greeted with catcalls and guffaws, but there was no riot, let alone bloodshed. At this date, the work seems to have deserved precisely this farcical mini-furor rather than inchoate fury, for it reveals the link between the postwar frenzy and the twenties' cult of the Absurd; Milhaud was, after all, a founder-member of "Les Six," though he had in more than one sense too large a frame to be accommodated within it. Musically, *L'Homme et son désir* preserves its effervescence. It is scored for a small orchestra of solo instruments—piccolo, flute, oboe, clarinet, bassoon, trumpet, harp—and string quintet, reinforced by a vocal quartet and a battery of percussion instruments, some of local provenance. Moreover, the band is arranged stereophonically in segregated groups, related to the levels of consciousness designated in the scenario. This encourages the illusion that the audience is involved along with the players, singers, and dancers; all are celebrants and, strictly speaking, performers. The music they make contains genuinely Brazilian elements, though the pseudo-African or Native American pentatonics and polymetrical ostinatos sound childish rather than ferocious. The effect is compounded by the intrusion of wordless voices, which transmute aboriginal rigor into a simplicity resembling the *enfantines* of Satie, Poulenc, and Koechlin. That the nondeveloping motives function polytonally again reinforces rather than obscures the wide-eyed, open-eared effect; tunes and rhythms, in their sappy sonorities, are so basic that tonal and metrical coordination seems unnecessary, even undesirable. The man's music of desire, whether passionate or tender, is obliterated by the bumping, banging, gnawing, and whistling noises of the percussive forest, though it is his human lust that drives the music to its climax over a pedal point of C sharp. This subsides to C natural as the sexy but healthy woman leads the man away, "always at a distance marked by her outstretched arm."[7] The end, with a primitive tune in F sharp major with flattened seventh, is unexpectedly gentle, whether it is signalling humanity's insignificance in the forest or whether it is merely admitting that the game of savages *is* a game.

Immediately after his return from Brazil to Paris Milhaud further exploited his South American experience. The best known of these works, *Saudades do Brasil* (opus 67), is accurately described by its title, being a suite of piano pieces celebrating various districts of Rio in appropriate dance forms—tango, samba, maxixe, Portuguese fado. Assembled in 1920, the sophisticated pieces fuse Spanish, Portuguese, Italian, French, and Native American popular genres, and again the persistent polytonality, far from being technically systematic, emulates the sonorities of communal fiesta. The melodic lines, being polytonal, sound screwily out of focus, as though in the melée of physical action; a demotic rite occurs as the dances are played—preferably by the composer on a not very grand piano—in a bar or café, not a concert hall. The composer-performer at once belongs to and is separate from the rite; although the dances are indigenous, each associated with a particular district of the city, the tunes are invented by Milhaud. Within a year he orchestrated some of the pieces for balletic purposes (opus 67b), with an effect more alienated, and therefore romantic, than the piano originals. They become theatrical illusion, rather than literally *saudades*—nostalgic reminiscences of strolls taken by Milhaud, alone or in the company of friends, around suburbs of Rio, along the Copacabana beach or, after a cable-car ride, through the lush vegetation of Painéras. All these regions are pervaded by pop musics that Milhaud found, in memory no less than in present reality, hauntingly immediate.

The more Milhaud transplanted Rio into postwar Paris, the more surreal it became, reaching its climax in a ballet shaped up in 1919. The composer's modest intention, in *Le Boeuf sur le toit,* was to make an orchestral potpourri of Brazilian pop tunes that continued to haunt him after he'd brought them home, along with collections of folk artifacts and indigenous instruments. Carnival festivities in Rio, especially ad hoc singing and dancing in the streets and in the clubs (where everyone sported harlequin costumes), captivated Milhaud; the lively rhythms, repeated in melodies played over and over again, were impressive in their monotony. Were we to think of *Le Boeuf* as concert music we might indeed find it "monotonous" in its repetitiousness; that we find it enlivening is because its monotony echoes Mircea Eliade's "paradise of archetypes and repetition" that anthropologists have noted in other indigenous musics.[8] The score that Milhaud produced in Paris (opus 58, 1919), at the turn into the giddy twenties, was not merely of an alien culture imported; it also revealed the pertinence of such South American exuberance to the sexual and cultural liberation of postwar Paris.

Milhaud's original notion was that his chain of Brazilian pop numbers, tied together by a repeated refrain until the dancers were tired or the night spent, might serve as aural background to a Charlie Chaplin movie—literally melding aboriginal and industrial techniques. Jean Cocteau decided to modify and stage-manage the enterprise as a show. He devised a scenario of typical ingenuity, creating a surreal escapade set neither in Rio nor in Paris, but in a New York bar during the Prohibition era. The cast included an African American boxer who smokes "a cigar as long as a torpedo"; an African American dwarf; a New York cop who carries his head under his arm (having mislaid it as an intellectual instrument, according to Milhaud); a red-haired prostitute who dances around the policeman in Salome-like gyrations; and a transvestite barman, "tout blanc, tout rose," who tickles the policeman. Nothing happens in the way of a plot, which may be why, when the piece was produced in London, it was entitled *The Nothing-Doing Bar*. Even so, the combination in a modern realistic setting of Milhaud's exotic music with Cocteau's action-to-no-end generates an outrageous virility, fringed with fright.

Cocteau's point may have been to define the relationship between the Brazilian "jungle" and the asphalt jungle that was the scene of old-time gangster movies. The positive, primitive impulses in this case prove stronger than the negations of war and mechanization, just as they do in Cocteau's scenario, in Milhaud's music, in Guy-Pierre Fauconnet's masks and costumes, in Raoul Dufy's dazzling scenery, in the antics of clowns and acrobats hired from the Médrano Circus, and, still more piquantly, in the notorious *Parade* of Cocteau, Satie, and Picasso in 1924.

In *Parade* the equilibrium between human motivation and the encroaching Machine is not only precarious but also potentially tragic; *Le Boeuf sur le toit* has a similar theme, but Cocteau defuses its tragic implications. In a very practical way the Brazilian street music of *Le Boeuf* turned into Parisian sophistication of the twenties, for a cabaret-bar was named after it and was patronized by avant-garde artists, including Milhaud.[9] Here the vivacious Jean Wiéner (who courageously sponsored avant-garde music, including Schoenberg's *Pierrot Lunaire*, in postwar Paris) played French-American jazz and composed irreverent music in homage to the "chers orchestres nègres" that had had so "bienfaisante" an influence on music in general.[10]

African American jazz is not, however, a direct influence on Milhaud's ballet, which instead uses the ad hoc techniques of Brazilian *chôros*—improvised music of the streets embraced within a nondeveloping rondo, wherein other street-tune episodes kaleidoscopically come and go. All the tunes are as raucous, rude, sexy, or seductive as are the streets of Rio at Carnival time, and the scoring is vulgar in more than one sense. We have noted the tie-up between the Rio streets during Carnival and a New York bar during Prohibition: an irony that has a mirror inversion in that Heitor Villa-Lobos, a Brazilian composer whose art-music is itself founded on pop-style *chôros,* had recently arrived in Paris and was consorting with avant-garde Parisians.

In 1923, the very year in which Villa-Lobos impinged on Paris, Milhaud produced the most famous, and enduring, of his quasi-Brazilian pieces. This was also a ballet, related to *L'Homme et son désir* in that it too addresses a creation myth. But although the immediate inspiration for *La Création du monde* (opus 81) came from Brazil, its mythology is African, a musical counterpart to the cult of black African visual art by Pablo Picasso, Amedeo Modigliani, and Fernand Léger. Milhaud, in his verbal *Etudes,* follows Wiéner in paying homage to African Americans and their "profoundly moving gift for a kind of melody that only people who have been long oppressed know how to utter."[11] Pointedly, he relates their African American destiny to that of the Jews in bondage in Egypt. Taking the cue from Stravinsky's *Soldier's Tale* (first performed in 1918), he scores his ballet for an ensemble resembling a New Orleans jazz band: flute, clarinet, two trumpets, trombone, an assortment of percussion instruments handled by one player, and a double bass— reinforced by what would have been a polite string quartet, had not alto saxophone been substituted for viola. Léger designed the scenery and costumes, characteristically introducing mechanistic motives into ostensible primitivism; the scenario, based on African folklore, was by Blaise Cendrars. African masks graced a masque of African earth-worship, though the piece is more than a product of the back to basics movement that for a while seemed a valid riposte to machine-dominated societies.

The direct influence of African American jazz makes a difference here, in comparison with Milhaud's other post-Brazilian works, for although this creation opens with obscure sonorities through which orgiastic rhythms deviously define themselves, the music grows more *civilized* the more life burgeons. Milhaud is a few years further away from Brazil, and his jazz proves to be lyrically nostalgic for a lost Eden, its blue notes being as heart-rending as the voice of the sophisticated Josephine Baker, who had recently taken Paris by storm. Polytonality occurs, but less brashly than in the earlier pieces, and the consummatory theme is generated by way of a European notion of unity—a highly syncopated, but formally "correct," fugue. The blue-tinged tune that surfaces from the fugue strikingly resembles those of George Gershwin, whose *Rhapsody in Blue* Milhaud must have heard performed by Paul Whiteman's concert band. So *La Création du monde* is closer to "art" (at least in a European sense) than is *Le Boeuf sur le toit*. A parable of primitive re-creation that is also sophisticated recreation, it deserves its reputation as the most convincing attempt to fuse jazz with art-music; yet at the same time it is once more a game, a "plaything": a dream of the rain forest that refreshes the spirit and senses without annulling the dubious legacy of "syphilization"—to call on James Joyce's brilliant pun. The end, again in luminously transcendent F sharp major with blue seventh, is benedictory.

La Création du monde is the most artistically "realized" of Milhaud's neo-primitive pieces, rather more so than his attempt to fuse his Brazilian new world with his old (Provençal) France. This attempt had its source in a work started in Rio and appropriately called *Salade* (opus 83), since it stirred together fragments of Braziliana, shook them up, and seasoned them with distant recollections of his childhood and adolescence in Aix-en-Provence. This "sung ballet in two acts" made no decisive impression in its original form, but proved highly effective in a revised version for piano and orchestra (opus 83b), dished up by Milhaud in 1926, to take on his first American tour (he played the piano solo). In this form *Le Carnaval d'Aix* delightfully fuses the indigenous with the exotic elements of Milhaud's muse, making a soufflé of Provençal peasant and urban dances, of musical portraits of commedia dell'arte characters that underline the significance, for Milhaud, of play and illusion, and of "souvenirs de Rio" riddled with blue false relations. The virility of the tunes and rhythms, in tinglingly scored polytonality, encapsulates Milhaud's global village ethnicity, no less than does the pretend folk-and-pop idiom of the 1936 work *Suite Provençal*—a set of arrangements of Provençal tunes that may sustain comparison with those of a classical baroque composer from Aix, André Campra. The latter found no contradiction between Provençal pop and *la Gloire* of Louis XIV; similarly, Milhaud reincarnated Old Provence in the sophistication of early-twentieth-century Paris, with intimations of the global village that eventually became timeless and placeless.

Although to have reanimated primitive sun and earth in the context of industrial technocracy is no mean achievement, it does not adequately indicate Milhaud's range. In the late twenties the universal aspects of his Mediterranean culture erupted in a trilogy of ritual operas on Claudel's translations and Catholic reinterpretations of Greek tragedy; recurrently, his religious impulse functioned in Jewish terms, culminating in the *Service sacré* of 1947 and the opus ultimum of 1972, *Ani maamin*. More pointed in relation to our "wilderness" theme is the Latin American trilogy comprising the opera-oratorio *Christophe Colomb* (1928), the more psychologically probing study of the tragic victim *Maximilien* (1930), and the full-blooded historical opera *Bolivar* (1943). To assess these monumental works, all dealing with tensions between worlds old and new, "savage" and "civilized," is difficult in the current state of our knowledge. They have been little performed, unsurprisingly given their massive scale, and only one has been recorded. The lucid density of Milhaud's many-layered polyharmony, and the works' hybrid status between opera, rite, and fiesta, suggest that they might be pertinent to our divided and distracted society. Milhaud was always a socially if not politically committed composer; the pity is that current attitudes and economics condone his ephemera while disavowing his major achievements. It may be that his youthful bombshells are the heart of the matter; they have worn better than most of the music of his second (American) career. Even so, one would like to know more about those big Latin American theater pieces, which ask questions about the place of the artist in our pluralistically fragmented world. That Milhaud should prompt us to re-ask these questions testifies to his potency, even though the questions remain unanswered, and are perhaps unanswerable.

NOTES

1. Darius Milhaud, *Ma vie heureuse* (Paris: Editions Belfond, 1973).

2. *Francis Poulenc, Selected Correspondence, 1915–1963,* trans. and ed. Sidney Buckland (London: Victor Gollancz, 1991), 270.

3. Paul Collaer, *Darius Milhaud* (Antwerp: Nederlansche Boekhandel, 1947).

4. Paul Collaer, *Darius Milhaud,* rev. and expanded (Geneva: Editions Slatkine, 1982).

5. Darius Milhaud quoted in Paul Collaer, *Darius Milhaud,* trans. and ed. Jane Hohfeld Galante (San Francisco: San Francisco Press, 1988), 63.

6. Ibid.

7. Ibid., 66.

8. Mircea Eliade, *The Myth of the Eternal Return,* trans. Willard R. Trask (New York: Pantheon, 1954), 162.

9. Darius Milhaud, *Notes without Music* (New York: Knopf, 1953), 128.

10. Jean Wiéner, *Sonatine syncopée: Pour piano* (Paris: Max Eschig, 1923), 1.

11. Collaer, ed. Galante, *Darius Milhaud,* 69.

PART THREE

The Jungle and the City

7

Heitor Villa-Lobos in Rio and Paris

KOECHLIN TRAVELED within legendary landscapes and *le forêt féerique* rather than in Old France, discovering vistas at once new and ancient. Milhaud youthfully visited real forests in an exotic land, wherein he garnered legends that could be relived in his French habitats. Those rain forests were in Brazil, a vast country that nurtured a composer even more fecund than either of the prolific Frenchmen. By the standards of a Bach or a Beethoven, Villa-Lobos is not a great composer; he is an extraordinary phenomenon who encourages reflection on the relation between an artist and the community, especially in a pluralistic society such as ours. His documentary significance is inherent in the nature of Brazil, which is neither a "new" country nor an "old" one.

For Brazil is several countries in one, embracing groups that still use crude tools and weapons alongside others whose horizons are flashing television screens and flickering computers. In the backlands, frontier justice of the type promulgated in the pioneering days of the Wild West still operates; even in the vicinity of Rio indentured labor not far from slavery persists, along with a subculture of juvenile criminals beyond any law, while at the same time plantation owners lead lives of (bad) fairy-tale affluence—"between quicksilver and disgrace, between the monstrous and the sublime," as the pop singer Caetano Veloso has put it.

When Villa-Lobos was born in the late nineteenth century this multiethnic, multicultural stewpot fermented less extravagantly than it does today, but it was already simmering. The date of his birth in Rio is usually given as 1887, though several alternative dates have been proffered. His lifespan did not greatly exceed his biblically allotted three score years and ten, yet time means little in the face of a fecundity as irresistible as Koechlin's *foehn;* nor is Villa-Lobos more limited by space than by time, for he has no defined ethnic identity. As a backdrop to his native land was a once great, now moribund, Native American civilization and a still extant, if almost extinct, peasant culture. In the foreground were vestiges of Hispanic Renaissance culture surviving from missionary days, along with more potent infusions from Spanish and Portuguese, and to a lesser degree Italian, French, German, and British, colonizations of the eighteenth and nineteenth centuries. In musical terms this embraced, within local folk and pop elements, traces of Renaissance ecclesiastical polyphony, Spanish *zarzuela,* Italian romantic opera and popular song, French vaudeville, *opéra buffe, chanson,* and *café-concert,* plus a few pockets of familiar Teutonic classics and a substratum of British salon and parlor music. Entangled with this European detritus was an African music precipitated from the slave trade, including the seeds of jazz, which in turn linked up with a mechanistic culture from the United States. Whereas in the work of Europeans such as Janáček, Bartók, and Stravinsky "primitivism" was absorbed into European traditions, in South America the various layers coexisted, side by side. So Villa-Lobos's imagination teemed with musical images of the Brazilian rain forest, of lost Native American cities, of Spanish and Portuguese colonialism, and of the North American skyscraper and roadhouse. In his appetite for life in the raw Villa-Lobos has points in common with Koechlin and Milhaud, while being still closer to his North American contemporary, Charles Ives. Both Ives and Villa-Lobos were musical democrats, relishing the multifarious; but whereas Ives made a new world materially and spiritually, Villa-Lobos countered his exuberance with passivity. Accepting the chaos of the contemporary scene, he was even less self-critical than were Koechlin and Milhaud. This must be why his music impresses most when it is most fortuitous.

While Villa-Lobos's fortuitousness may be his weakness as a European-style artist, it is his strength as a "phenomenon." Though he picked up much that was of value to him during his belated student days in Paris, it does not follow that his most technically accomplished works are the most rewarding. The first four string quartets, for instance, hold their own with those of Milhaud in metamorphosing Debussyan and Ravellian dreams into South American *saudades,* sometimes gingered up with a whiff of Bartókian aggression, but they pale in comparison with exactly contemporary works that assert Villa-Lobos's aboriginal nature. An oft-repeated but probably apocryphal story tells us that when asked with whom he wanted to study in Paris, Villa-Lobos supposedly retorted, "*You* are going to study *me;* I am not here to study, but to demonstrate my achievements." Certainly, he had much to demonstrate, for the wellsprings of his creation had little to do with European academicism. He had acquired most of his musical skills by ear while improvising on many instruments; he had a charismatic command of the piano and exceptional expertise on cello and guitar. As a lad he had joined, during more or less continuous carnival seasons, with Brazilian village and city-street musicians in jam sessions wherein any number of performers, singing or playing on any traditional or ad hoc instrument, improvised randomly, with no more than a pulse, a metrical pattern, a chord sequence, or a snatch of remembered tune to keep them going, if not together. Such activity was more a way of life than a form of music, for the musicians created Mircea Eliade's "paradise of archetypes and repetition" that offered a continuum to live in.

The Brazilian name for such music-making was *chôros,* with some of the implications of our chorus in that it was a communal activity. Strictly, the Portuguese word *chôrar* means to weep, which probably covers any inarticulate cry. Villa-Lobos participated in such improvised song-and-dance sessions on feast days and relished formlessness as the natural condition for music made in the heat of the moment, the basic materials being derived from Native American sources. In *chôros,* form and meaning are never specific, but coexistent at the moment they occur, in the sounds uttered by voices and instruments, and in the gestures of bouncing bodies, wafting arms, skipping feet. It is thus hardly surprising that Villa-Lobos's works in *chôros* style are composed music with slapdash notations. Often, a definitive score does not exist, since Villa-Lobos rejoiced in maximum prolixity of detail borne on maximum corporeal momentum. Ives too believed that completion was an illusory virtue, so that many of his works remained in provisional notation for many years, and sometimes until his death. The difference is that Ives's notations were provisional because he was a Beethovenian seeker, unwilling to pre-empt conclusions, whereas Villa-Lobos's notations were haphazard because he didn't know, or care, where he was going. Everything was grist to his voracious mill.

Although Villa-Lobos was an improvising composer, he had some conservatory training in Rio during adolescence and also picked up, by way of his acute ear, clichés of European music audible around the city. Spanish, Portuguese, Italian, and French "light" music offered material from which to concoct sleekly tailored salon pieces for piano, in the category now known as Easy Listening. There's nothing wrong with that, if the music is as graceful to fingers and ears as is the *Suite floral,* published in 1916 but mostly written much earlier. He knew what he liked: Italian romantic opera, especially that of Puccini, frequently performed in Rio; romantic piano music, especially that of Chopin, Liszt, and Rachmaninoff; and the music of the Russian nationalists, including the "primitive" Moussorgsky, the "amateur" Borodin, and the "sophisticated" Tchaikovsky. This partiality for the Russians made sense, given their sectional empiricism, which—as Debussy and Ravel also recognized—was appropriate for a world in flux. Half a dozen years before he went to Paris Villa-Lobos had created carefully notated music that provided evidence that his *chôros* music, dethroning will and intellect, might contribute to the work of the European avant-garde, as represented by Stravinsky, Janáček, and Bartók. Whatever technical know-how Villa-Lobos acquired from art composers during his Parisian years (1923–30), his most significant creations were still conceived in the spirit of *chôros*.

Among Villa-Lobos's pre-Parisian works is the *Sexteto mistico* of 1917, for the exotic combination of flute, oboe, saxophone, celesta, harp, and guitar. The tone colors suggest a debt to French romanticism and impressionism, the splashing harp and tremulous celesta being redolent of Debussy and Ravel, and perhaps of Vincent d'Indy, whose *Cours de composition musicale* the adolescent Brazilian had studied. But what distinguishes the work from its European prototypes is the empiricism it shares with the music Villa-Lobos improvised with his friends in Rio's streets. The brief phrases, radiantly colored and vivaciously rhythmed, bubble in present spontaneity rather than unfold in sequence. The music works because, not in spite of, its innocence, which incorporates within a French salon the folk-like or even animal-like cries of the wind instruments, while the sophisticated celesta and the at once romantic and primitive harp could be affiliated with the rain forest, in dialogue with a simultaneously folky and artful guitar. Although the work is not called *chôros,* the word *mistico* in the title hints at some such intuitive alchemy.

Even more out of this (modern materialistic) world is the comparably scored *Quatuor* for flute, alto saxophone, celesta, harp, and female voices, written in 1921. Here the harp and celesta still splash impressionistically, while the wind instruments recall Debussy's magical *Syrinx* for solo flute (written on the verge of World War I) and Ravel's paganly piping Pan in *Daphnis et Chloé.* These exotic figures are now not legendary, but real, in a Brazilian rain forest, and when the wordless voices appear in the second movement they transmute nature into realms more "mystical" than those of the *Sexteto mistico.* For all their empiricism the three movements of the *Quatuor* form a whole: an instrumental first movement in which a prelude and postlude frame a duet for flute and harp; a second movement dominated by the ste-reophonic voices, which disembody the first movement's physicality; and a dancing finale that, in becoming a "continuum," paradoxically negates tem-porality. The piece does not end, but stops.

In the same year Villa-Lobos started a work that is literally transitional in that he took it with him to Paris, where he finished it in 1926. Perhaps Villa-Lobos took his time over the piece because he intuitively knew how impor-tant it was as a demonstration of his talents, for *Rudepoêma* is a single-move-ment, twenty-minute work for piano solo, the impact of which has not been dimmed by the passing years. Whereas the *Sexteto místico* was written as a serenade for the pianist Arthur Rubinstein on his first visit to Rio, *Rudepoêma* was written for Rubinstein to play and was described by the composer as a "portrait" of the pianist—apparently viewed as an ultimate *homme sauvage*. The piece was also a portrait of the wilderness through which Villa-Lobos had traveled between his eighteenth year and his midtwenties and, one sus-pects, also a portrait of Villa-Lobos himself. It brings the fetid Brazilian rain forest into the concert hall, threatening "civilization" in the process, as it pounds in the polymetrics of fiesta through the pretonal yells of the crea-tures. It is difficult to believe that this aptly titled *Rudepoêma* predates by more than twenty years the evocations of wildly holy nature in Olivier Messiaen's piano music. Given the prodigality of Villa-Lobos's invention, the lack of conventional structure and the relishment of the empiricism of *chôros* en-hances the excitation. We're swept pell-mell between the vociferous denizens of the forest, the Native American "savages," "civilized" Portuguese colonists valsing in the salons, and a Chicago-style barrelhouse pianist in a club. No single work of Villa-Lobos so powerfully encapsulates his polymorphous paradoxes. Sadly, the piece is seldom played—more, one suspects, through ignorance than because of its hair-raising difficulty. Rubinstein, the dedica-tee, played it frequently but did not issue a recording. There are now several adequate substitutes.

Villa-Lobos was hotly engaged on *Rudepoêma* when, in 1923, he arrived in Paris. That this proved a vintage year for him was attributable more to a sense of liberation than to the cultural shot-in-the-arm provided by the French capital. Alongside the cataclysmic *Rudepoêma* he produced a work for the exiguous medium of voice and violin: a suite of three songs with texts by Mario de Andrade, a poet who was also an ethnomusicologist, drawing on folklore. The songs are supposed to be sung by a small girl in a Brazilian vil-lage. In the corporeal action of the first song she strolls, or sometimes scuttles, down a dusty village street, followed by a black crone bearing a bundle of clothes on her head. The second and third movements are not narrative, but explosions of childish babble. Throughout, the voice part is closer to folk styles, or even to real kids' rhymes, than to concert music; calling for searing articulation, flexible rhythm, and ambivalent pitch, it shifts between human lyricism and arbitrary noises appropriate to forest creatures. If the violin part sounds more like folk fiddle than concert violin, it has analogies with the fiddle part of Stravinsky's *Soldier's Tale,* a work, written in the war year of 1918, that still haunted Parisian music of the twenties. But Villa-Lobos's violin part has nothing to do with Russia ancient or modern, nor with incipiently American jazz; the violin line in this suite is as indigenously and ingenuously Brazilian as the voice part, in duo with which it creates a "jungle" music still of surprising potency. The first movement incrementally repeats diatonic figures, like a child's rhyme; the second mingles fragmented words and wordless vocalise as it gravitates from human articulacy toward the unnotatable hubbub of nature; in the third song the girl seems to *become* a forest creature, giving vent to avian squawks and screeches and beastly growls and grunts. The collocation of child and forest becomes an act of rebirth.

Another, larger-scaled work written in the vintage year of 1923 stands, with *Rudepoêma,* as an apex to Villa-Lobos's recreated primitivism. It is called simply *Noneto,* an analogy with the *Sexteto* and the *Quator.* The composer's title is inaccurate, however, for the piece is scored for eight solo instruments: flute, oboe, alto saxophone, clarinet, bassoon, horn, piano, and celesta; the ninth part could be either the wordless mixed chorus or the large percussion ensemble, including Brazilian instruments. These amorphous forces haven't quite the rudimentary "reality" of the Suite for Voice and Violin, but are closer to it than *Rudepoêma,* which was written for a mechanical contrivance (the piano) that is sophisticated, if not necessarily "civilized." Any equal-tempered keyboard, operated by a single performer, may lend itself to bravura, but an unpremeditated concourse of sound-sources, like that of the *Noneto,* offers rewards proportionate to the risks. In *Noneto* Villa-Lobos brings off an inspired fusion of the Brazilian rain forest with the asphalt jungle, by way of a Latinization of jazz improvisation for a rather Big Band. The savagely sophisticated piece has no beginning, middle, or end, for its incremental climax obliterates time. When the human voices belatedly but thrillingly enter they are not merely, if at all, human but are manifestations of the "breath" of life. The *Noneto* achieves what "tribal" pop aims at, but usually misses.

The works that Villa-Lobos entitled *Chôros* mostly date from the twenties. It is not clear why he always used the plural form of the noun, unless it was to suggest that a *chôros* was not a single "work" of art but an ongoing activity, always present *in potentia*. The pieces may be scored for anything from a single guitar or piano to a symphony orchestra, though an orchestra, usually needing a conductor, would have less freedom to improvise. The process of *chôros* applies most effectively to a small group of soloists like those Villa-Lobos had participated in back in Brazil. An enlivening instance is *Chôros no. 2* for flute and clarinet, written in 1924. Clarinet was the instrument Villa-Lobos usually played in *chôros* groups, since it was more easily transportable than a cello, the instrument on which he was most expert. In this piece the two players are not making an artifact dependent on formalized devices like canon, but are indulging in duologue at once competitive and mutually inspirational. In ludic rivalry, they throw sparks off one another in the act of per-form-ance. Although such music is difficult to play convincingly from a score, the version Villa-Lobos wrote down preserves the raw edge of spontaneity until it abruptly expires—on a bare fourth.

A few years later Villa-Lobos devised a similar caper for two string instruments—the *Chôros bis* of 1928, for violin and cello. The players explore reiterated metrical figures and soaring cantilenas, intermittently erupting into seemingly unpremeditated cadenzas. The motives are Native American, though Villa-Lobos's virtuosity is timeless and placeless. The multiple stoppings and harmonics sometimes enable two players to sound like an orchestra; in competition and interchange two individuals may "stand for" a community.

The same principle operates in the *Quintette en forme de chôros,* also of 1928. This is scored for the conventional wind ensemble of flute, oboe, clarinet, horn, and bassoon, though the French horn had originally been a cor anglais, of the same family as oboe and bassoon. The substitution of the French horn no doubt guaranteed more frequent performances, though Villa-Lobos was probably also keen to demonstrate that an orthodox set-up need not dampen his enthusiasm. This wind quintet behaves like an improvising *chôros* ensemble, especially in the first section when the players tease one another into incrementally wilder virtuosity of a primitively heterophonic, rather than polyphonic-harmonic, nature. This is not polite "chamber music," for nature's wind instruments blow their hearts out, canalized by slowly revolving ostinatos. Humans and nature are in dangerous equipoise; fragments of quasi-Brazilian tunes meld with creature noises, the humans being no less haphazard than the beasts.

In the seventh *chôros* (one of the first to be written, in 1924), a heterogeneous ensemble of flute, oboe, clarinet, alto saxophone, bassoon, violin, cello, and tom-tom hints at a social order for human beings within the disorder of nature. For while the wind instruments emulate wild things of the woods, the Native American melodic motives create harmonic tensions that, whether diatonically concordant or chromatically luxurious, sound urban, and in that sense social. The work encapsulates the often chaotic pluralism of modern communities, which is why Villa-Lobos's exoticism is relevant to us today. In this case the pseudo–Native American chant has the last inarticulate word.

One wouldn't expect Villa-Lobos to bring off an illusion of communal improvisation when writing for full orchestra, though he has an impressive shot at it in the eighth *chôros,* conceived in Paris in 1925, but completed after he had returned to Rio in 1930. One thing follows another in this music, with the same unpredictability as was favored by the young Villa-Lobos and his mates as they prowled through village or city streets. The opening might be real Brazilian folk music, with polymetrical patterns on percussion, through which solo instruments—especially saxophone and contrabassoon—entwine melodic twiddles that, although notated, sound extempore, since the poly-meters and heterophony are too complex to be accurately performed. Nor is accuracy desirable, for this fiesta is not an act of communication from a composed composer to his public. This is why Villa-Lobos, although employ-ing a conductor, minimizes the role. This conductor is more a master of cer-emonies, who like a circus ringleader herds the polyrhythms into a commu-nal dance (a *caracaxa*) that seems to be presently happening *over there,* not in mythical reenactment, like the dance of brigands at the end of Ravel's *Daphnis et Chloé.*

The middle section is more harmonic in texture and regular in rhythm, sounding relatively urban, even urbane. But the forest is still minatory, and the wind instruments' babbling birds and barking beasts are not effaced by the human junketing. There's an affinity with Ives's *Central Park in the Dark* (1898–1907), which juxtaposes a park (or "walled garden"), where human beings congregate socially in inchoate night and nature. Central Park was less scary in Ives's time than it is today, but one isn't surprised that, even then, it fostered improvisation in uncoordinated meters. Villa-Lobos doesn't, like Ives, segregate human from nature but produces a chaotic effect by submit-ting to experience pell-mell, once more reminding us that the root of the word *experience* is in the Latin *ex periculo,* meaning from or out of peril. It's understandable that the third section should reseek a balance between rain forest and city. We're swept back to Africa in a *batuque,* a dance of African origin, but although horns howl, a solo piano makes a show of politesse. A solo pianist, as *Rudepoêma* had demonstrated, may be a one-person band, with chaos under his hands, if not always in his head's control.

Chôros no. 9, also for large orchestra, was written in 1929, the composer's last year in Paris. Less outrageous in starting from urban rather than rural fiesta, it initially resembles an Ives march. A solo bassoon, wriggling out of the march, reminds us of the famous high bassoon line in Stravinsky's *Le Sacre du printemps,* but proves to be a lone Native American luring us not deeper into the rain forest, but into the bewildering byways of the nocturnal city. In Ives's music a solitary Native American, lamenting in a city bar or a café resounding with a solo flute piping a French valse, would seem grotesque, possibly ironic. Villa-Lobos, though contrarious, is hardly ever ironic, even when this French café tune carries us into an American roadhouse, with fetching tunes and lush harmonies redolent of Gershwin. Even so, the lone Native American has the last word, or nonword, as solo bassoon unwinds an incantation with the baleful fascination of a snake charmer. The music's Africanism sounds northern, perhaps Moroccan, and this is not an impossible conjunction, since Villa-Lobos, ears avid as ever, visited Morocco from Paris. The meandering bassoon in the coda sounds forlorn, and the final dance wears the illusory mask of Carnival: a Latin American man, ignorant of where he is and still more of where he's going, is surrogate for us all.

While Villa-Lobos's wildest works—particularly his *chôros* pieces—are those that wear best, they are also those most dependent on the white heat of inspiration. It didn't worry Villa-Lobos that he poured out a vast stream of pieces on the nonprinciple of hit or, more commonly, miss. Even discounting the multitudinous unpublished pieces he semi-improvised or semi-composed for guitar, estimates of the number of his compositions recorded in musical dictionaries vary between 700 and 1,500; he admitted to having lost count around the 1,000 mark, though he hazarded that a tally of around 2,000 would be a not ungenerous estimate. Nor did he differentiate between works that came out, like the "wild" pieces, *sui generis;* those spawned in the parlor, saloon, or cocktail lounge; and those cast, like the well-known Guitar Concerto, in a romantic-academic mold appropriate to the North American concert circuit, on which Villa Lobos's music was liberally performed during his last two decades. The relatively small body of Villa-Lobos's *published* music for guitar neatly illustrates the social categories of his work. The *Suite popular Brasileira*—published in 1908 but probably written and certainly improvised a decade or more earlier—is unabashed salon or saloon music such as the adolescent composer had improvised in bars and cafés. Each movement bears a dual title—Valse-Chôro, Mazurka-Chôro, Gavotta-Chôro, and so on—indicating that his improvising form is being domesticated in a European art form. The *Twelve Études,* on the other hand, written in Paris in 1929, offer a notated form of the Brazilian composer's extemporization in his native haunts, reveling in his virtuosity; especially remarkable are the sultry and sulky eleventh and the fiendishly difficult twelfth. On the brink of a third category stands the *Five Preludes* composed in 1940: pieces that make a useful contribution to the limited repertory for solo guitar, while lacking the panache of the *Études*.

Villa-Lobos's "categories" cannot be tabulated chronologically. Throughout his life he made music in all these genres impartially, asking only that the music had a function when and where it happened. Unsurprisingly, his pluralism is most evident in his songs, wherein the conventional division between "folk" and "pop" scarcely exists. During the first and second decades of the twentieth century he produced masses of pop songs for voice with guitar or piano. The manner is theatrical, often Puccinian, though the songs are more comfortable in a café than in a theater. They are satisfying to sing and pleasing to play ("Confidencia" of 1908 is typical), while neither having nor desiring personal identity. Yet while he was producing these anonymous numbers Villa-Lobos was also making art songs like the *Miniaturas* of 1907–16, some of which are sound pictures of considerable subtlety. "Chromos no. 2," for instance, has a nostalgically jazzy piano part, and in "Chromos no. 3" whole-tone harmonies and lazily lilting rhythms depict the dreamy listlessness of the girl in the swing. The final song evokes the reverberation of bells. Only a few years later Villa-Lobos is writing song cycles such as *Epigramas ironicos e sentimentais* (two sets, 1921 and 1923), which are as ungrammatically aphoristic as the "advanced" piano and chamber works of the same years. Especially startling is his account of a Midsummer Night's Dream, wherein, through the stillness of the night, a crazy moth (*Louca mariposa*) beats frantically against the windowpane, with ad hoc illumination from fireflies. The technique is inconsequential—appropriately so, since all the tiny poems (by Ronaldo de Carvahlo) are about life's ephemerality, whether it be manifest in a chance occurrence like this mad moth or in a laconic description of volatile breeze or riffling water. The brief aphorisms on our moral duplicities have a comparably defusing effect; in these strange little songs ephemerality becomes a kind of acceptance, making an antiphilosophy of momentariness.

Villa-Lobos was unabashed by his pluralism. Of half Spanish and half Native American descent, he would produce corny Palm Court music with no ethnic identity alongside a piece, such as "A lendo do coboclo," of which the main point is its ethnicity. This last piece, based on a legend about a mixed-blood like himself, depends on rhythmic excitation rather than melodic appeal or harmonic event and dates from 1920. During this same period Villa-Lobos entitled a piano work *Saudades das selvas Brasileiras,* probably in response to Milhaud's then well-known *Saudades do Brasil.* The Frenchman's dances are reminiscences of urban and suburban Rio; Villa-Lobos's two dances—respectively in E flat major and A major, a devilish tritone apart—evoke the wild woods. Yet for all his identification with the idea of wilderness, and notwithstanding his youthful pilgrimage into it, (grown-up) Villa-Lobos found his main impulse in the *bifurcation* between wilderness and civilization. If from one point of view he was the *sauvage homme,* who might redeem a fallen world, from another point of view he saw himself as a modernist, steering his country into conformity with the American Dream. In the twenties he musically fulfilled the vision he had of himself as the "Red Redeemer"; when, at the twenties' close, he returned home to Rio he made music that simultaneously sustained Europe and America, in the context of Brazil's indigenous traditions. This was partly a consequence of his inner evolution but was specifically the result of external circumstances. His return to Rio coincided with the dictatorship of Getulio Vargas, with which Villa-Lobos identified himself.

Resettled in Rio, Villa-Lobos did not relinquish the writing of his popular songs, though he gave them a more explicitly national and political slant. The *Modinhas e cançoes,* appearing between 1933 and 1943, are more conventionally formalized than the often startling songs of the twenties. Some of them are direct transferences of traditional material—such as "Cantilena," a house slave song from Bahia, wherein an age-old vocal lament is spun over a piano part emulating bells and drums; or, as comic complement, "A gatinha parda," a child's tune about a lost cat, vividly imitative and simultaneously comic and pathetic, even melancholic. The thirties songs are political in making an appeal for national unity; Villa-Lobos's *"mestizo"* state is manifest in that the numbers are variously classified as Hispanic-French, Italian-Spanish, Portuguese-Italian, Hispanic-African, and even Hispanic-English. The songs with the deepest cultural roots tend to be the most musically potent, but the main point is that a *mestizo* condition may testify to, rather than against, national unity. The interdependence of the genres is most effectively revealed in the songs with piano or guitar accompaniment called *Serestas.* Significantly, this cycle had been started in the crucial Parisian year of 1923, but was substantially added to over the next two decades, as a conscious contribution to Vargas's campaign for unification. So the songs' several identities are not mutually exclusive. Some are genuine folk songs, of rural peasant origin; others exploit the ditties of urban beggars, carters, factory hands, and shop assistants. Some ("Cancao da folha morta" and "Modinha") are overt café music; a few (the raucous "Cancao do carreiro") are as fiercely Brazilian-Hispanic as the "wild" pieces of the Paris years. However unpredictable the manner, the songs are so direct in impact that they count as people's music, preferably to be sung by a loud tenor or savage soprano. Being social gestures, as well as political acts, they have no need of further categorization.

For obvious reasons, church music was the most official manifestation of Vargas's establishmentarianism. The dictator courted Villa-Lobos, realizing that his near-superhuman energy could be an asset in the reorganization of the country. For all his pluralism, Villa-Lobos embraced Roman Catholicism, the accredited state religion, and made the choral music of the Golden Age of Catholic ecclesiastical music a linchpin of his educational, as well as religious, system. The Christian God, the Brazilian nation, the bloody heritage of the Aztecs, and the power of the present secular authority were simultaneously celebrated when, in 1936, Villa-Lobos was commissioned to compose *Missa Sa' Sebastiano* in honor of Rio's patron saint. As with the early salon pieces for guitar, Villa-Lobos gave each section of his mass a double title—one, in Latin, traditionally liturgical, the other, in Portuguese, indicating local and patriotic identity, with reference to Sebastian's virtue, glory, and martyrdom, all of which succored the Brazilian nation.

Whereas the works of the twenties vociferously proclaimed Villa-Lobos's individuality, the church music of the thirties effaces it, as is appropriate to liturgical function. The St. Sebastian mass is written in pure Palestrinian polyphony in three parts, the lines flowing either by step or through the intervals sanctioned by sixteenth-century precedent. The rite may be sung either by boys', women's, or men's voices, the music's sobriety inducing deference as well as reverence. It is a typical Villa-Lobos paradox that a composer so remarkable for lawless startlement should also be capable of such depersonalized humility; even so, Villa-Lobos makes "Palestrina style" a part of his own culture, just as the Brazilian Catholic church found a place for strains from the magical cults of African Macumba. A Brazilian composer makes expert Roman polyphony because the Roman church has become endemic to his society; traditional spiritual grace survives even though the vocal range extends that of orthodox ecclesiastical style. Similar qualities distinguish smaller contributions to Catholic liturgical polyphony made by Villa-Lobos over the thirties and forties; especially beautiful is an *Ave Maria* of 1938, set in Portuguese in five parts and capped, ten years later, by another setting of the Latin text. Such devotionally functional music, expertly written for a cappella voices, was also attuned to presently emergent Brazil, encouraging conservatism and even subservience to Europe, yet blossoming, in the Latin *Ave Maria,* from austere modality into a self-congratulatory, jubilant AMEN.

Although Villa-Lobos's Catholic church music is peripheral to the mainstream of his work, we may note, during the thirties, a parallel shift toward conservatism in his concert music, notably in the nine *Bachianas Brasileiras* he composed between 1930 and 1945—dates that exactly coincide with Vargas's reign. In these works Villa-Lobos synthesized the empirical techniques of *chôros* with those of Bach, the European composer he loved most. Although Bach's Protestantism was superficially alien to this (or almost any) Brazilian, there are profound affinities between Bach's compositional principles and Villa-Lobos's. For Bach's unbroken beat—usually at about the speed of the human pulse—and his unified figurations affirm a faith that has qualities in common with the wholeness and "going-on-ness" of the musics of communal fiesta: as Percy Grainger, another *sauvage homme*—of the Australian Outback rather than of the Amazonian rain forest—pointed out, he being a vehement anti-Christian, not merely of an alternative Christian denomination. Alone among the European masters, Bach has been consistently pillaged by jazz and pop musicians seeking a "paradise of archetypes and repetition" parallel, in an industrial environment, to those that flourished in "primitive" cultures. Bach's unity embraced diversity in the rich complexity of his harmonic polyphony, and in this Villa-Lobos cannot compete with him. Nonetheless, he was justified in claiming that, since Bach is the most universal of the great composers, a modern composer may adapt his affirmations to his own more mundane ends. This is what Villa-Lobos attempts in the first of his *Bachianas Brasileiras,* composed in 1930 and scored for eight cellos—the singing instrument, like a sublimated and extended baritone voice, that Villa-Lobos loved most and played best.

Around this date Villa-Lobos made several arrangements, for massed cellos, of preludes and fugues from Bach's Forty-Eight. Very fine they sound, given Villa-Lobos's love of Bach and expertise on the cello, though this does not mean that the first in the series of *Bachianas Brasileiras* is also Bachian pastiche. Again, Villa-Lobos gives each movement a double title, one to indicate its Bachian baroque universality, the other in reference to its Brazilian topicality and locality. Thus the first movement is headed "Intoduçao-Embolada," the baroque "introduction" pointing to the continuous motor rhythm and unbroken figuration that relate it to a Brandenburg concerto, while "embolada" tells us that the tunes gambol in the spirit of Brazilian fiesta. Although not intricately contrapuntal, the music is in eight real parts, as is the slow movement, which attains a Bach-like fusion of sustained melody with textural density, while at the same time rending the guts with harmonic nostalgia. This *modinha* is a sentimental, urban, Italianate pop song from a Portuguese nineteenth-century tradition, which can claim something like Bachian universality, since retrospection becomes a positive virtue, even a substitute for Bach's faith. Listening to this *modinha*—which however popular in manner is Villa-Lobos's own invention—one can better understand the faith necessary to build Brasilia, the miraculous new city, in the midst of the wilderness, while also sensing, in the music's piercing melancholy, how vulnerable the New City is, how frail in the face of the omnivorous "jungle" that may reduce complex human artifacts to an empty shell.

Only in the finale of *Bachianas Brasileiras no. 1* does Villa-Lobos assay a straight Bachian fugue. Its theme has a syncopated playfulness such as Bach often relished (in, for instance, the Jig Fugue), and although Villa-Lobos's fugue doesn't display the interdependence of polyphony and homophony typical of Bach, it proves that the Brazilian was a natural folk polyphonist who in this piece uses the classical device of augmentation so spontaneously that we respond to it not as an intellectual ploy but as an inevitable event. Similarly, in the ninth *Bachianas Brasileiras,* composed in 1945, Villa-Lobos creates from the Bachian convention of a fantasia and fugue for organ something that reminds us less of Lutheran church music than of a ritual sung by Brazilian Native Americans. Although this work is usually heard in the composer's arrangement for string orchestra—in which form its sonority is impressively organlike—it was originally written for a large a cappella chorus, and its grandeur is fully revealed only in this version. The string version was made only because the vocal one proved extremely difficult to perform. A recording by the BBC Singers under Odaline de la Martinez has demonstrated, however, that the choral form is as practicable as it is magnificent.[1]

Like the choral part of the *Sexteto mistico,* the ninth *Bachianas Brasileiras* is wordless; "mystically" colored vowels and consonants become a living-and-breathing symphony of creatures human and nonhuman. Even so, compared with the *sauvage* works of the twenties, this music is Europeanized, as well as ostensibly Bachian. Its convention of fantasia and fugue opens with pedal notes around which undulate stepwise-moving or pentatonic vocalise reminiscent of the wordless choral episode in Delius's *Song of the High Hills,* which also whirls in ecstatic (if nordic) nature worship as a backdrop to human venturesomeness. But Villa-Lobos's vocal fugue is Bach-like in structure, with a diatonic theme lilting in conjunct motion, like the la-la-laing refrains in Delius's *Mass of Life.* Only the 11/8 time signature and the tipsy syncopations and rumboid cross-rhythms relate Bachian precedents to South American fiesta, especially when the diatonic theme is slipperily chromaticized. License is disciplined in an imposing coda, wherein augmentation is again used to consummatory effect. This fugue is "European" in having an unanswerable end, as well as a beginning and a middle.

Although there is a case for considering the ninth *Bachianas Brasileiras* a masterwork of twentieth-century choral music, it is not the most celebrated piece in the series. That honor belongs to the fifth, composed in 1938, which is scored, like the first, for eight cellos, but with the addition of a soprano soloist. The opening section, called "Aria cantilena," is a wordless vocalise, though its "middle" has words by Ruth V. Correa, while the second and last movement is set to a text by Manuel Bandeira. That the beginning of the work is wordless is not fortuitous; when copyright problems loomed, Villa-Lobos, ever the pragmatist, cheerfully abandoned words and reinforced the vocal line with first cello. In this form the aria triumphed, not only musically, but also sociologically and economically, for the vocalise has attained the status of a pop hit, graduating to TV commercials. This is far from being a sneer. The tune is magical, marvelous, and memorable—a supreme hit. That Villa-Lobos could thus sunder the ultimate barrier between art and commerce offers further evidence of his crucial place in his (and our) cultural scene. The words for the middle section are about the rapt, out-of-this-world state induced by Brazilian twilight. When the *modinha*-style vocalise returns, hummed in a truncated da capo, we realize that this melody makes words unnecessary.

Although the second, *danza* movement hasn't the magic of the vocalise, its words confirm Villa-Lobos's habitual message, for a woman carols in the forest, her love song entwined with, and often indistinguishable from, that of the blithe birds. There is nothing Bachian about this, except that it is still in eight real parts and balances the soloist's cross-meters against a motor rhythm. Compared with the works of the twenties this piece is artistically formalized, reflecting not only its Bachian affiliation but also its alignment with Italian, French, Spanish, and Portuguese concert musics. This, too, is an aspect of Villa-Lobos's significance as a "pluralistic" twentieth-century composer.

The relation between the *chôros*-style works (mostly of the twenties) and the *Bachianas Brasileiras* (mostly of the thirties) is neatly revealed by comparing the 1924 *Chôros* for flute and clarinet with the 1938 *Bachianas Brasileiras* for flute and bassoon. The Bachian piece still relates to the "old Brazilian serenade" wherein two or more singing instruments converse, calling to one another as though they were human creatures or beasts or birds or even reptiles or insects. This notion is modified when the intertwining melodies attempt canonic imitation, momentarily sounding like civilized Bach himself, in the open spaces of the savannah rather than in the labyrinthine forest. Even so, the second of the two movements is less disciplined than the first, for the flute takes off in whirligig cadenzas, like a bird beating its wings against the threat of imprisonment. Since the bassoon is inspired by the flute to its own weightier agility, it would be oversimple to identify either instrument with wilderness or civilization. The point is rather that for Villa-Lobos, and perhaps for modern humans in general, the states of wilderness and civilization are interdependent. That this piece is extremely demanding on the performers, both in technique and in sheer physical endurance, bears on the nature of Villa-Lobos's music, which is at once *play* and *contest:* a synonym for the "battle of life."

If we reflect on how Villa-Lobos's music evolved through the (wild) twenties and the (more disciplined) thirties, we'll understand how, as a phenomenon, he relates to our situation in the "Western" world. Exhausted by several centuries' dominance of head and will over heart and body, Westerners have been breaking barriers between art, folk, jazz, and pop musics, seeking an Eternal Return. Although we cannot, and should not, relinquish our "Faustian" heritage, we can and should rediscover what it means to live, *for the time being,* in the present moment. So, in assessing Villa-Lobos's place in our world, we must return to the point we started from: the childhood he celebrated in his vintage works of the early twenties. When, in mature years, Villa-Lobos became the state-sponsored father of Brazilian music in being appointed, by Vargas, director of the state educational system in music, the wheel came full circle. In a psychological sense his music was child-oriented from his earliest days, so his specifically educational work makes a public statement on the basis of his most private impulses.

How, in between making his multitudinous compositions fulfilling so many different social functions, Villa-Lobos found time to embark on so many giant educational projects defies explanation. His catalogue of published pieces and arrangements of traditional material, for use by the young at every stage of development, is immense, and by no means were all his ventures committed to the durability of print. Since most everyone has a voice, choral music was central to this educational enterprise, and Villa-Lobos's choral arrangements of folk songs were sung, often under his charismatic direction, by hundreds, occasionally by thousands, of children and adults. Choral communality became a political as well as a religious testament, culminating in a monster concert reputedly given, in the open air, by a choir of forty thousand children and an orchestra of a thousand. (Can this really have been possible?[2]) But for Villa-Lobos himself, as distinct from his political masters, such grotesque public statements were ancillary to a desire and a need to promote music in school and home. Appropriately arranged, choral settings of folk material could be domestically performed, which is why, between 1932 and 1949, he published vast collections of "educational" part songs and rearranged many of them as piano pieces under the title *Guia prático:* all skillfully devised as "teaching material" that excites the sonorous imagination while at the same time drilling the fingers. We must remember that for the young people who played the pieces the tunes were their lifeblood, sung and danced to on the streets. Even more than the adult *Serestas,* Villa-Lobos's children's pieces live in their immediacy, which sets feet prancing and fingers twitching. Only Bartók's *Mikrokosmos* can rival Villa-Lobos's *Guia prático* as teaching material. Regrettably, the Western educational system has to a degree recognized the former while remaining oblivious of the latter.

Although Villa-Lobos regarded *Guia prático* as an educational system, there were no barriers between his teaching material and his "art" music. Two comparable collections of piano pieces, *Cirandas* and *Cirandinhas,* are less tied to an educational function, though their titles indicate that they are based on children's rhymes and tunes. The earlier cycle, *Cirandinhas* (1925) presents tunes straight, with almost Satiean economy. They are mostly negotiable by reasonably talented children, though the quite lengthy setting of a rare slow melody, "Lindos olhos que ela tem," calls for a delicate balance of sonorities if it is to register as the mini–tone poem it is. In the *Cirandas* of 1928 other or the same children's song games are mutated into elaborate pieces in which virtuosity serves not to show off the player's skills but to create what Villa-Lobos called an "atmosphere." This—though the pieces are recital music—may be related to the "continuum" within which musical fiesta functions. If the *Cirandas* haven't the distilled poetry of the earlier set, they are superbly laid out for the instrument, and their "atmospheres" reveal the often tragic implications of the (unspoken) verses. Many of the implicit tales will have been familiar to the children from the days when they were bounced on their mothers' knees; in the more frequent quick numbers in either cycle the words are less significant, for we are involved with the children more in action than in narrative, frolicking vicariously in the cross- and counter-rhythms of popular song and dance.

Although the years of Villa-Lobos's deliberate dedication to "educational" music coincide with the dates of Vargas's presidency, he produced music for or about children at every stage in his career, since the truth of childish instinct was his basic theme. The earliest instance of a suite based on children's games goes back to 1919–20, predating *Cirandas Brasileiras*. A suite of piano pieces infantile in mindless merriment, *Carnival das crianças Brasileiras* links real childhood with the pretend-childhood of Carnival, allowing festive antics to impart an exhibitionistic panache. How inseparably inner and outer, private and public impulses are linked is revealed when, ten years later, Villa-Lobos transmuted the little pieces into a fantasia for piano and orchestra, comparable with the fantasy for the same forces that Milhaud made, in 1926, out of his Brazilian *Salade*. Milhaud called his piece *Le Carnaval d'Aix;* Villa-Lobos's *Carnival das crianças Brasileiras* becomes, in its orchestral version, *Mômeprécôce*, in reference to Momus, the king of Carnival, and to the *gamins* and *gamines* who sing and dance in the guise of commedia dell'arte characters. While the original piano pieces are music "for" children, the piano and orchestra piece, needing a conductor, has become concert music, though this is countered by the solo pianist acting, even mimicking, the masked young folk.

Once again Villa-Lobos obliterates distinctions between children's play and adult art and can do so because of the nature of the world he lived in. We think we have put away childish things, and might even congratulate ourselves on having done so. Yet when we reflect on the catastrophes our self-conscious literacy has landed us in, we begin to understand why many of Villa-Lobos's educational works tend to overlap—children being small savages—with the wilder works of his early, vintage years. It is therefore appropriate that, rounding off this survey of Villa-Lobos's work, we should return to those years, and in particular to the two suites of piano pieces composed in 1918–19 and 1921, to which he gave the title *A prole do bebé*. These were among the works that Villa-Lobos took with him to Paris. The most famous piece in the first set—a portrait of Pulcinello, a doll and Carnival character—sounds like a sketch for the astonishing *Rudepoêma* (which was completed in Paris), while the second cycle is perhaps, with *Rudepoêma* and the *Noneto*, the composer's most audacious work. Although the pieces draw on children's songs and dances, this is no longer music for practical use by children, though it wonderfully stimulates their potential. Each piece is a small tone poem of high textural sophistication, creative of both mood and physical activity.

The pieces' ambivalent position between folk pop music and art is evident in that they emulate, in the first suite, not actual children but their surrogates in the form of dolls, and in the second suite not real birds and beasts but toy imitations of them, presumably in a fairly affluent nursery. Villa-Lobos's habitual equivocation between play (something *done*) and art (something *made*)—finds here its deepest manifestation, demonstrating how toys may be a defense mechanism against an inimical world. Consider the hard textures and very Native American, peg-legged cross-rhythms in the portrait of the paper cockroach; or the little cat who, though fabricated of cardboard, meows piteously in undulating semitones that, with the aid of cunning pedaling, may give an illusion of microtonal whining. These caterwaulings are haloed in ripe chords of ninth, eleventh, and thirteenth; so physical is the music that the small feline is incarnate not only in the sounds it utters but also in the tension of sheathed claws that occasionally strike in spitting glissandos. The jazzy flavor of the harmony, with its resonantly spaced tenths, underlines this equipoise between surface elegance and dangerous depths. The end, when the melodically wailing thirds and fourths are boosted by acerbic chords of the thirteenth, encapsulates the piece's point, for the pathos of the subsiding meows is cancelled by a fortissimo B flat in the middle register, echoed in a gong tone in the lowest reach of the keyboard. Far from being music for performance by children, this music identifies the child "lost" in a city apartment with modern humanity's uneasy stance in an industrial society. A kid's kitten hides the heart of a jungle jaguar, and it's unclear whether the child or the cat is the more distraught.

Similar astonishments occur throughout the cycle. The papier mâché mouse has an infantile, plain diatonic ditty engulfed in contrarious rhythms, figurations, and note clusters, revealing the pathos of smallness in a too-big world. The little rubber dog undulates in 11/8 time, sensual in harmony but forlorn in jagged rhythms and creaky timbres, while the leaden ox lives up to its Taurean nature by lumbering around in dislocated samba rhythms over a range covering seven octaves. Strangest of all is the little cloth bird who, having winged its way from the Amazonian forests to a Rio nursery, makes Messiaen's *oiseaux exotiques* of thirty years later sound like domesticated parakeets. These whirring trills, stuttering repeated notes, chittering note clusters, and screeching glissandos prove that keyboard virtuosity, however far beyond a child's technical competence, need not be alien to a child's imaginative world. Technical audacity may be an act of self-discovery relished by the young at heart; discovery may induce fright as well as delight—as in the marrow-freezing repeated notes and dryly champing chords in the piece describing the little glass wolf—the scariest and longest piece in the suite, significantly placed last.

This disturbing music tells us that these audible toys are "playthings" in a sense very different from Milhaud's Brazilian ballet, *L'homme et son désir*. In *A prole do bebé* cat, dog, bird, bull, wolf, and the other creatures, though "little" and "toys," initiate rites that carry the young, and us with them, through the perils and paradoxes that are the stuff of life. This survey of Villa-Lobos's oeuvre has followed a roughly chronological order, but it inevitably climaxes in these extraordinary pieces about childhood, which were, indeed, among the very pieces he bore to Paris, way back in 1923, in order to remind moribund Europeans of what life basically was, and still could be, about.

Villa-Lobos's most deeply characteristic music is his work of the early twenties, that which is most firmly rooted in Brazilian sources. Yet it would also seem that his essential achievement is to have refashioned those sources in terms of the polyglot, technological, industrialized society that is epitomized in the new city of Brasilia. The music Villa-Lobos composed over his final decade has something to tell us about this evolution. Is the "modern city" victorious? If so, is the victory unequivocal?

These questions may be misleading, since some aspects of "European" encroachment are not conducive to modernity. During his final decade Villa-Lobos composed several a cappella settings of religious (Roman Catholic) texts in which the modal polyphony accords, as did that of his earlier liturgical music, with the conventions of Renaissance ecclesiastical music. Yet the sounds are reborn. Settings of texts by the sixteenth-century poet-priest Padre Jose de Achista—especially a Nativity piece, "Praesepe," for mezzosoprano solo with a wordless chorus in limpid homophony—have a modal purity as strange as it is serene. Most remarkable of all is *Bendita sabedoria,* commissioned by the Collegiate Chorus of New York University and first performed in New York City, hub of modern technocracy, in 1958, the year the composer died. The Latin texts from Psalms and Proverbs are aphoristic fragments of biblical lore, and they are set in a modal homophony so concordantly transparent that it induces awe. In his final year Villa-Lobos transmutes the church-and-state-sanctioned idiom of his earlier church music into the innocence of the child-savage he fundamentally was. Although the style would seem to be remote from the startlements of the *Prole do bebé* piano pieces that, early in his career, represented his heart of hearts, the candor and the "newborn" feeling are the same. Villa-Lobos's pagan and Christian identities finally prove to be allied; he can never have doubted that we must become as little children if we are to enter the Kingdom of Heaven.

During the last year of his life Villa-Lobos also composed his final string quartet, the seventeenth. Though this music isn't as "purged" as the devotional *Bendita sabedoria,* it has something of the same transparency, savoring the classical purity of the string quartet medium in a way distinct from the regionally folky veins of the early and middle string quartets. Lucently written for the medium, it is, if often rhythmically energetic, basically concordant, owing something to Renaissance choral polyphony, to the seventeenth-century string *ricercar,* and to Bachian fugue. Here is further evidence that, way back in his youth in Rio, Villa-Lobos had educated himself on Vincent d'Indy's *Cours de composition musicale.*[3] In toto, Villa-Lobos's series of seventeen string quartets is, if less enigmatic and less profound than Shostakovitch's superb sequence of fifteen, impressively affirmative. The quartets, like several other aspects of Villa-Lobos's music, deserve to be better known.

Yet if, in his final Catholic church music and in the last four of his string quartets, Villa-Lobos discovered a magic fountain that linked his primitivism to his sophistication, the bulk of his late music was oriented toward New York, whence most of the works were commissioned by famous soloists or maestro conductors. The most revealing instance is the sequence of five piano concertos composed between 1945 and 1957. Written in the tradition of the big romantic piano concerto, and unselfconsciously emulating Tschaikovsky and Rachmaninoff, they were essays in a style relished by mass audiences in an urban metropolis, the convention being congenial to Villa-Lobos in that he could see himself, the composer-soloist, as a loner, mustering the orchestral tutti into an industrialized "tribe." In fact, Villa-Lobos didn't often himself play the solo parts, and several of the concertos were commissioned by virtuoso pianists who were awed by his personal charisma and perhaps by the dazzling pianism displayed in the solo pieces written in the twenties, notably the notorious *Rudepoêma.* If these concertos compromise between the Brazilian rain forest and the asphalt jungle, there is a sense in which that is what all Villa-Lobos's characteristic music is about; certainly he was aware that in the concertos he was forging a hybrid between a very old and savage fiesta in *chôros* style and a virtuoso concerto in the romantic tradition. He built each work on the same four-movement plan: a substantial allegro; a slow movement (usually andante con moto or poco adagio); a scherzo, leading to a cadenza, in which the soloist takes over, refashioning and sometimes developing the material, and instigating an exuberant, usually triumphant, finale that transforms a modern concert hall into a place of celebration. As in a classical-romantic concerto the order of slow movement and scherzo may be reversed, but the pivotal position of the cadenza is constant.

This concept—between fiesta, which is communal, and sonata-style conflict, which segregates the soloist—entailed problems that Villa-Lobos hadn't entirely foreseen. The massive first concerto makes gestures toward

Tchaikovsky and Rachmaninoff that don't quite come off, since the vast first allegro is constructed on the mosaic principle of the composer's *chôros*-style pieces; sheer energy suffices, and the Big Tune remains just around the corner, rather than fulfilled. Still, the composer's invention is either unquenchably voluble or prodigally invigorating, according to one's point of view; and the enormous cadenza before the finale has an experiential logic, since it takes over material from all the movements, leaving us in no doubt that, if there is a conflict, it is masterminded by the soloist—in effect, if not often in fact, Villa-Lobos himself, who had arrived, long ago, in Paris, to take over the "civilized" world. The effrontery takes one's breath away, leaving one openmouthed as well as open-eared, but perhaps too battered to be fully rewarded in musical terms.

The second concerto, composed in 1948 for the Brazilian pianist J'ao de Sousa Lima—a close friend of the composer and a pianist of comparable aplomb—comes nearer to achieving Villa-Lobos's hopeful compromise between *chôros*-style fiesta and a romantic piano concerto for the American concert hall. The opening allegro is content to be festively ceremonial, uninhibited from start to finish, and so persuades us momentarily to accept "tribal" identity. Against it, the spacious slow movement (the only one in the five concertos marked "lento") evokes a new-old world in a hypnotically syncopated pulse, from which slowly germinates a genuine Native American song ("Ens Mokece"), bringing lyrical consummation for Villa-Lobos as soloist-composer, yet also propelling the aboriginal into the modern world. This time, the Big Tune, such as we anticipate in Rachmaninoff, comes off, and is no less effective for being without the Russian's scruff-of-the-neck importunity. So a romantic concerto-conflict seems to have occurred, and to have been resolved, as in the first concerto it is not. Significantly, Villa-Lobos dispenses with a scherzo but makes the *cadença*—ambiguously marked "quasi allegro"—a movement in its own right, signaling the soloist's victory, not through technical bravura, but through the very *process* of improvisation. Although the cadenza is notated, it sounds as if it is being invented here and now, telling us that "civilization" is most likely to be attained, or rediscovered, through the inner strife of an individual man or woman capable of Villa-Lobos–like spontaneity. This embryonically brooding cadenza generates an allegro finale that is merrily triumphant, culminating in a Big Tune that is indubitably romantic, yet also folkily guileless, if not entirely guiltless.

Two other aspects of Villa-Lobos's attempt at hybridization between his ethnic identity and "Noo York"—in the sense the city acquires in Gershwin's

Porgy and Bess—call for comment. During his New York years, when Villa-Lobos tried himself out in any mask his pluralism offered, he came into contact, but crossed swords, with Hollywood, since MGM commissioned him to do a score for a movie version of W. H. Hudson's marvelous *Green Mansions*, which, in dealing with Rima, the forest-child of nature, embraced a basic Villa-Lobos myth. The score he produced was in the luscious, late romantic vein of his full-scale operas, such as his version of Lorca's *Yerma*, and was therefore not intrinsically antipathetic to the tastes of Hollywood moguls. Even so, the movie business couldn't take the score, which was tidied up, presumably to make it, in their view, more commercially viable. Villa-Lobos, a man by temperament as impetuous as his music, furiously reclaimed his score and transformed it into a symphonic poem for very large orchestra and voices, with texts by his friend Dora Vasceoncellos, then appositely the consul-general representing Brazil in New York. In its form as concert music, this *Poem of the Amazonian Forest* is even more of a hybrid between art and industry than are the piano concertos. It works effectively, but is not a Villa-Lobos masterpiece, being a negative instance of hybridization.

Yet hybridization has a positive aspect also, since Villa-Lobos's significant place in the contemporary scene depends on the difference between what musical culture means to him and South Americans and what it means to Europeans and North Americans. We have noted that the technical sophistication of Villa-Lobos's wildest (and best) works does not deprive them of an innocence that links them to children's games, to rural and urban fiesta, and, we may add, to the "eternal present" of Latin American jazz. In this last context it is pertinent to note that the Brazilian singer-poet-pianist-composer Tania Maria should, as pop musician, complement Villa-Lobos as art musician. "Normally," she has remarked, "when you are Brazilian and you play music people want it that you always seem very happy and very high. My music is an invitation."[4] Her songs live in fiesta's timeless moments, embracing rain forest and village alongside the cocktail lounges and discos of Rio, as does the (often very happy and very high) music of Villa-Lobos. The sambalike polymeters and the harmonic and figurative luxuriance of Maria's piano sometimes sound similar to Villa-Lobos's pianism—or at least they did on her jazz-oriented discs issued before she gravitated into heavier—probably more lucrative if less musically rewarding— rock. Although she cannot approach the imaginative audacities of Villa-Lobos's *Rudepoêma* and the second *Prole do bebé* suite, the energy sparked by her piano is Villa-Lobos–like in its fusion of hazy opulence with crystalline clarity, as well as in its global-village multifariousness.

It is improbable that Tania Maria was consciously influenced by Villa-Lobos, though no educated person of her generation could have escaped his impact on the Brazilian school curriculum. Native American, Portuguese, Spanish, French, Mexican, Cuban, Caribbean, and American musics meld in her work, as in his. In both, environmental immediacy is mated to technical sophistication to mutual advantage. This helps us understand why it doesn't matter that Villa-Lobos's huge output includes a substantial amount of dross. He seldom thought of his creations as "good" or "bad," asking only whether, in their given context, they *worked*. His music was predestined by its purposes, and there is a great deal of it because it is the fruit of (in his words) "Une terre immense, ardente, et généreuse."[5] That Villa-Lobos and Tania Maria arrive at a similar point by contrary directions may even have some relevance to the future of music. Although he could never have been a Beethoven, we have seen that Villa-Lobos has genuine affinities with Bach, as have several jazz and pop performers indifferent to the Viennese classics. It may be that Western civilization is rediscovering an ongoing performance culture comparable with that in which the juvenile Villa-Lobos "had his being" and that this discovery is necessary before we can hope, or deserve, to produce another Beethoven.

NOTES

1. Heitor Villa-Lobos, *Chamber and Choral Music,* BBC Singers, Odaline de la Martinez, Lontano Records CD LNT 102.

2. This story has been often repeated, in books as well as on liner notes. Villa-Lobos's "gargantuanism" is part of a long Latin American tradition and is closely paralleled by the no less legendary "monster-concerts" organized by the New Orleans pianist-composer Louis-Moreau Gottschalk.

3. It was at Vincent d'Indy's Schola Cantorum that Villa-Lobos made his notorious rejection of academic tuition. Rather surprisingly, d'Indy, aristocrat, autocrat, Roman Catholic, and anti-Semite, was amiably disposed toward Villa-Lobos and attempted to tame his ungrammatical excesses. When Villa-Lobos returned to Brazil he adapted several aspects of d'Indy's *Cours* to the scheme of music education he embarked on at the behest of Vargas.

4. Tania Maria, liner notes to *Live,* Accord CD 112552.

5. Heitor Villa-Lobos quoted in liner notes to *Villa-Lobos par lui-même,* Choeurs and Orchestre National de la Radiodiffusion Française, Heitor Villa-Lobos, notes written by Pierre Vidal, English trans. Denis Ogan, EMI CZS 767229 2.

8

Carlos Chávez in Mexico City and New York

IN PARIS AFTER World War I, Europeans recognized that Villa-Lobos's new-old music had something which they had lost and were worse for the lack of. Similarly, Americans after World War II found refreshment, if of a less sparkling vintage, in the more streamlined qualities of the Brazilian's later music. Yet in the context of Western civilization he remained an alien; he was admired precisely because he was different. It is possible, however, that rain forest and wilderness may have a more intrinsic relationship to what, given the disintegration of Western values, we cannot help being; this is palpable in the life and work of Carlos Chávez, whose land lies between Brazil and the United States. Born in Mexico City in 1899, Chávez was to Mexican music what Villa-Lobos was to Brazilian music: his country's most potent creative talent and the instigator and director of its state program in musical education.

Like Villa-Lobos, Chávez was of *mestizo* stock, his maternal grandfather being Native American. Yet although from the age of five he was familiar with Native American culture, he was not, like Villa-Lobos, a complete rebel. He studied piano and violin enthusiastically, playing almost exclusively European music; from childhood onward he composed romantic piano pieces a long way after Schumann, a famed teller of fairy tales. Even so, he eschewed formal training, maintaining that academic instruction nullified spontaneity. Both the similarities and the distinctions between Chávez and Villa-Lobos mirror the differences between their cultures. Brazil was perpetually in revolutionary ferment as it struggled, with the dubious help of a succession of dictators, from an agricultural society toward an industrial one; but it did not seek a decisive "new start" such as Mexico embarked on when, in 1910, the dictator Porfirio Díaz was overthrown. The consciously proletarian, Russian- and Marxist-inspired New Era, established in Mexico by 1921, became the mainspring of Chávez's career and of his art. José Vasconcelos, the charismatic minister of education to the New Era, was adept at countering the pragmatic realism of left-wing political philosophy with a passionate regard for aesthetic values. He fostered the work of the mural painter-propagandist Diego Rivera and appointed the avant-garde architects who, in collaboration with Rivera, made Mexico City a visual wonder of the modern world. Complementarily, Vasconcelos spotted Chávez's talent and commissioned him to create a ballet—at once social ritual and political propaganda—in celebration of *El fuego nuevo*. Disorganization, abetted by competitive administrative squabbles, saw to it that the ballet was never produced. Even so, the seal had been set on Chávez's national and eventually international fame, for as a result of his friendship with Vasconcelos, Chávez became a contributor to the national revolutionary paper *El Universal* and, furthering his journalistic work, went to live in New York between 1926 and 1928. Close ties established with Copland, Edgard Varèse, and Henry Cowell fostered kinship with progressive American music and politics alike, whereas Villa-Lobos's contacts with North America were delayed until later in his life. During the years in which Villa-Lobos was enlivening Parisian sophisticates with his bombshells about children and savages, Chávez was becoming a responsible musical politician, investigating connections between music and industrial electronics. He published a remarkably advanced pamphlet on this subject.[1]

Mexico City is an industrial oasis in a land of forests and deserts; New York City is an asphalt jungle with its own problems of alienation and oppression. The Mexican Chávez and the New Yorker Copland recognized this consanguinity, and it is not surprising that their musics should have qualities in common from which Villa-Lobos's sensual fecundity is remote. The reasons for this are rooted in Mexico's history, about which its greatest poet-philosopher, Octavio Paz, has written in *The Labyrinth of Solitude:*

> Man collaborates actively in defending universal order, which is always being threatened by chaos. And when it collapses, he must create a new one, this time his own. But exile, expiation, and penitence should proceed from the reconciliation of man with the universe. Neither the Mexican nor the North American has achieved this reconciliation. What is even more serious, I am afraid we have lost our sense of the very meaning of all human activity, which is to assure the operation of an order in which knowledge and innocence, man and nature, are in harmony. If the solitude of the Mexican is like a stagnant pool, that of the North American is like a mirror. We have ceased to be springs of living water.[2]

Chávez's importance in Pan-American life was thus dependent at once on his place in the cultural-political scene and on his art's response to the equation between primitivism and industrialism. A youthful work, created in 1926, is explicitly entitled *Caballos de vapor*, in which the phallic horse is harnessed to industrial energy in music that fuses tropical exuberance of line with mechanized motor rhythm, though the piece is far more than an imitation of factory noises such as was offered in once-notorious orchestral works of Arthur Honegger and Alexander Mossolov. Chávez too wrote purely instrumental works, one of them entitled *Energía*, in the same genre, though a more valid parallel would be with the (also contemporary) percussion-dominated works of Varèse that find common ground between factory noises and fiestas.

Chávez made no distinction between the archaic and the modern elements in his art, as we may note in his early ballet, *Los cuatro soles*, which, if less electrically charged than Stravinsky's epoch-making *Le Sacre du printemps*, is the only work of the twenties that carries Stravinsky's radicalism a stage further. For *Los cuatro soles* is radical in the basic sense that it searches for the wellsprings of being in the four elements of water, air, fire, and earth, each representing a mythological stage in the human story. All four elements, allotted a movement each, end violently: water in a flood, air (wind) in an ice age, fire (sun) in volcanic eruption and torrents of lava, and earth (where we are now) in self-asserting desperation. Chávez's characteristic techniques—monodic modal incantation, geometric pattern-making, hypnotic repetition, pounding, often polymetric rhythms—are deployed in an irresistible surge toward cataclysm, with whooping horns and blaring trombones. That the sound of this aboriginal music should sometimes resemble the sounds that Copland was creating in contemporary New York points to the link between the communality of fiesta and a machine society. Chávez's sinewy, diatonic modal textures may have sprung from the sun-baked deserts and monolithic rocks of Mexico and from the seemingly ageless stylizations of Mexican folk musics; but they also belong to modern America, insofar as savagery is latent within the steel girders of a machine-made world. It is not only Copland's deliberately Pan-American works, such as *El salón México*, that remind us of Chávez; there are echoes too in his Wild West ballets and, at a deeper level, in the stark abstraction of works like the *Piano Variations* and the *Short Symphony*. In this context tough American jazz and basic Latin American pop represent a crossover between old and new.

Despite its harsh balance of contradictory forces, Chávez's music operates on our human behalf. In the last movement of *Los cuatro soles* orgy is effaced by a moment of quietude—a monody for solo violin, leading into a humanely choral, as well as orchestral, epilogue. Chávez's chorus shouts in massive homophony and antiphony, with a ferocity comparable with that of genuinely primitive fiesta which, "for the time being," becomes ours. Occasionally the ostinato patterns of the chorus recall the childlike simplicities of Milhaud's *L'Homme et son désir*, adumbrating a human renewal, though we are not tempted to describe any of Chávez's music as "a plaything." His metamorphoses, in danced and choreographed forms, tend to be painful, as are his purely instrumental works.

A case in point is the piece that made Chávez internationally famous, the *Sinfonía India* of 1935. This is not a symphony in the European sense but a one-movement dance-ritual comparable with Villa-Lobos's *Rudepoêma* or *Noneto*, though without the *chôros*-like abandon of those works. Compared with the Villa-Lobos pieces, *Sinfonía India* seems deliberately to evoke lost states of being, calling (exceptionally for Chávez) on real Native American tunes and aiming at an "auralization" of the Mexican deserts. Chávez, more intellectual than Villa-Lobos, consciously explores the implications of his *mestizo* condition, seeking the putative identity of the "lost Indian" and even of ancestral Aztec civilization.

There is a prophecy of this in Chávez's first symphony—known as *Sinfonía de Antigona* because it derived from music Chávez had written for Jean Cocteau's adaptation of Sophocles' *Antigone* when it was produced in Mexico City in 1932. The work is neither a symphony nor a symphonic poem, and it carries no literary program analogous to Sophocles' play, though it reflects the drama's moods of rebellion and exaltation and is thus in tune with postrevolutionary Mexico. The musical techniques differ little from those of Chávez's overtly Mexican works. Again, the themes are modal, with a preponderance of stepwise movement interspersed with leaps of minor thirds, fourths, and fifths, rather than of major thirds and sixths. Chávez claimed that such melodic formulas were Aztec in origin, though he must merely have meant that they were archaic, since he admitted that almost nothing is or can be known about Aztec music before the Spanish conquest. Certainly in this symphony a huge orchestra—piccolo, flute, alto flute, oboe, cor anglais, three bassoons, contrabassoon, heckelphone, E-flat clarinet, three B-flat clarinets, bass clarinet, eight horns, three trumpets, three trombones, tuba, a galaxy of orchestral and exotic percussion instruments, with the usual complement of strings—make a hieratic music reinvoking a legendary, pre-Columbian world and impart to it a steely rigor appropriate to our times.

During his middle years Chávez "civilized" this aboriginality without tempering its energy. Indeed, there are anticipations of this process in his music of the early twenties. In the Sonatina for Piano of 1924 we find techniques similar to those in his early ballets, presented in starkly abstract terms. No native tunes or dance rhythms are called on, and if comparison with other musics is possible it can only be with "white note" Stravinsky and with the cubist pattern-making of Satie—if one can imagine the Frenchman's chaste linearity imbued with the Mexican's ferocity. The sonatina, naggingly reiterative in its modal patterns, eschews development, is without modulation in the European sense, and is structured in tight mirror formation. The white note dissonance quota is high, the sonorities unflinching; even when the patterns are momentarily shifted out of tonal focus, the effect of rocky imperturbability is sustained. One might be tempted to think that the steely grandeur of this work was dependent on its lasting, chronometrically, for so short a time. Such an account is belied, however, by the masterpieces of Chávez's middle years, which are on a monumental scale, yet do not deny the compositional principles he'd established.

Supreme among them is the Concerto for Piano and Orchestra, written between 1938 and 1940, at the onset of World War II. Chávez had prefaced his concerto with Preludes for Piano, which seemed to be a preparatory study for it. All ten preludes are severely linear, often in two parts, one for each hand; white note, pandiatonic formulas prevail, though the moods vary between pentatonic (perhaps Balinese?) grace in the fourth prelude and propulsive, gritty momentum in the last, longest, and most difficult piece in the cycle. The concerto itself has the usual three movements, but the first is on a vast scale, propelled over an unbroken span of twenty minutes. There's an affinity with the consistent pulse and figuration of classical baroque music, especially that of Bach, this being validated by the same technical-philosophical principles that prompted Villa-Lobos to embark on his *Bachianas Brasileiras*. Chávez's conception is, however, far grander, devised for piano and orchestra operating on equal terms. As usual the lines move mainly by step and by leaps of primary intervals, both in the massive slow introduction and in the bounding allegro, wherein the lines have the tensility of steel. Although the piano's clattering figuration may recall neo-classic Stravinsky and perhaps percussive Bartók, its direct roots are in the pattern-making of (still extant) communal fiesta. Despite its length, the movement neither develops nor flags, as its wide-flung string polyphonies intertwine with canonic woodwind and brass, driven by implacable, often polymetrical, percussion. The piano, being an instrument simultaneously polyphonic and percussive, serves as catalyst; the climax is not worked up to, but spontaneously occurs as the soloist's cascading scales and whirling trills coalesce with the gongs, bells, and keyed percussion of the orchestra. A piano concerto thus becomes a synonym not for duality between an individual and the community, as it had been to varying degrees in the classical and romantic piano concerto from Mozart to Rachmaninoff, but rather for a potential union of Paz's solitary man with the world he inhabits. Momentarily, the music achieves that heroic "reconciliation of man with the universe" that, according to Paz, is essential for human salvation.

That is a bold claim, not belied by the hardly less massive slow movement and finale. The molto lento is as immobile as the first allegro is compulsive. Piano and harp initially duologue in stepwise-moving modality, which becomes magical when the piano floats into dissonant two-part counterpoint, sharp as broken glass. Here, sevenths and ninths are percussive, and chromaticism is alien to the idiom, which is so exiguous in texture that it is sometimes virtually monophonic, with a piano line doubled at unison or octave by a wind instrument, often an icy flute. Pedal points, supporting canons usually on fourth-founded motives, prohibit development, so the movement's calm is unsullied. When the slow movement merges into the finale, however, corporeal action is again rampant, though the tumultuous moto perpetuo has been generated from the modal immobility of the lento. The turbulent "going-on-ness" precludes climax; the finale inexorably *continues* until it explodes in cascading glissandos and whirligig trills. If this is a public fiesta, it is also an artistic apotheosis that Chávez can pull off.

It is significant that no one has more acutely defined the "total originality" of this concerto than Copland. Commenting on Chávez's music, in general, Copland said it is

> strong and deliberate, at times almost fatalistic in tone; it bespeaks the sober and stolid and lithic Amerindian. It is music of persistence—relentless and uncompromising; there is nothing of the humble Mexican peon here. It is music that knows its own mind—stark and clear and, if one may say so, *earthy* in an abstract way. There are no frills, nothing extraneous; . . . above all, [it is] profoundly non-European. To me it possesses an Indian quality that is at the same time curiously contemporary in spirit. *Sometimes it strikes me as the most truly contemporary music I know, not in the superficial sense, but in the sense that it comes closest to expressing the fundamental reality of modern man after he has been stripped of the accumulations of centuries of aesthetic experiences.*[3]

Only another composer of genius, from the neighboring United States, could have so precisely and profoundly described aspects of this concerto that make it a masterpiece of our century. It ought to be as frequently performed as the central masterpieces in Stravinsky's oeuvre, for it is hardly less powerful in impact, and of no less documentary significance. That it is seldom played is probably attributable to the very non-European quality to which it owes its importance. A big piano concerto is expected by concert promoters and by most keyboard virtuosos to be emotively romantic and self-indulgently exhibitionistic rather than, like Chávez's concerto, classically austere and self-transcendent.

Few modern composers—Copland himself being one of them—attain the sheer originality of sound that Copland here ascribes to Chávez. We have referred to affinities between the two men; these have little to do with their having been friends and colleagues, but much to do with consanguinity of mind and concatenation of circumstance. Both composers cultivated an austere linearity, whether in orchestral writing or in metallic piano sonorities. The hard yet lucent textures of Chávez's pianism in his concerto complement the glittering sonorities of Copland's Piano Variations of 1930, a keywork of its and our time, and the sharp yet massive sonorities of the great Piano Sonata that Copland produced in the year of Chávez's concerto, 1940. Only whereas Copland's figurations are cabinned, cribbed, and confined in the girders of a New York skyscraper (unless they escape into thin air above the empty plains, as in the Piano Sonata's extraordinary finale), Chávez's figurations *go on* inexhaustibly, spacious as the Mexican deserts, if no less lonesome. Mexican Chávez and New Yorker Copland alike assert humanity's irremediable solitude, whether it is—to return to Paz's *Labyrinth of Solitude*—the random solitude of industrialism (that of "hotels, offices, shops, movie theaters," which is "utter damnation, mirroring a world without exit") or whether it is that of elemental humanity, whose "feeling of solitude is a nostalgic longing for the body from which [he or she is] cast out," for "a return to the golden age" in which "is implicit the promise of salvation."[4] For both modern and elemental human "solitude and original sin become one and the same. . . . They constitute the golden age, an era which preceded history and to which we could perhaps return if we broke out of time's prison. When we acquire a sense of sin we also grow aware of our need for redemption and a redeemer."[5] We noted that Villa-Lobos thought of himself as a potential redeemer; Copland, in suggesting that Chávez's Concerto for Piano and Orchestra plumbs to "the fundamental reality of modern man after he has been stripped of the accumulations of centuries of aesthetic experiences," sees Chávez as a redeemer in a starker and more elemental sense: a tribute as noble as it is justifiable.

Although the piano concerto is the high point of Chávez's potentially redemptive art, he continued to explore both the deeper recesses of Western humanism and the animistic wellsprings he found in nonindustrialized cultures; this is not surprising since the burden of Paz's book is that the one is necessary to the other. The Concerto for Violin and Orchestra of 1947 is the major work wherein Chávez's "European" humanity comes to terms with his Mexican aboriginality, as is appropriate to a stringed instrument often regarded as a sublimated human voice. Although we think of the "Chávez sound" in terms of wind instruments and percussion, or of the polyphonically percussive piano, Chávez tells us that his first love among instruments was the violin: "Ever since my early childhood, . . . when by chance I first had [a violin] in my hands, I felt some kind of devotion and mystery about that perfectly shaped and finished thing, consisting of two completely separate elements, violin and bow, that had to be close together and rub against each other to produce sound and music."[6] Responding to the violin's magical unity-out-of-duality the boy Chávez composed, "around the age of ten, various small pieces for violin and piano," while the violin sonata of 1924 (the year of the trenchant Sonatina for Piano) was one of the earliest works he admitted to his "canon."[7] His love as well as experience of string instruments was fostered when, in his and the century's late twenties, he founded and directed the Orquesta Sinfoníca Naçional de México. He became a magnificent conductor, especially of his own music, but also of that of other twentieth-century composers. Whereas Villa-Lobos was, as a conductor, charismatic but undisciplined, Chávez was a total professional.

The solo part of Chávez's violin concerto sings—as one would expect of a composer whose music is rooted in stepwise movement, in the primary intervals, and in the distinctions between one interval and another. But Chávez's violin concerto is no more a conventional example of the genre than his piano concerto is a typical romantic effusion. Designed on a large scale, if not as long as the piano concerto, the violin work combines quasi-vocal lyricism and corporeal energy with a formal austerity that reflects the geometric Aztec architecture that so fascinated Chávez. Played without a break, the concerto has four sections that follow classical precedents in comprising an introduction (A), an allegro with two (closely related rather than oppositional) themes (B), a slow movement (C), and a scherzo-finale (D). Where the work departs from classical models is in that these materials are arranged in mirror formation: ABCD DCBA, so that the recapitulation reflects the exposition. Moreover, since the themes of this recapitulation are themselves mirror inversions of the themes of the exposition, the recapitulation is itself organic evolution, if not development. In this reconciliation of the unexpected with the preordained we may detect another instance of Chávez's Paz-like harmony between "knowledge and innocence, man and nature." The contrast with Villa-Lobos could hardly be more extreme: the Brazilian is a force of nature; the Mexican is a man in almost mechanistic control.

The opening of the violin concerto is electrifying. Solo violin pierces silence with a long-held tone that then winds into a lyrical *cantilena*, supported by modal polyphony on woodwind and horns. The textures are severe, despite the soloist's lyricism. As in the piano concerto, organum-like fourths and fifths prevail, though contrary motion between the organums and the singing bass propels the music in hieratic solemnity. The allegro that erupts out of the introduction is Bachian in its consistently figured moto perpetuo. If there is also a resemblance to neoclassic Stravinsky, Chávez's counterpoint is less dissonant, and there is no hint of parody in the occasionally out-of-focus polymodality. Again, Bachian going-on-ness and fiesta are allied.

The slow movement that floats out of this communality is solitary in being at first unaccompanied cantillation for the soloist; this might be folk monody, liturgically flavored. The exiguous wind parts are slow-moving, not far from drones, until the soloist suddenly takes off in a birdlike cadenza—the bird suggesting a liberated human spirit rather than a *oiseau exotique.* The quasi-liturgical theme returns on solo horn to lead into the scherzo-finale, dancing in asymmetrical rhythms. This is the only passage in the concerto to suggest Mexican fiesta, though no folk tunes are quoted.

A long, hair-raisingly difficult cadenza for the soloist—of extreme metrical intricacy and in multistopped polyphony—forms the pivot of the concerto's palindrome, stressing humanity's crucial position within nature's order. From this point, the music reverses itself, both in the order of its events and in their linear shapes. The soloist, interweaving with woodwind, transforms the monody of the slow movement into polyphony, but is then mute, to dramatic effect, as a slow ostinato implacably measures off time. The soloist, levitating in a complement to the bird-cadenza, propels the music toward a recapitulation of the moto perpetuo allegro and of the slow introduction, freely inverted into a chorale. The soloist's virtuosity doesn't imperil the heroic stance of the end. Throughout, the rigorous formal devices—the mirror-disposed structure and the mirror inversion of the themes—are as audible as the geometric symmetries of Aztec architecture are visible.

Chávez made more overt compromises with Western humanism, especially in the fourth symphony of 1952, which he presumably called *Sinfonía romántica* in reference to its European affiliations. Yet its effect is not radically distinct from that of the works so far discussed, for although the first movement is sonatalike in having two groups of themes, they are not contrasted in character or key, while the evolution of the movement is strenuously contrapuntal. Not only the linearity but also the rhythmic momentum and stark scoring relate the music to the two concertos of the previous decade. So does the integration between the three movements, all pervaded by a motif of falling fifth to fourth to tonic—that rudiment of vocal modality from which much of Chávez's music stems, as does that of an in some (but not all) ways very different composer, Ralph Vaughan Williams.

Wind instruments, often canonic, dominate the slow movement, an aria the theme of which, derived from the seminal motif, is ritualistic rather than romantic. This modal, quasi-liturgical polyphony contrasts with the rambunctious finale, centered on the youthfully optimistic key of A major. This movement compromises with sonata in being a double rondo with two themes in alternation. But they don't interact in sonata style; once more, contrapuntal evolution takes the place of dualistic development. According to Octavio Paz, such a reconciliation of opposites is profoundly Mexican: "The bloody Christs in our village churches, the macabre humor in some of our newspaper headlines, our wakes, the custom of eating skull-shaped cakes and candies on the Day of the Dead, are habits inherited from the Indians and the Spaniards and are now an inseparable part of our being. Our cult of death is also a cult of life, in the same way that love is a hunger for life and a longing for death."[8] This rondo-finale, if cruder, is hardly less exhilarating than the coda to the last movement of the piano concerto. Exploiting the same downward-hurling scales, whirring trills, and street-band raucosities, it carries Mexican fiesta into revels at once hilarious and ferocious. Copland's *El salón México* reminds us how closely linked this may be to urban America, though Copland's intentionally "light" piece is brilliant tourist music, in comparison with Chávez's authenticity.

The Europeanizing tendencies in the music of Chávez's middle years contrast with the music of his late phase, in which he sought a revival of the primitivism of his early years, more basic in the sense in which he described a keywork of the sixties, *Xochipilli*, as, in its subtitle, "an imagined Aztec music, for piccolo, flute, E-flat clarinet, trombone and six percussion players." The preponderant percussion and shrieking or blurting wind instruments hark back to the pretend-ritual music of *Sinfonía India*, but create from pentatonic pattern-making and polymetric geometry a music more abstract, and therefore "modern," in sound. Since—as Chávez points out in his preface to the score of *Xochipilli*—we know nothing about Aztec music except what we can gather from the study of pre-Cortesian instruments in museums, such an exercise was doomed to be abstract and academic. This doesn't matter since a literal re-creation, were it possible, would be futile; there is no chance of our feeling or behaving like long-defunct Aztecs. The music Chávez builds on these premises—and "builds" is an appropriately Aztec metaphor—is mainly monophonic or heterophonic, but occasionally contemplative, if not lyrical. An "imagined Aztec music" is bound to omit more than we who have a Western heritage can readily dispense with. Mere abstraction must tend to aridity.

Nonetheless there is characteristic mental, as well as corporeal, energy behind *Xochipilli*, as there is in the series of experimental works that Chávez called *Soli*. *Soli I* dates back to 1933, the year after *Sinfonía India;* the title indicates that each instrument in the ensemble of oboe, clarinet, bassoon, and trumpet is featured in the four-movement suite. Although the sonorities and figurations relate to Native American musics, there is a further link with black jazz improvisation, wherein one thing leads to another with little or no reference to preordained principles. In the first movement all the instruments autonomously "unroll in a constant process of renewal,"[9] paradoxically but significantly making "new life" from what had once been a "paradise of archetypes and repetition." Not until the sixties, however, did Chávez carry this nonprinciple of nonform to fruition.

In *Soli II*—for the conventional wind quintet of flute, oboe, clarinet, horn, and bassoon—all four movements bear conventional titles: Sonatina, Rondo, Prelude, and Aria. These titles must be ironic, since *Soli II* is the apex of a series of experiments in nonrepetitiveness carried out between 1933 and 1961, when this work was first performed. While the stinging sonorities are comparable with those of Chávez's pandiatonic works, the lines are much more angular, with sudden spurts and savage pounces. Chávez denied any parallel with Schoenbergian chromaticism, though he admitted that one of the aims of serialism had been to evade imprisoning repetitions of pitch. This new linearity in Chávez's music has more to do with late serial Stravinsky than with Schoenberg, and probably owes still more to Varèse.

A yet more pertinent analogy is with Free Jazz, which surfaced during the sixties. This music, too, eschewed thematic patterns, chord sequences, and defined keys, trusting to the moment for emotional if not intellectual coherence. The difference is that Chávez's nonrepetitive freedom was not improvised in the heat of the moment but merely sounds as though it was. *Soli IV,* commissioned in 1964 and premiered in 1967 for horn, trumpet, and trombone, is an extreme example, the experimental nature of which is evident in Chávez's informing us that he has deliberately evaded the major thirds, fourths, fifths, minor sevenths, and octaves that had been the fundaments of tonal music. "Melody and melodic counterpoint proceed freely," he remarks, "each 'antecedent' producing a 'consequent,' that in turn becomes the antecedent of a new consequent. It is music that continuously evolves from itself. In this sense, the entire piece constitutes a single, long, main 'theme.'"[10] So fanatical a desire to escape from the "paradise of archetypes and repetition" that had nurtured Chávez along with Native American musicians may be intellectually comprehensible but seems imaginatively perverse. There is, however, a parallel between these dislocated squawks and grunts and the abstraction of advanced Free Jazz, which was *meant* to be a music of *hommes sauvages* reborn in an urban technocracy.

The recipe of Free Jazz could sometimes—in the hands of a genius like Ornette Coleman—effect miracles; more commonly it induced tedium. Chávez's nonimprovised nonrepetitiveness is seldom tedious since in notating the music he allowed himself opportunity for second or even third thoughts. Even so, the notation of nonrepetitiveness seems a contradiction in terms, and we should probably regard these *Soli* as experiments toward that "imagined Aztec music," rather than as intrinsically significant artifacts. Again Chávez emerges as a disciple of Octavio Paz in that his powerfully leonine head nourished his heart when his experiments of the sixties culminated, in 1968, in a theater piece commissioned by Amalia Hernández, director of the Ballet Folklórico de México. Significantly, *Pirámide* returns to the theme of Chávez's first ballet, *Los cuatro soles,* written more than forty years previously, for the scenario, devised by the composer himself, is based on creation myths of the four elements, projected into a series of "plastic-dynamic ensembles."[11] Primitive forms of life sing and dance "to suggest the passing of the human race from chaos, myths, superstitions, discoveries etc., to an ideal reunion and cooperation of peoples of all places."[12] This is Paz's prescription for regeneration writ very large; yet Chávez brings it off, not because he creates putative Aztec music, but because dancers and musicians convince us that, *for the time being,* they are gods and goddesses. Such is the incandescence of this work that Chávez's godly Four Elements struggle from chaos through "the discovery of fire, the development of architecture (symbolized by the building of a pyramid), and the getting together of men and women of all epochs and places, dressed in all sorts of costumes, dancing the final general dance."[13] This is the ultimate manifestation of Chávez's mating of art with science, and of artifact-making humanity with the presumptive laws of nature. Here, at least momentarily, he fulfills Paz's hopeful prophecy and the juvenile dreams that Percy Grainger embraced in his "imaginary ballet," *The Warriors.*

Moreover, it is significant that, as with the early *Los cuatro soles,* the final section of *Pyrámide* is choral and that its choral writing sunders barriers between the animal and the human; voices chatter, gibber, scream, wail, and whimper while preserving musical identity. Although these ululations owe much to Chávez's experience of ethnic musics—especially Javanese and Polynesian—he has made a creature music pertinent to us in being dislocated, screwy, even prehuman in impulse, yet also assertive of our and the animals' mutually supportive rights. That in theater music of fairly recent years such "extended vocal techniques" have become common doesn't affect the fact that Chávez, first in the field, made music that is indubitably—in Ezra Pound's phrase—"news that STAYS news." It is easy to understand why this should be so. The human infant, like the birds and beasts, utters its own language. Even after this first language is obliterated, we can never wholly forget it; or if we do so, it is at our own peril. Unfortunately, *Pyrámide,* like Chávez's great piano concerto, is seldom heard or seen, and we need his help if we are to understand the desperate ecological issues that confront us today.

NOTES

1. Carlos Chávez, *Toward a New Music: Music and Electricity,* trans. Herbert Weinstock (New York: W. W. Norton, 1937).

2. Octavio Paz, *The Labyrinth of Solitude: Life and Thought in Mexico,* trans. Lysander Kemp (New York: Grove Press, 1961), 26–27.

3. Aaron Copland, *Music and Imagination* (Cambridge, Mass.: Harvard University Press, 1953), 91–92, emphasis added.

4. Paz, *The Labyrinth of Solitude,* 204, 208, 207.

5. Ibid., 206.

6. Carlos Chávez, liner notes to *Concerto for Violin and Orchestra,* CBS LP 32 11 00 64.

7. Ibid.

8. Paz, *The Labyrinth of Solitude,* 23.

9. Carlos Chávez, liner notes to *Chávez, Soli I, Soli II, Soli IV,* Columbia/Odyssey LP Y 31534.

10. Ibid.

11. Carlos Chávez, liner notes to *Pirámide: Ballet in Four Acts,* Columbia LP M 32685.

12. Ibid.

13. Ibid.

PART FOUR

Mountains and Machines in New-Old Worlds

9

Carl Ruggles in New England, Edgard Varèse in Old France and New York

AT THE END OF THE NINETEENTH CENTURY the old-new world of Latin America struggled for an identity in the context of wilderness; much of North America, however, was rapidly industrialized and directed its culture toward technology. But it is misleading to think of North America as mainly a technocracy, for this is to ignore the physical immensity and diversity of the continent. While the United States, in particular, may be powered by its industrial cities, the wilderness of its continent is omnipresent; sparsely populated, even unpopulated, areas of vast extent efface the antlike energy of Blake's "dark satanic mills." This is evident in the two poles between which spark the music of the greatest—certainly the most representative—American composer thus far, for if the music of Charles Ives manifests a Whitmanesque, ubiquitous love of humanity and of every facet of the visible, tactile, and audible world, he was also a solitary, alone with nature, seeking (like Thoreau at Walden Pond) a transcendental order within the flux. Ives's greatness lies in the strong if precarious equilibrium he preserved between these opposite poles. Carl Ruggles, a composer of the same generation (born in 1876), with a similar New England background, neither sought nor achieved such an equilibrium. He was an American mystic who sang of "the wind-struck music man's bones were moulded to be the harp for"—to quote Robinson Jeffers's philosophy of "inhumanism."[1]

A descendant of a very old New England whaling family, Ruggles had, as a New England pioneer, qualities relatable to Herman Melville, author of *Moby-Dick*. Musically, he was a "natural," no less than was Villa-Lobos; he picked up instruments with empirical facility and at the age of six was playing a violin self-fabricated from a cigar box. Such ad hoc ingenuity resembled that of Charles Ives's remarkable father, George, with the difference that, since the Ruggles family was affluent, Carl soon contacted genteel music in Boston and had formal lessons on violin and in composition—the latter from the then esteemed John Knowles Paine. Briefly, the young Ruggles worked for a music publisher before proceeding to an Ivy League university—in his case to Harvard, not, like Ives, to Yale.

But although at Harvard Ruggles received a conventional training under Walter Spalding, he soon espoused the causes of composers such as Wagner, César Franck, and above all Debussy, in whom he recognized, as did Varèse, a true revolutionary. Upon leaving the university, Ruggles was liberated by the financial support of a generous patron; working independently of all coteries, he rejoiced in being a solitary in New England, where so much that had made America was rooted. Although his music, unlike that of Ives, contains no direct reflection of a social world—and no quotations from religious or secular populist sources—it was still preoccupied with the new. Settled into his home in his native Vermont, Ruggles became reclusive, albeit far from a hermit, since he was socially outgoing and a brilliant raconteur. In humorous toughness Ruggles resembled Ives, who had become a close friend. Unlike Ives, however, he shielded his music from the contagion of the world; papering his study with the exquisite calligraphy of his own manuscripts—so that he could "see where he was" at a given moment—he was literally enclosed within his own creation, while the chaos of the American scene, so passionately embraced by Ives, passed him by.

This bears on the distinctions between the techniques of the two composers. Ives's eclecticism—his near-simultaneous use of modal, diatonic, and chromatic aspects of the past and present—is part of his immediate awareness of his environment. Ruggles, however, was neither eclectic nor profuse. In a very long life he composed only a handful of works that are as consistent in style as Ives's protean music is inconsistent. Ruggles's idiom is comparable with only one aspect of Ives's multifarious art—the freely evolving, unsystematized polyphony in which he expressed both his freedom from the past and his desire for identity with nature. From Ruggles's music all those tune-filled, time-dominated, harmonically codified conventions that auralize the values of society are banished. His art was dedicated not to humanity or society but to the "inscape" of his own spirit, in the context of the windswept natural world.

Ruggles started composing at about the same time Schoenberg had arrived at his "free" atonal phase, which was a rejection of the public values of the past in favor of personal response and "expressionistic" immediacy, even if this meant confining oneself to works of small dimensions. It is improbable that Ruggles knew Schoenberg's music intimately, although as a self-conscious harbinger of the new he would have been aware of its nature. Certainly the two men had much in common. Both were amateur painters who, in their visual artifacts, sought the expressionistic moment of truth. Both, in their music even more than in their painting, found that the disintegrated facets of the modern psyche could be reintegrated only in a mystical act—such as the one the Woman, in Schoenberg's *Erwartung,* experienced in the moonlit forest glade. Schoenberg, as a Viennese Jew, had an ancient religion and the spirit of Beethoven to help him; Ruggles had only the American wilderness and the guilt-ridden austerities of Puritan New England. So he sought freedom—from tonal bondage, from the harmonic straitjacket, from conventionalized repetition, from anything that sullied the immediacy of experience—even more fanatically than did Schoenberg. His chromaticism started from the Wagnerian identification of the world with the self, but when the burden of consciousness proved too great to be borne, his harmonic chromaticism sought a linear release. The sequences of *Tristan* impel the music forward yet engender frustration in that each sequence returns to the point it started from. In Schoenberg's "free" atonality and in the chromatic polyphony of Ruggles, there is a minimum of repetition, for each piece is a new birth. *Self-*consciousness evaporates as the lines soar.

The implications of this are evident in the earliest work that Ruggles admitted to his exiguous canon—*Angels,* originally written in 1921 for six trumpets, but revised for four trumpets and three trombones (or four violins and three cellos) in 1938. This is his only work to have affinities with classical precedents; within an ABA ternary structure and an A flat key flavor it uses vocal intervals in a close harmonic texture, creating a neobaroque brass sonority. That this does not remind us of the ceremonial and public aspects of the baroque is due to the music's hermetically indrawn character and perhaps to its veiled sonority, all the instruments being muted. Metrically, the polyphony is elusive because the rhythms of the individual parts flow in triplets and tied syncopations across the duple pulse; harmonically, the texture is ambivalent because each line oscillates chromatically around a nodal point. Both tonally and rhythmically the apparently constricted lines aspire to freedom, and it is in this aspiration that their "angelic"—their superhuman, or in Ruggles's and Jeffers's sense, "*in*humanist"—quality consists.

Despite the quasi-vocal and incipiently tonal bases, the harmony created by these chromatic oscillations and elliptical rhythms is uncompromisingly dissonant. By the time of the chamber-orchestra piece *Men and Mountains*

(1924), Ruggles's characteristic idiom, which did not substantially change for the rest of his life, was defined. The harshness of the harmony, with its preponderance of minor seconds, major sevenths, and minor ninths, is Schoenbergian; but in place of Schoenberg's indrawn density Ruggles cultivates a clear, open resonance by way of a polyphony that bounds and springs. There is a peculiarly American quality in the simultaneous hardness of harmony and liberation of line, in which the reiteration of tones is discouraged though not, as in Schoenbergian serialism, prohibited. The violence of the harmony suggests the American axe in the pioneer's wilderness and the savagery within the mind that the axe came to represent; yet this sadistic pain becomes itself an agent of freedom as the lines burgeon. This is marvelously manifest in the slow movement, entitled "Lilacs," for the lyricism of this does not evoke only the heavy-scented spring flower but also the passionate heart—the appoggiatura-laden harmony that would drag down the singing lines, though song proves triumphant. Historically speaking, Ruggles's chromaticism is not far from Delius's; yet the tough energy of his lines and harmonies transforms a personal melancholy into an epic celebration of organic process. Delius is a belated and weary, if strong, humanist; Ruggles is a nature mystic in a society crassly antimystical. Yet paradoxically Ruggles's nature mysticism is also his Americanism, his "newness," his integrity. Only against the backdrop of the American wilderness can we understand how his "inhumanism," like that of the poet Jeffers, conditions his identity with the immensity, terror, cruelty, and beauty of the natural world. Perhaps there can be no European artist strictly comparable with Ruggles or Jeffers, for most of Europe is too populous for inhumanism to be meaningful. The term is not, of course, equivalent with antihumanism, but refers to a recognition, at once humble and proud, of human insufficiency, divorced from animate and inanimate nature.

The title of the piece was borrowed from Blake's "Great things are done when Men and Mountains meet." The nature of these great things is defined in a work for string orchestra, *Portals* (1926), which bears an inscription from another bardic poet, Walt Whitman, who proclaimed that it was the duty of "the known to ascend and enter the unknown." In this piece there are two themes, one (the known?) strenuously human, with fierce tritones, leaping sevenths, and doubled dots, the other (the unknown?) remotely floating in a flexible triple rhythm. Texturally the piece is all melody, in twelve real parts. The two themes collide, grow toward a climax, break off unfulfilled, tentatively start again. At the second climax the lines whirl in grinding dissonance until a brief, distant coda telescopes the notes of the themes vertically in an immense spread chord that fades to silence. Again, process is an act of birth, both painful and natural. Wilderness is an act of therapy, as pain is freed, but not resolved, in space and silence.

Given his commitment to free expressionism, Ruggles's compositions tend to be brief but concentrated. His longest work is the seventeen-minute *Sun-Treader* for a very large orchestra, composed between 1926 and 1931. The wildly bounding first theme, riddled with minor ninths, major sevenths, and tritones, epitomizes Ruggles's pioneering strife and heroic aspiration. Against it is poised an indrawn theme developed in close polyphony. The two themes alternate, and ultimately interact, always pressing onward toward a tightened recapitulation while remaining unresolved, still "treading" toward an un-known future. The title, *Sun-Treader,* was applied by Robert Browning to Percy Bysshe Shelley, apostle of both spiritual and political liberation; it is pertinent too that Ruggles's only major vocal work, *Vox Clamans in Deserto* (1923), is based on poems by Browning and Whitman. The desert, or wilder-ness, is here explicitly invoked; and the motivation behind *Evocations,* writ-ten for piano between 1937 and 1943, is similar, for each short "chant" emerges from silence, independent of a social context, and evolves to and from a single climax, with a minimum of repetition. (The second chant has a twelve-note theme.) That Ruggles originally scored these pieces for piano solo may sug-gest that he was seeking an un-Ivesian concision and clarification, or it may merely mean that, unperturbed by the relationship between composer and public, he was making a "short score" to be worked up later, as occasion of-fered. The pieces work as piano solos, for the resonances are both powerful and luminous. Even so, the idiom is not pianistic, and the orchestral version that Ruggles produced very much later, in 1971, sounds predestined.

Ralph Waldo Emerson, confronted by an earnest female transcendentalist who informed him that she "accepted the Universe," is said to have retorted, "Madame, *you better had.*" Charles Ives also accepted the universe, the taw-dry and trivial along with the heroic and sublime. Ruggles, on the contrary, concentrated exclusively on an identification of his own consciousness with the processes of nature. His achievement has qualities we may call heroic, though his positive virtues were limited by his exclusiveness—perhaps even, musically, in comparison with Ives, by his lack—in his music, if not in life—of humor. It may not be fortuitous that throughout his long life his compo-sitions, with the momentary exception of *Sun-Treader,* got progressively shorter as well as fewer. His significant output is restricted to eight works for orchestra, refined and revised over many years. When he died in 1971, soon after he had orchestrated *Evocations,* he left a few unfinished sketches, mostly dating back many years, but his last completed work remained *Organum* for large orchestra, composed as far back as 1944–47. One assumes that the title refers not merely to the fact that the piece is, like medieval organum, in essence linear, but also to the organic nature of its compositional principle. Although Ruggles impresses with his unabashed dedication to the Sublime, one may query whether isolation—his fundamental theme—could always and forever be inspirational. In *Organum* the evolutionary polyphony seems dammed by the viscidity of the orchestral sonorities, and if the lines cannot take wing, their violence becomes self-defeating. Perhaps this was why Ruggles did not, in the last quarter-century of his life, assay another major work. What he had to say was valid and, within limits, important; but the relative failure of *Organum,* and perhaps also the aphoristic restriction of *Evocations,* hint that "inhumanism" was not enough. Our current obsession with ecological issues may modify that view; in any case Ruggles's quantitatively small contribution should qualitatively survive.

Carl Ruggles created an aboriginal American music starting from the twilight of Old Europe, as manifest in the "free" atonality of the Viennese Schoenberg. Edgard Varèse, a Frenchman of the same generation (born in 1885), came from the oldest of European civilizations but, having settled in the United States and become an American citizen in 1916, devoted himself assiduously to the making of a New World music. Significantly enough, the world war that had disabled Europe was raging at the time when Varèse became an American citizen, and he called the first work he admitted to his ultimate canon *Amériques,* not so much because it celebrated his new geographic home as because it created a new world of sound.

At the Paris Conservatoire he had been a pupil of the "civilized" but musically and politically progressive Albert Roussel as well as of the conservative Vincent d'Indy and of the organist Charles Widor. Such bastions of tradition Varèse rejected when he immigrated to the States, and it was another French composer, his friend and colleague Claude Debussy, who fired his search for a new music in a newfound land. As a young man Varèse admired Debussy above all composers "for his economy of means and clarity, and the intensity he achieved through them, balancing with almost mathematical equilibrium timbres against rhythms and textures—like a fantastic chemist."[2] Analytical work on Debussy's techniques, undertaken many years after that statement, has given backing to Varèse's hunch about the mathematical and quasi-chemical nature of Debussy's structures and has similarly endorsed Varèse's view of the techniques of Satie, who, according to Varèse, "wrote some rather remarkable music, such as the Kyrie from his *Messe des pauvres*

[1895], a music which always reminds me of Dante's *Inferno* and strikes me as a kind of pre-electronic music."[3]

Satie's directionless harmonies might perhaps be more accurately related to Dante's purgatory than to his inferno, but one can see that they have reference to a lost or "fallen" state. In any case Varèse saw Debussy and Satie as starting points for his own experiments toward the new: since if one liberates the chord from antecedence and consequence, as they did, the next step must be to liberate the individual sound. This is not just a technical procedure; it is also a new, and at the same time a very old, musical philosophy. Varèse was probably the first art composer to reject the Renaissance conception of art as individual expression and as a communication from one being to another. Bypassing twelve-tone serialism (which he shunned as a musical hardening of the arteries because of its commitment to fixed, equal-tempered pitch), Varèse made manifest the prophecies of his friend Ferruccio Busoni in his *Entwarf einer Neuen Aesthetick der Tonkunst* (1907). He was a composer at once magical and scientific, prophetic respectively of Messiaen and of Karlheinz Stockhausen, demonstrating that these apparent opposites are complementary in that they offer a revelation, rather than an incarnation, of natural law. To live in a mathematical universe must tend to efface the self; and it is to the point that Varèse, who as a youth had scientific training and hoped to become a mathematical engineer, should, in naming one of his works *Arcana*, relate the revelation of natural order to the activities of the alchemists.

Varèse's sophisticated music is thus also primitive in that it consists of nondeveloping patterns and clusters of sounds of varying timbre and tension, rather than of harmonies that can be grammatically construed, in a European sense. These sounds interact in a manner that Varèse compared, in detailed if inaccurate analogy, to rock formation and crystal mutation. He claimed that as a child he had been "tremendously impressed by the qualities and character of the granite" found in his native Burgundy: "I used to watch the old stone cutters, marveling at the precision with which they worked. They didn't use cement, and every stone had to fit and balance with every other."[4] So construction, for Varèse as for Debussy, was spatial rather than temporal; and while harmonically conceived music achieves purposeful order by the development of themes in time and by movement toward and away from a tonal center, Varèse achieves his "opening of space" through the contrasts of rhythms and timbres that, insofar as they behave like crystals, seem to be as impervious to the dictates of the human will as is nature itself. When asked about the form of his compositions, Varèse turned to an analogy with crystallization. Quoting Nathaniel Arbiter, a professor of mineralogy at Columbia, he said, "'The crystal is characterized by both a definite external form and a definite internal structure. The internal structure is based on the unit of crystal which is the smallest grouping of the atoms that has the order and composition of the substance. The extension of the unit into space forms the whole crystal.'"[5] For Varèse, musical forms were as limitless as the exterior forms of crystals, splitting into different shapes and groups that constantly change in contour, direction, and speed. To encourage forgetfulness of self seemed, for Varèse, a necessity if we were to escape from the chaos of individuation; he believed that his music was modern as well as primeval, since it was magical in action but at the same time related to scientific principles and to a machine-dominated civilization. Certainly the percussive noises and mechanistic patterns in his music have affinities with the sounds of city life. The artist's task is to help us perceive the mathematical order and beauty that lie within apparent disorder and chaos, if we have ears to hear.

Since Varèse's music is nonharmonic in the functional sense, it may make sense in purely percussive or in purely linear terms. An example of the former is *Ionization*, written in 1931, scored for thirteen players on a large variety of hissing, banging, and scraping instruments. The effect is primitive and orgiastically exciting in that noise—both that of natural occurrences like hurricanes, earthquakes, and volcanic eruptions, and the human-generated noises of the asphalt jungle—comes into its own. We respond to it spontaneously, much as Debussy invited us to identify with the rising sun; yet if noise is for Varèse a force of nature, and therefore sometimes savage or vicious, it can also be human-directed, a *release* from horror. For if *Ionization* does not have a post-Renaissance sense of temporal progression, it has a spatial awareness of periodic time, and even a control of climax in that the pitched percussion instruments (piano, chimes, glockenspiel) finally take over, as the unpitched hissings, bangings, and scrapings slow time's pulse into a seemingly endless reverberation. Pitch becomes an ally of silence, for as pitched instruments gain ascendancy, the exacerbations of wailing sirens—which remind us of air raids and police cars and similarly scary manifestations of an industrial world—lose their potency. At the end the silences get gradually longer—an effect possibly borrowed from the bell-tolling final pages of Stravinsky's *Les Noces*.

As in the Stravinsky example, this inconclusive conclusion is both Eastern and a consequence of the Decline of the West. A modern composer, Varèse maintained, must magically discover, through activity of the mind, nerves, body, and senses, the aural order inherent in nature; but this composer must be a scientist in that such a discovery can emerge only from knowledge of the ways in which sounds behave. This is evident in an example of the totally linear dimension of Varèse's music: a work called *Density 21.5*, written for the inauguration of Georges Barrère's platinum flute, 21.5 being the density of that metal. The scientific title presumably indicates that the experience is dependent on the metal's "aural reality": a process that happens as melismatic arabesques oscillate around nodal points and incantatory repetitions change almost imperceptibly. The effect has affinities with some Asian musics and certainly with the European re-creation of non-Western melody in Debussy's monodic *Syrinx*, written on the eve of World War I in 1913, a piece that Debussy hoped would be played, not in a formal concert, but in the dark outdoors, for whomever might overhear it. Yet at the same time Varèse's investigation, in *Density 21.5*, of pitch relationships and dynamic levels is intellectually planned, for tensions and density are gradually neutralized, as they are by the encroaching silences at the end of *Ionization*.

In most of his works Varèse combines the linear techniques of the flute piece with the polyphony of timbres and rhythms typical of *Ionization*. The longest of his early works, *Intégrales*, written in 1924, sounds like a collage of the noises of city life, reverberant with sirens, horns, drills, and the din of traffic. Its asphalt jungle does not sound merely arbitrary, however, because it is not; grandeur accrues from its impersonal, clearly defined, three-part form. In the first section two vertical chord formations change neither in sonority nor in dynamics, and a variable melodic pattern oscillates around a single tone. Each of these elements is a noise that does not seek "development," though it may undergo crystal-like mutation. The section ends with a huge shimmering cadence chord in which the two vertical chord structures and the one linear pattern occur simultaneously. The second and third sections similarly allow basic "polarities" to coexist and interact, with an effect comparable with those passages in Ives's music that bring together the aural disparities of the world around us. But whereas Ives is content to be humanly amorphous, Varèse assays the scientist's exactitude, an attempt doomed to failure since an artist must admit to human fallibility. Nonetheless there is splendor, as well as excitement, in Varèse's attempt to rival the processes of nature. Maybe only God can make a tree, but a human being may at least make sounds behave like crystals.

Varèse was singularly consistent, whether he was adapting traditional fugal techniques to his own nonharmonic, incantatory ends (as in *Octandre* of 1924) or whether he was writing for a full symphony orchestra abetted by forty percussion instruments and a phalanx of exotica such as sarrusophone, heckelphone, contrabass clarinet, and contrabass trombone, as in *Arcana* (1927). Such mammoth forces are in a sense a belated survival of the monster orchestras of Mahler and Schoenbergian expressionism, though Varèse's aesthetic is, as we have seen, anti-expressionist. The title of this work comes from the *Hermetic Astronomy* of Paraclesus, and while it refers to the pseudo-science of alchemy, it also implies that the generator of change—the transmuter of base metal into gold—is the human imagination. Varèse described the work as a passacaglia on the eleven- (not twelve-) note figure that opens the work, but the structure is neither thematic nor harmonic. The recollections of "normal" music that bubble to the surface—fragments of street and military tunes, as in Mahler's symphonies, as well as recollections of Stravinsky's *Firebird, Petrouchka,* and *Le Sacre du printemps*—are un- or at the most semiconscious. The true form of the work is the arch of tensions it creates from its passacaglia "crystal," absorbing the arbitrary noises of the asphalt jungle. Formidable though the work is, its hybrid nature renders it less convincing than pieces in which Varèse concentrates on smaller, more "scientifically" abstract forces, though he learned from it when, a little later, he extended his explorations into electronic music.

Varèse was perhaps the first to explore outer space musically. A space traveler is a pioneer in a sense previously inconceivable, and Varèse came to feel that his works of the twenties—which remain landmarks in the century's music—were inevitably aborted by the lack of electronic acoustical resources that would make feasible an infinite variety of pitches and timbres. In those days, few took him seriously, which may be why he gave up composition between the midthirties and the early fifties. The development of magnetic tape encouraged Varèse to compose again and led to a revival of his early works. Henceforth composition, whether through indirect human agency or through electronics, was for Varèse "process," since he was "fascinated by the fact that through electronic means one can generate a sound instantaneously. . . . For instance, in the use of an oscillator, it is not a question of working against it or taming it, but using it directly, without, of course, letting it use you. . . . To me, working with electronic music is composing with living sounds, paradoxical though that may appear."[6]

Nothing could be further from the mathematically determined electronic music of a composer such as Milton Babbitt, who, as Varèse put it, wanted to exercise maximum control over certain materials, as if he were *above* them. Varèse himself wanted to be *in* the material, directly generating music by electronic means: "I think of musical space as open rather than bounded."[7]

This still leaves artistic and moral responsibility with the composer. A bad musician with conventional instruments will be a bad musician with electronics, for a "thorough knowledge of the laws governing the vibratory system, and of the possibilities that science has placed at the service of the human imagination is an additive, not a destructive factor in the art and science of music."[8]

In 1953 Varèse reappeared as a composer with a work specifically called *Déserts*, for orchestra and prerecorded tape. He explains in a preface that the work was conceived for two different media that are complementary. One medium is sounds humanly produced on conventional instruments; the other is real sounds that instruments cannot reproduce. He wrote the work as a whole, composing the conventionally notated music while bearing in mind the nature and character of the taped interpolations that he was preparing. He recorded sounds on a tape machine that he took around with him in both the natural world and in the fabricated industrial environment. After being electronically "processed," these sounds were ready for fusion with the notated score. The score of *Déserts* thus consists of two distinct elements, of which the first is a live instrumental ensemble consisting of several varieties of flute, oboe, clarinet, horn, trumpet, trombone, tuba, piano, and percussion, all of which evolve on shifting planes and volumes, not on a traditional system of intervals or even a fixed one. This space traveling is associated with the human element, for which Varèse's term is "presence." The taped interpolations—the second element—are associated not with presence but with distance, with the nonhuman aspects of the universe. The first taped interpolation has natural forces such as winds and waters as well as the industrial sounds of hissing, grinding, and puffing, but all are filtered by electronic devices. The second taped interpolation is both mechanical and human, for although it is taped it is played by an ensemble of percussionists who provide a link between human and nonhuman forces. The third interpolation uses taped industrial noises and fragments of human-operated percussion simultaneously. The interplay of the human and the nonhuman generate increased intensity, and the higher the intensity the briefer the section. The music reaches a climax in the third interpolation and the fourth instrumental section, after which it dissolves into silence.

Varèse said that the word *Déserts* is to be understood as suggesting not merely deserts in a geographical or physical sense—whether of sand and sea or empty city streets—but also deserts in a psychological sense. It speaks to the loneliness of the human condition and the unreachable inner space of the mind. The honesty with which Varèse explores this basic modern theme explains why *Déserts* is frightening as well as impressive: the rhythmic dislocations, the piercingly high and growlingly low sonorities create an audible cosmos wherein factory, subway, and airport noises merge into the sounds of forests, birds, and beasts. The dissonant heterophony, the microtonally wailing portamentos, and the immensely slow metrical organization create what is very rare—a *new sound,* yet this new sound reminds us of something immensely ancient, the imperial court music of Japanese *gagaku* that flourished in the eighth and ninth centuries. The lyrical continuity of classical Indian music or the mellifluous sonorities of Balinese gamelan are remote from this music, which is at once highly sophisticated and cruelly barbaric. The flute and oboe set the teeth on edge, being tuned to the maximum degree of distonation; yet the *gagaku* voices are emotionally deflated, singing of the most gruesome occurrences in a deadpan moan. Although Varèse was well-versed in Eastern musics, it is unlikely that the affinity between *gagaku* and his *Déserts* was consciously contrived. American twentieth-century and Japanese ninth-century violence have deep tentacular roots; indeed Varèse's most remarkable prophecy may be that so many years ago he aurally "realized" the interdependence of American and Japanese technology—now a most potent factor in economic life. This prophetic intuition again testifies that art matters: for Varèse's music in *Déserts* remains, if frightening, unafraid. If the music tells us that the human ego has lost touch with the natural order, the admission helps us to live again. Varèse's *Déserts* bears even more directly on the crisis of modern humans, as defined by Octavio Paz, than does the music of Chávez.

At least Varèse never forgot that people have hearts and senses. His first completely electronic work, the *Poème électronique,* composed for the Brussels Festival in 1957, proved to be an end as well as a beginning, for he was to compose no more music. Moreover, the work was performed in a pavilion especially designed by Le Corbusier. The human voice is introduced into taped sounds that include both processed natural noises (*musique concrète*) and vibrations produced by pure electronics. Varèse described the work as "ordered sound" rather than as music, thereby suggesting that while all music is ordered sound, not all ordered sound is music, at least in the orthodox sense. But although he has extended boundaries by admitting an infinite variety of pitches and timbres instead of the few that are conventionally accepted, and although these sounds are mathematically controlled by graphs, creating a sound universe half scientific and half magical, nonetheless the ordering agency is still human. It is a human voice that cries from the vast prison of space, and objections that the human voice cannot be miscible with the electronic sounds surely miss the point. The piece is uncannily disturbing in much the same way as Reg Butler's sculptured *Unknown Political Prisoner*, a visual artifact that made an immense impact around the same time as Varèse's piece. Varèse's *Poème électronique* has been equally forgotten, partly because it was the product of specific conditions that cannot easily be duplicated and partly because Varèse's electronic music was technically rudimentary compared with the marvels that professional electronic composers now toy with. Even so, it is Varèse's electronic music, especially *Déserts*, that almost alone with that of Stockhausen "*stays* news." We still don't know whether it marks the wilderness's triumph over the beleaguered *human* spirit or whether it signifies the beginning of our passage through the wilderness, to whatever dimly imagined future.

NOTES

1. Robinson Jeffers, "The Wind-Struck Music," in *The Collected Poetry of Robinson Jeffers*, ed. Tim Hunt, vol. 2, 1928–38 (Stanford, Calif.: Stanford University Press, 1989), 521.

2. Gunther Schuller, "Conversation with Varèse," in *Perspectives on American Composers*, ed. Benjamin Boretz and Edward T. Cone (New York: W. W. Norton, 1971), 35.

3. Ibid.

4. Ibid., 36.

5. Edgard Varèse, "Rhythm, Form, and Content," a 1959 lecture given at Princeton University excerpted and edited by Chou Wen-chung in "The Liberation of Sound," in *Perspectives on American Composers*, 30.

6. Schuller, "Conversation with Varèse," 38.

7. Ibid., 38–39.

8. Varèse, "Rhythm, Form, and Content," 29.

10

Harry Partch in the Desert, Steve Reich in the City

THERE IS A POWERFUL affirmation behind Varèse's bringing together aural disparities. Starting from his observation of natural phenomena in his Old France, he related those observations to the scientific technology of the New World, finding a form of social justification in that people and machines need one another if wilderness and chaos are to be kept at bay. Harry Partch, a senior American progressive, sought the same ends by opposite means since, born in a new world, he found a path forward by rejecting mechanization, and even industrialism itself.

In the harmonic system of Europe's classical music, octaves, fifths, and thirds are incommensurate in their pure form—"pure" intonation is possible only in the monophony of angels. If Harry Partch, born in 1901, is the most radical among the grand old pioneers who sought for a distinctive New World order, the reason is that for him Just Intonation was not merely a technical matter but also an article of faith and an implicit criticism of the Western world. For Partch, the equal temperament that, since Bach, had made the glories of Western music realizable was literally a fall from grace to disgrace. Westerners had created musical artifacts of extreme sophistication; for so-called primitive peoples, on the other hand, there is no artifact in the form of a score. The discovery of sound sources in the world out there, and their metamorphosis into *instruments* by means of which natural and supernatural forces may speak, is itself an act of creation. In this sense the medium is indeed the message.

Harry Partch, reared in the parched and parching wastes of the California and Arizona deserts, was favorably placed to begin again, *ab ovo*. He disowned such music as he had composed in conventionally European guises because he believed that Westerners, and collaterally their music, were on the wrong track. His renovated new music was about as old as music could get, for Partch, like the Native Americans among whom he lived, made it for instruments designed and built by himself, out of materials from the local environment. The beautiful instruments project the spirit of place and speak truth in that their intonation is as pure as may be, with minimal deference to harmonic exigencies. The players, moreover, need to be worthy of their instruments, for how they stand and move is almost as important as the sounds they utter. This would have been entirely intelligible to Partch's Native American colleagues, and if for him as a white West Coast American the music was inevitably a mask, it was far from being a passive imitation of Native American chants and dance ceremonies or of the Japanese kabuki theater, Chinese opera, and African song-and-dance rituals that he knew and relished in San Francisco. Partch's instruments, glamorously named cloud chambers, diamond marimba, kithara, harmonic canon, and the like, emit sounds relatable to that global California scene, being as distinct in timbre as in tuning from those of Western music.

Music was Partch's lifework in a literal sense. His rediscovery of the word and the body in what he called a "corporeal" music countered the pretensions of Western civilization and the cheats and deceits inherent in its commodity and consumer ethics. Moreover, Partch had the courage of his convictions, abandoning civilization for some years to ride the roads and rails as a hobo. This was not a gesture conformable with Beat poets like Allen Ginsberg and Lawrence Ferlinghetti or "on the road" novelists like Jack Kerouac and William Burroughs; it was genuinely a consequence of the Great Depression years through which Partch bummed around, washing dishes while mulling over new-old theories of music theater, for the revival of which he could find no financial support. Eventually, he garnered backing to produce his book, *Genesis of a Music* (1949), which expounds in vigorous and lucid prose the sociological, ideological, mathematical, and acoustical basis of a justly intoned monody opposed to the artificial temperaments of Western music and to the (as he thought) bogus civilization that had produced it. What this meant to him is beautifully expressed in a poem dedicated to him by his disciple and surviving heir, Lou Harrison:

> Thus we compose continuance from his start
> More fully than for centuries.
> Such history perhaps must follow from him
> That tune & tuning shall conjoin.[1]

This is an affecting testimony and an implicit prophecy, written in 1973, the year before Partch's death. If the prophecy has not been completely fulfilled, this is not merely because support for Partch's music, as distinct from his theory, did not accrue. Reasonably he could hardly have expected it to, since the fulfillment of his ideals would have implied the demise of the society from which he sought succor. Most people are reluctant to commit suicide, which is what Partch himself did insofar as there was a flaw in his own "philosophy," as well as in that of the maligned Western world.

This gradually becomes evident in the journals and diaries describing his hobo years.[2] These are written in tough, flexible prose without self-pity and leave us in no doubt that for Partch life and music were one. Personal reflection mingles with snatches of hobo speech and song, presented in rudimentary notation that demonstrates how "words *are* music," in rock-bottom America no less than in ancient Greece, in the Middle Ages' Gregorian chant, or in Provençal troubadour song. Partch's start as an authentic American rather than a pseudo-European composer occurred when, in 1941, he refashioned some of this aural graffiti in a piece called *Barstow*, after the place that spawned it, and scored it for his own intoning voice, accompanied by his adapted, justly intoned microtonal viola, and by ad hoc percussion, all played by himself. Never did music spring more "corporeally" from word and body.

More ambitiously, he capped this in 1943 with *U.S. Highball*, a musical retrospect of his hobo years. Here Partchian instruments enact both the railway trains and the bums as characters, and the text, chanted or intoned by a tramp called Mac, consists of the names of stations culled from a journey east from San Francisco to Chicago mixed up with fragments of hobo dialogue, Mac's random musings, and snippets of advertisements and wayside graffiti. Snatches of pop songs on car radios, bar tunes, and hillbillies float in and out of this hobo's journey-to-no-end; naive pentatonic cries sound wistful against the corny seventh and ninth chords of the vamping guitar-bass, disembodied yet weirdly magnified on Partchian percussion. This is rudimentary music of the American rural wilderness and urban wasteland.

U.S. Highball is directly about the disintegration of urban civilization and the pathos of the outcast's search for the wellsprings of life. In Partch's later work the positive and negative aspects of the situation are more sharply differentiated, the rebirth of (pre-Christian) vitality being opposed to the mechanization and bureaucracy-ridden sterility of the modern world. Partch epitomizes this duality by calling some of his works "satyrs": they are satires, in the modern sense, of the present, but they also reinvoke the ancient Greek satyrs who were a source of potency. So although Partch doesn't accept a scientific-mathematical universe as did Varèse, neither does he present a simple case of white against black, morally (and perhaps racially) speaking. He offers not a churlish lament against industrialization, but a passionate appeal that industrial power should serve life rather than death. This comes out even in works that have no explicit theatrical connotations. Thus he describes *Even Wild Horses* as a "dance for an absent drama. Music and dance enter the consciousness through the gate to illusion, lost recollections, and dimly seen prophetic projections. This music might be considered as autobiographical by almost anyone, in darkly humorous moments."[3] While the music is often surrealistically funny (it includes the "Afro-Cuban Minuet on Happy Birthday to You"), the innocence of the dadaism releases energy. Significantly, the music starts from aspects of primitive music that have found a place in the commercial world, and the point is not to reinforce the clichés of samba, rumba, or conga, but to reveal again, as the jazzy or pop stereotypes revert to the wilder wails and grislier grunts they sprang from, the mysterious power that makes for life.

Partch's most sustained, very well written statement of his aims comes in his verbal prelude and postlude to *The Bewitched*, which is probably his most convincing piece, theatrically and musically. It was written in 1956 for the University of Illinois campus and first performed there on March 26, 1957, during the period when the university gave a home to both Partch and his instruments. The text contains few articulate words, and the instruments effect the action no less than the mimes and dancers. A group of Lost Musicians, aided by "an ancient Witch, a prehistoric seer," dadaistically and unmaliciously debunk fake products of twentieth-century mechanization and intellectuality: "A Soul Tormented by Contemporary Music finds a Humanizing Alchemy" (the title of scene 4) or "The Cognoscenti Are Plunged into a Demonic Descent while at Cocktails" (the title of scene 10). At the end the Lost Musicians find that they already know, in their clownish innocence, the only truth that is humanly apprehensible, for "perception is a sand flea. It can light only for a moment. Another moment must provide its own sand flea."[4] So twentieth-century satire merges into what Partch calls slapstick, linking contemporary nonvalues to concepts so old they seem eternal. Humans who yell, moan, or grunt in jazzy abandon or hysteria may become indistinguishable from hooting owls, barking foxes, and the wild cats of the woods; in returning to nature they may rediscover their true selves. The long, wailing chant at the end of the prologue therapeutically evokes an age-old quietude that is nonetheless pregnant with longing. Significantly, it is based on a chant of the Cahuilla Indians, who live in the southern California desert.[5]

Partch followed *The Bewitched* with three other "satyrs" or, as he also called them, "American musical comedies." *Revelation in the Courthouse Park* (1960) transplants the Bacchae of Euripedes into suburban America; *Water! Water!* (1961) presents an American city that, drought-afflicted, desperately appeals to a water witch—a risky course since the floods released by a black jazz band prove so copious that a baseball game has to be abandoned, and Civilization topples in rain and ruin. *Delusion of the Fury* (1961), the last of Partch's global village musicals, grimly lives up to its title and is worldwide in reference. In all these theater pieces words are no more than semiarticulate, while the instruments are makers of magic, as were, in the depths of the forgotten forest, the first strings ever plucked or stroked, the first horns or pipes ever blown into, the first bells ever clanged, the first drums ever walloped.

All Partch's works, whether modest blessings on the house or ambitious assaults on our technocracies, are magic that is supposed to affect our personal behavior and communal discourse. Herein lies the rub, for the sharp intelligence of Partch's approach and the vigor of his prose cannot disguise a damaging naiveté. It is true that post-Renaissance science and technology have much to answer for in terms of human weal; but it is also true that post-Renaissance "consciousness" alone made possible a Shakespeare and a Beethoven, and that when once they have been "invented," we cannot pretend they are expendable. Although Partch protested that he had no wish to oust alternative notions of music and life, that, given his premises, must have been self-deceit. There is even inconsistency in his *wanting* to give notated form to a concept that is in principle "performance music." The dreary distrust of Western values currently rampant in some (especially American) universities might even be construed as Partchian doctrine carried to ultimate imbecility. No wonder Partch was left with a sense of failure—incorporated in the title of his collection of essays and journals—*Bitter Music.*

There were crudely practical reasons why Partch's "corporeal" ideology and his forty-three-tone-to-the-octave system of intonation could not reach fruition. For his instruments could be developed only in rich (usually industrially sponsored) academic institutions such as were philosophically anathema to him, so that his global village, ideologically a home for everyone, was rendered elitist. The more inescapably this came home to him the more curmudgeonly became his response to the academic institutions that, however inadequately, supported him, and the more his well-wishers suffered from his jeremiads about the malignancy of the society he was heir to. The dignity of his prose was not transferred to his conduct of personal relationships, and one consequence of this is that it is difficult to know just how good Partch is. The designedly semiarticulate texts of the theater pieces do not, on the evidence of their reprinting, offer much purely literary nourishment, for the obvious reason that they were not meant to exist apart from their visual and musical extensions. Equally, the music, though all recorded, was not meant to stand as concert music per se. In musical terms there are arid stretches as well as marvelous moments, and the latter (mostly in *The Bewitched*) need theatrical projection for total effect. It would seem that the flaw in Partch's philosophy lay in its simplistic nature, notwithstanding the sharp rigor of his mind. What he asked for—a handmade ritual relevant to a mass-produced world—could never happen in urban life; and he wasn't prepared to accommodate what is to what might be.

It may be significant that the most musically beautiful moments in Partch's work occur in his score to *Windsong* (1958), a film version of the Apollo and Daphne story, wherein the human is metamorphosed into nonhuman nature. Partch instruments create a collage of sounds, aural cuts complementary to the visual cuts of the film—musical images suggested by "dead trees, driftwood, falling sand, blowing tumbleweed, flying gulls, wriggling snakes, waving grasses."[6] Here Partch carries to an ultimate end the element in Varèse's work that is concerned with wildernesses within the mind and without. The sounds are remarkably similar, though Varèse achieves his "natural" effects through scientific technology, which Partch affected to despise. Paradox is inherent in that Partch's most congenial medium proved to be film.

Although Partch was himself in part responsible for his nonfulfillment, the legacy he left has to be reckoned with, and this is not easy, since there are so many problems involved in recreating his works. Lou Harrison, the California composer who has to a degree assumed Partch's mantle, was on the mark in saying Partch "told us the truth about tune, as Kinsey did about sex. In ancient things we hunt eternity—their dust is incense, & beyond them we hear old melodies surely learned from angels in gardens."[7] That in turn reminds us that Partch may genuinely claim to have something in common with Yeats, a far greater artist whose translation of Sophocles' *Oedipus* provided the text for Partch's first venture into music theater. One of the most fascinating items in the published collection of Partch's journals is the account of his meeting with Yeats, who approved of his "corporeal" view of music. Partch reciprocally hazarded that Yeats's much-vaunted unmusicality—his inability to "carry a tune"—was really evidence of his aural acuity, which would not tolerate the "false," because tempered, intervals of Western tradition.[8] Well, maybe. But not even for Yeats's ear could the entire heritage of Western music be thrown on the trash heap; and Harry Partch was no Yeats nor even, as a corporeal composer, a Michael Tippett or a Harrison Birtwistle.

Harry Partch opted out from industrial civilization in a literal sense, though his attempt to create a "tribal" music theater was frustrated by the paradox of his not being a member of a tribe. A quarter of a century later Steve Reich came near to success in such an enterprise. Born in 1936 in New York City, Reich received a conventional education in philosophy at Cornell University and in music at the Juilliard School, reinforced by work, at Mills College in California, with Milhaud and Luciano Berio. He seems to have felt no need to disown "Europe," since he knew, as a Jew and as a member of the polyglot industrial metropolis, that the "Faustian" Western tradition could not be for him. His real musical education was in Ghana, where he studied African drumming, and in Bali, Berkeley, and Seattle, where he worked on gamelan. His early music was consistently percussive, sometimes requiring only a few pairs of clapping hands for its realization. All his work was "performance" art in that it became a composition only in the process of "forming it through." In New York's Soho during the seventies, the skill of the "process" whereby Reich's notated linear and metrical patterns acquired aural flesh and blood as their repetitions drew slightly out of phase, enlivened both body and spirit. As the players habitually worked as a "group," in the same spirit as do pop and tribal musicians, the audience (which might more aptly be called a congregation) was involved in a physical act.

The climax to this phase of Reich's work was in *Drumming*, a ninety-minute extension of a single metrical cell, devised in 1971 for Reich's group to execute on tuned bongos, marimbas, and glockenspiels (deputizing for African xylophone-type instruments), with the addition of wordless voices functioning much as do singers in African tribal musics. Of course we are not, in listening to *Drumming*, indulging in a ritual act comparable with those indulged in by Africans; but we are participants in a corporeal and mental activity closer to a ritual ceremony than to an orthodox concert. The piece has been much performed, presumably because it fulfills a need for people living in big cities, dedicated to head and will rather than to body and senses. Nor is it surprising that Reich should have supplemented this acoustic music with electronic resources appropriate to industrial societies. A piece called *Electric Counterpoint*, written in 1987 for the guitarist Pat Metheny, presents the live guitarist soloing to the accompaniment of tapes prerecorded by himself on two other guitars and two electric basses. The work opens with a continuum of figurations similar to those that in real tribal musics initiate activity, out of which emerges a theme derived from central African horn music. This theme builds into an eight-voiced canon: a togetherness that again emulates the "processes" of African music, wherein everyone plays or sings the same song at slightly different times. Excitation accrues from overlap between the voices: a process that is sociological, even psychological, in that it implies that the "I" wants to "belong," yet is stimulated by the fact that he or she cannot quite do so. Since the soloist plays patterns triggered by the interlocked prerecorded parts, the music subsumes the private into the public life and finds personal fulfillment, if not individual identity, in the process. Although the work has three movements—fast, slow, fast—it is not sectional, since the slow movement halves the tempo without changing the pulse, while the third, returning to the original tempo, adds a new motif in triple time, but ends by ironing out the polymeters and reasserting the original modality. This is as much a beginning as an end; given the conditions in which people in industrial cities live, Reich has offered physical and nervous stimulation, in hopeful simulation of African tribal music.

Reich's other ethnic root, his Jewishness, wasn't deeply explored until 1981 when he produced *Tehillim*, a work involving melody instruments and voices as well as percussion. The original version was for a chamber group, which was expanded to full orchestra for performance by the New York Philharmonic. While this may signify Reich's acceptance into usual concert repertory, it doesn't affect the concept of the music, since the strings mostly hold drones while the musical substance is provided by wind instruments, tuned percussion, and voices whose patterns, though more lyrically defined than in Reich's earlier music, still create a continuum wherein communal life may flourish. A further development is that these voices utter words and that both the melodic patterns and the metrical proportions are derived from the words' inflections. The texts, from the Hebraic version of the Psalms of David, fuse Christian with Jewish eschatology, but do not aim at personal expressivity. The piece is rather an act of praise, which often suggests the drone-founded cantillation and tintinnabulation of Pérotin, music master of Notre Dame in the twelfth century, whose scintillating textures are much relished by Reich. Given the pre-Renaissance and to a degree non-Western characteristics of Pérotin's music, it is understandable that *Tehillim* should also remind us of near-Eastern secular fiesta which, transported to New York, still provides a potent affirmation, springing from word and body, in which audience or celebrants may vicariously share. So sunny a sonority and so ebullient a rhythm might seem too simple to be true—were it not that the performers, exhibiting self-obliterating skill, carry us with them, gratefully alive rather than, as with some heavy metal and minimalist music, amnesially dead.

Reich's music, like that of other minimalist composers, now shares the racks in record shops with sundry types of tribal pop music, which suggests the change in social function his music stands for. He is not merely, or at all, making concert music, but rather the kind of music theater Harry Partch abortedly aimed at. A striking instance is offered by *Different Trains*, for live string quartet and prerecorded tapes, a work that, like *Electric Counterpoint*, calls on electronics while at the same time being derived, like *Tehillim*, from human speech. A new element is an autobiographical dimension, for the different trains referred to in the three movements belong respectively to Reich's unknowing childhood, to the retrospective awareness of his middle years, and to his present and his potential future. When he was a baby, Reich's parents separated. So both could keep contact with the young Steve, he was recurrently shunted by train, in the care of a governess, between New York and Los Angeles. To reanimate this remote past Reich collected tapes of his now aged governess's voice, of the voice of a still more ancient African American Pullman car attendant, and of the museum-preserved sounds of American railway trains of the thirties and forties. A collage made from these tapes prompted the metrical and linear patterns of the notated string quartet music that, in being also train music, is a long way from the world of the Viennese string quartet, since it evokes a journey, without end, and still present in the mind. As memory becomes here-and-now, the abstract pattern-making of Reich's early work acquires topical and local meanings, which in the second movement merge into the mythic aspects of his Jewish heritage.

For while these trips between New York and Los Angeles were thrilling to the infant Reich, he couldn't help but think, looking back from the eighties, that had he been in Europe during those years, "as a Jew I would have had to ride very different trains."[9] With this in mind he prepared a taped collage: of the speech of Holocaust survivors now living in the United States and of European trains of the same vintage. In both the first (American) section and the second (European) section the music for string quartet—that most "civilizedly" European of media—springs from the rhythms of the declaimed or wailed words. Reich explains, "The speech samples as well as the train sounds were transferred to tape with the use of sampling keyboards and a computer. Kronos then made four separate string quartet recordings which were combined with the speech and train sounds to create the finished work."[10] The rounding-off movement, headed "After the War," follows without a break, capping the distant and the middle past with present survival—music more jazzy in pulse, clearer in texture, in which the string quartet is even recognizable as such. Yet although the spoken phrases remind us that the musical Nazis loved to listen to Jewish singing, we are promised no millennium. The caroling "girl with the beautiful voice" is irremediably dead; voices question whether the war is "really" over; and even the once-glamorous American trains are on the way out. We end with a joke: the Pullman car attendant of the first movement praises his train for being "crack," which in his day meant "best"; now the word has different connotations.

So while *Different Trains* is process music existing in an eternal present, it embraces past and future in the forms of memory and desire and is not extrapolated from history. Indeed, it is unusual in being ritual that admits to the possibility of change, and even growth. It thus helps us to evade a lemminglike suicidal state, and momentarily to escape, if not discount, the tyranny of ego and will. Its exhilaration and terror don't obliterate us in amnesia, let alone euphoria, for conscience and choice remain among the possibilities of consciousness. The only other composer who can challenge Reich in this respect is John Adams, especially in his opera *Nixon in China*. Perhaps these men are social moralists of music rather than composers in the traditional sense. They may be the more welcome because great composers in the old sense are less likely to have a close relationship to the community than was once the case.

Minimal music on the whole mistrusts old age since both technically and philosophically it finds its most urgent priority in relearning the "momentariness" of children—in the sense defined by the wisely childlike G. K. Chesterton: "[Children] always say 'Do it again,' and the grown-up person does it again until he is nearly dead. For grown-up people are not strong enough to exult in monotony. But perhaps God is strong enough to exult in monotony. It is possible that God says every morning, 'Do it again' to the sun; and every evening, 'Do it again' to the moon. . . . It may be that He has the eternal appetite of infancy; but we have sinned and grown old, and our Father is younger than we."[11] A good minimalist, like Reich, may have a peculiar ability to "exult in monotony": to sing in the wilderness, rejoice in the desert. It may not be an accident that one of Reich's most ambitious works is a choral and orchestral setting of lines from William Carlos Williams's poem "Desert Music" and that his work goes some way toward accommodating Reich's "process" to the kind of "communication" people expect in concert halls. The music encourages us to belong to and respect a community, and for that matter the earth. Williams referred to his desert music as "protecting music," adding that

> I could not help thinking
> of the wonders of the brain that
> hears that music and of our
> skill sometimes to record it.[12]

On this basis Reich's *Desert Music,* though not a "great" work, indubitably matters.

NOTES

1. Lou Harrison, *Joys and Perplexities: Selected Poems of Lou Harrison* (Winston-Salem, N.C.: Jargon Society, 1992), 41.

2. See Harry Partch, *Bitter Music: Collected Journals, Essays, Introductions, and Librettos,* ed. Thomas McGeary (Urbana: University of Illinois Press, 1991).

3. Harry Partch, liner notes to *Even Wild Horses* on *Plectra and Percussion Dances,* Gate 5 Records, issue C, HO8P-1321, H08P-1322.

4. Harry Partch, liner notes to *The Bewitched: A Dance Satire,* Gate 5 Records.

5. Ibid.

6. Harry Partch, liner notes to *Windsong* on *Thirty Years of Lyrical and Dramatic Music,* Gate 5 Records, Issue A, N80P-7421, N80P-7422.

7. Harrison, *Joys and Perplexities,* 94.

8. Partch, *Bitter Music,* 166.

9. Steve Reich, liner notes to *Different Trains,* Electra/Nonesuch CD 9 79176-2.

10. Ibid.

11. G. K. Chesterton, "The Ethics of Elfland," in *G. K. Chesterton: A Selection from His Non-fictional Prose; selected by W. H. Auden* (London: Faber and Faber, 1970), 186.

12. William Carlos Williams, "The Desert Music," in *The Desert Music and Other Poems* (New York: Random House, 1954), 90.

11

Peter Sculthorpe in the Australian Outback

The North American deserts, wherein Steve Reich distantly heard a "protecting music," are ancient, but the deserts of Australia, a land more newly inhabited by migrating Europeans, are still more ancient and are still tenuously occupied by a people with a heritage even longer than that of North America's indigenous inhabitants. The Gagadju of northern Australia, living in the immense area now known as Kakadu National Park, have been there for more than forty thousand years. This healthy folk succored by a hospitable environment was ravaged by willfully cruel rapacity and diseases of body and mind witlessly inflicted by Europeans and other interlopers. Today, of the Gagadju only a few elderly elders survive; when they die, their mainly oral traditions—the Song Lines with which they demarcate their homes, the Dream Time that their souls inhabit—will vanish with them. Australia, shorn of its native population attuned to the environment, became a wasteland, a wilderness densely populated only in a fringe of Western-style civilization scattered around the coasts. But although Westerners, given their technological know-how, triumphed in their acts of destruction, they failed to impose a Western image on the "conquered" folk. Reluctantly these Westerners have been forced to admit that, while the indigenous population needed technology to thrive in a changing world, the new settlers had something to learn, in spiritual as well as ecological terms, from the original inhabitants. The continent the European settlers called Australia is still embryonic, having even less written history than the United States, wherein the Native Americans represent the Europeans' aborted conscience. The Australian aborigines, less engulfed by the "advance" of white technocracy, proffer an even more potent moral yardstick; as the Western world erupts in political, social, psychological, and environmental terms, Australia may find profit as well as loss in the force of their warning, and even in the depths of their despair.

The uncompromising nature of the Australian experience makes the issues clearer than they are in the United States, where so may cultures have fused or mingled. White Australian artists are aware that they have no choice but to make, in Robert Creeley's words:

> The poem supreme, addressed to
> emptiness—this is the courage
> necessary. This is something
> quite different.[1]

Images of emptiness and space have pervaded Australian visual arts for more than a century, and both their potency and their relevance to modern society have been widely recognized. Painters such as Sidney Nolan, Arthur Boyd, and Russell Drysdale were internationally celebrated well before Australian writers had worldwide esteem. Nowadays we honor several fine Australian poets, from A. D. Hope and Judith Wright to Les Murray, as well as a novelist, Patrick White, who may claim a place among the century's supreme writers of English prose. His novels—especially *Voss, Riders in the Chariot,* and *A Fringe of Leaves*—are Australian in theme and have discovered rhythms of the English language native to the antipodes. Yet these aboriginally Australian books are also profoundly disturbing testaments about the modern world, there and elsewhere; and although White's stature is unique, there is now a "school" of novelists (often also poets) whom we may think of as his heirs—for instance, Peter Carey, David Malouf, and Rodney Hall (whose *Just Relations* is an accurately entitled study of Australia's inner tensions).

Moreover, there is increasing evidence that Australian music is beginning to discover the universal within the topical and local. In this respect Peter Sculthorpe is one of the most important of living composers, whether or not he may count as "great." Interestingly enough, he was born just off Australia's furthest edge, in a region (Tasmania) that is geographically and climatically similar to Europe, whence came the first outsiders, mostly convicts who were themselves outsiders from the civilizations of Europe. In their new world the European settlers were, though not overtly rebellious, bemused, since they knew neither where they were nor where they were going. Such artists as emerged in this raw new world fretted to get back to Europe. Although Australian light and air were priceless gifts to visual artists, and although Australian climatic conditions favored the development of vigorous vocal chords and powerful diaphragms, exceptionally gifted painters and singers—of whom Australia spawned many—almost without exception returned or escaped to Europe, both for training and in furtherance of their careers. Creatively, conventional Australian music of the nineteenth and early twentieth centuries was even more subservient to European (especially Teutonic) models than was American art-music of the same period. But whereas in the United States social groups soon became large and homogenous enough to nurture cultural traditions in a home-away-from-home, Australia remained an apparently irredeemable wasteland for Western-educated artists.

Even Sculthorpe himself, who was born late enough (in Launceston in 1929) to profit from a slowly evolving antipodean tradition, felt the need, having already graduated from Melbourne University, to study further in England, and in Oxford at that. His strength was such that there, in so ancient an environment so far from home, he discovered his true identity. He began, as had no Western-schooled composer before him, to make a music distinctively Australian; and although there is now an impressive phalanx of such composers, none rivals Sculthorpe in revealing a national identity that is also pertinent worldwide. From his early youth Sculthorpe nurtured a near-addiction to the writings of Joseph Conrad, a Polish expatriate who wrote brilliantly in a foreign language and, as a sea-faring man, was obsessed with the primeval terrors of the wilderness (whether in immense foreign continents or on the open sea) and with the anguish of alienation and the hazards of colonization.

Two apprentice works from Sculthorpe's Oxford days merit mention, both for their intrinsic quality and for their prophetic nature. The Sonatina for Pianoforte of 1954 was his first published work issued on a grant from the University of Sydney. On the page the music betrays affinities with twentieth-century European musics—perhaps the spikey textures of Stravinsky's World War I music, certainly the linear economy and rhythmic vitality of Bartók's *Mikrokosmos*. Even so, the piece, though called "Sonatina," is not in sonata form, nor is the music parasitic. It accords with Sculthorpe's description on the score: "for the journey of Yoonecara to the land of his forefathers, and the return to his tribe." This is what all Sculthorpe's music is about, and the real hero is not the aboriginal Yoonecara but Sculthorpe himself—and you and I, insofar as we all live in a world that has lost touch with our ancestors. Although this piano sonatina wasn't a deliberate attempt to create a modern aboriginal music, its sounds and structures are aboriginal in that they function not by development, but by the juxtaposition of tersely delineated figures, whether hieratically slow or briskly metrical. When chords occur in the grittily linear textures they tend to be sharply dissonant though basically concordant, telescoping (for instance) falsely related minor and major thirds in the manner of Copland. The sonatina is not—as its modest title indicates—a major achievement, but it is remarkably assured for an early work. People seem intuitively to have realized this, for the piece has been much performed.

In the following year Sculthorpe wrote a work far more significant in relation to his future. *Irkanda I* is conceived monodically, being an "auncient chant" for solo violin. The violin is of the string family, which Sculthorpe associates with human expressivity; and the piece works by accretion, as tiny cells are slowly mutated. Melodically, the technique follows aboriginal music in being based on incremental repetition; syncopations, extensions, and truncations create rhythmic movement without progression; harmonic progression—insofar as harmony may be latent in a single line and patent in a violin's multiple-stopping—is evaded by prevalent drones and ostinatos. For all these reasons the work is more "Australian" than the piano sonatina, though there are still European imprints, of which the most obvious is a debt to Bartók's Sonata for Solo Violin, while the deepest springs from Sculthorpe's early addiction to the music of Ernst Bloch, whose Jewish monodic lament could be metamorphosed into aboriginal lament in the Outback. Certain Sculthorpe fingerprints—wailing seconds, major or minor, oscillations between diminished fourths and thirds major and minor, microtones, glissandos, shivery tremolandos, and hazy harmonics—have parallels in Bloch's string writing, especially in *Schelomo* for cello and orchestra (1916) and the acutely entitled *Voice in the Wilderness* (1926) for the same forces. Even so, the perfervid dolor of Bloch's Hebraic lament, bearing the burden of European centuries, is poles apart from Sculthorpe's forlorn evocation of the self in the Outback.

Irkanda is an aboriginal word meaning "a remote and lonely place." Unsurprisingly, this violin work became a prototype for a series of pieces thus entitled, climaxing in *Irkanda IV* for solo violin, string orchestra, and percussion both conventionally orchestral and aboriginal. This landmark in Sculthorpe's evolution was composed in June 1961; he had returned to Launceston from Oxford in December 1960 to be with his father, who was approaching the end of a terminal illness. The piece probably owes its emotional charge to its being a requiem not only for his father but also for the past his family stood for—and even for "Europe," insofar as in this work several European ghosts are laid to rest. The solo part, passionately rhetorical in personal feeling, relates Jewish Bloch not only to Central European Béla

Bartók but also to the Jewish but Europeanly "civilized" Mahler, both directly in chromatic valediction and indirectly in parodistic hints of urban tangoid and gypsyish demotic musics. Structurally the piece works, as does *Irkanda I*, by slow mutation rather than development. The Outback engulfs the self as the solo violin's chant wavers between diminished fourths, major and minor thirds, and augmented seconds, with all the tonal ambivalences thus implied, while the orchestra evokes an eternal emptiness by way of telescoped concords, often *sul tasto* or *tremolando*. The music induces a human distress more lacerating than anything in Sculthorpe's earlier work. This was an abyss he had to descend into, in order to find its opposite, for during the sixties he embarked on another series of works radically different from, and even opposed to, the *Irkandas*.

Sun *Musics* I-IV established Sculthorpe's international reputation probably because some of them, being scored for full orchestra, lent themselves to usual concert repertory, though they transformed the familiar medium of symphony orchestra into a gigantic percussion ensemble. Whereas the *Irkandas* are melodic expressivity in essence, the *Sun Musics* have virtually no sustained melody or harmonic evolution. Brass, woodwind, strings, and percussion are used in static blocks, creating sunscapes that recall the paintings of Nolan and Drysdale. There was, of course, a European precedent for this in Stravinsky's once-notorious *Sacre du printemps*. Any composer of Sculthorpe's generation must have reeled under it, though Sculthorpe's more direct debt was to Varèse, thereby synthesizing impulses from both the Old World and the New. We noted, in the chapter on Varèse, how he, a Frenchman who settled in New York, created a revolutionary music that abandoned Western progression and development in favor of quasi-architectural blocks of sound. Carrying Debussy's fragmented lyricism, static harmony, and impressionist color into the harsh milieu of industrial New York, he discovered analogies between mathematical engineering and presumptively eternal laws of nature. The parallels he drew between his musical structures and crystal and rock formation are metaphorical rather than descriptive, but there is no doubt that his music offered a formidable alternative—harking back to the linear and metrical structures of primitive musics but looking forward to the mathematically preordained structures of electronics—to the vagaries of human passion.

Sculthorpe had already explored "primitive" sources in depth and was by this date familiar with developments in electronics. Although he did not exploit such techniques in *Sun Musics*, he has admitted that his sun sonorities were consciously influenced by the growth of electronic music during the sixties. His position was not far from that of Varèse, who, as we noted, virtually gave up composition during the forties and fifties, waiting for the development of electronic resources to provide the infinite gamut of pitches he needed. Sculthorpe made do without them, but, inspired by the electronic experiments of the sixties, exploited audible dimensions of the visual arts, especially by way of the collage techniques of film. It is pertinent to note that Sculthorpe's *Sun Musics* have been effectively used as background to documentary films about Australia and have been staged as ritual ballet. Whereas in the *Irkanda* series we have a music of what Sculthorpe described to me as the "self alone in time and space," the *Sun Musics* present, by way of techniques affiliated with nonhuman electronic music, a world devoid of human population—except insofar as the quasi-visual sounds come to us by courtesy of the composer's listening ear and watching eye. In these works the Outback's sun is far from benign, and as musical (and human) experience they are not richly sustaining. Yet although wilderness, per se, could hardly nourish, Sculthorpe's unflinching acceptance of the Australian desert was necessary for him. Only when he had accepted it on its own terms could he confront humanity's place in it.

The visual qualities of the *Sun Musics* bear on Sculthorpe's fascination with another kind of otherness: that of Asian musics, especially Japanese and Balinese. Given the Asian influences latent in Bloch's works, this was not a totally new development, but the alignment with Japan and Bali has more direct relevance, given their geographical proximity to Australia. Their "philosophical" implications also provide positive succor to the "paradise of archetypes and repetition" of aboriginal musics; it cannot be fortuitous that while many of the linear strands (rather than themes) in the *Sun Musics* are affiliated with aboriginal chant, others are based on Japanese court incantation, and the latter seems as appropriate as the former. A wind quintet with percussion, written in 1968 and entitled *Tabuh-tabuhan,* lives up to its Balinese title in evoking gamelan. In its pentatonic burblings and seductive sonorities, *Tabuh-tabuhan* creates, as Sculthorpe told me, "relaxed sensuous pleasure." Scarred and seared by the desert wilderness, we may momentarily escape into daydreaming that, if evasive, is therapeutically necessary. Sculthorpe's Asian themes become a means whereby he tempers the stress and distress of his ritual mourning, which returns, with enhanced intensity, in the works of the seventies. Significantly enough, they are scored for strings.

Given his partiality for the expressive humanity of the string family, it is not surprising that Sculthorpe has been a prolific writer of string quartets, even though this European medium is the very heart of the tradition he'd needed to efface. Two string quartets from his middle phase are in this context complementary. No. 6 (1965) has much of the tense energy of Bartók but adapts his motivic mutations and incremental rhythms for Australian ends, letting in air and space. No. 8, on the other hand, springs from aboriginal lament and Zen-like pattern-making, timbre, and color. Both East and West thus come to terms with aboriginality.

The same happens in the *Lament for Strings* of 1976, and even more impressively in the *Sonata for Strings,* written two years later. This is not a sonata, except in the root sense of being music sounded, as distinct from sung, as in a cantata. Nonetheless the piece is built on a basic duality, for the body movements of aboriginal dance interlock with harmonically static sections the composer calls chorales. Neither mobile dance nor immobile chorale progresses or wants to progress. Alternation rather than altercation creates an eternal present that might resemble minimalism except that the constituent materials are maximal in melodic, rhythmic, and even harmonic charge. Texturally, the dance sections are tough, while the Zen-like chorales are far from passive relaxation. Sculthorpe has suggested that this may be a legacy from a period in the late sixties when he lived in a Japanese Zen monastery. What John Cage said of American artists would seem to apply to this Australian: "The movement with the wind of the Orient and the movement against the wind of the Occident meet in America and produce a movement upwards into the air—the space, the silence, the nothing that supports us."[2]

But if the Sculthorpe experience is *solitudinous,* it has another dimension that, at the opposite pole of Zen Buddhism, embraces the everyday world—much as Patrick White precariously balances his Australian explorers, saints, simpletons, and oddballs against the chatter of suburbia. This aspect of Sculthorpe's work centers around his music for documentary film, beginning in 1962 with *The Fifth Continent,* a radiophonic work for speaker, orchestra, and film with a text—declaimed in its first performance in 1963 by the poet James McAuley—from D. H. Lawrence's Australian novel, *Kangaroo.* The scene is set around the World War I memorial of a small town called Thirroul, on the Pacific coast near Sydney. Much later Sculthorpe adapted, from this threnody for the local dead, a short, purely orchestral elegy that he called "Small Town." This is old-style frontier music, in which the deaths honored become not merely topical and local but also the death of the heart inherent in Sculthorpe's Australian laments. This may explain the poignancy of the corny oboe tune, displaced just off the beats of the loping harp accompaniment. This is a beguiling Australian complement to the shanty town tunes in the film and ballet scores of Copland, who especially admired the passage in Sculthorpe's score wherein two heterophonic bugles blow a last post. Again, there is a visual analogy; "Small Town" is dedicated to Drysdale, whose suburban landscapes it evokes.

A more substantial piece in the same vein, *Port Essington,* encapsulates Australian history in recounting two attempts to establish a settlement: the first one was launched in 1824; the second, begun in 1838, was abandoned in 1849 after appalling hardships. According to Sculthorpe, failure was inevitable because the new settlers could not adapt to their new environment. The garrison soldiers, for example, persisted in wearing their uniforms for winter—the season in England—during the hot Australian summer: a crude manifestation of Sculthorpe's basic theme of the loss of an organic relationship between humans and the natural world. The work, significantly scored for Sculthorpe's humanly expressive strings, traces through its six sections the spiritual as well as the material history of the continent. It opens with the Outback, scrawnily evoked in string ostinatos played *con ferocità* and proceeds into a series of variations on a quasi-colonial melody, played by a salon style trio in a demotic idiom that reflects the passage of time—from a Handelian Augustan Gentleman to a Mendelssohnic Victorian Lady in a salon to an Elgarian Representative of an Edwardian Outpost of Empire. Ironically enough, this settlers' song is itself a permutation of an *aboriginal* melody that Sculthorpe has used recurrently in his work; and all the permutations it passes through are embraced within the aural context of the Outback, including its birds, beasts, insects, and reptiles, as well as the natural sounds of wind and—occasionally if rarely—water. Throughout, both the latent aboriginal song and the settlers' mindlessly twittering pastiche is broken by rhythmic disruptions and harmonic dislocations; and it is not a matter of "good" aborigines against "bad" settlers. The drawing-room music rends the heart, partly because its (basically aboriginal) tune is so haunting and partly because its aural realization is so frail as to sound unreal, even slightly ridiculous. So not only the aborigines are defeated; the new settlers also sound—as they actually were—pathetically vulnerable. The evolution of the work—from the empty land to the indigenous population to the encroaching aliens to the "Estrangement" and back to the emptiness—is a myth of the human psyche, as well as a canned history of Australia. The piece is not finally depressing, perhaps because the aboriginal tune sounds clearest in the last variation, which is in traditionally heavenly E major. As a whole, *Port Essington* bears the same relationship to a toughly abstract piece like *Sonata for Strings* as Copland's ballets and film scores bear to the "absolute" music of his three superb piano works, the *Variations* of 1930, the *Sonata* of 1940, and the *Fan-*

tasy of 1957. The more accessible pieces spell out motifs latent in the abstract pieces, in forms more readily communicable though no less musical.

Port Essington was composed in 1977. In subsequent years Sculthorpe's concern with solitariness has revealed how everyday life is contained within, and itself contains, solitariness. Three major works chart the process of maturation, beginning in 1974 with *The Song of Tailitnama,* for soprano solo, six cellos, and percussion—an ensemble that embraces the basic elements of Sculthorpe's art. The voice, which vocalizes but also sings the words of a rock wallaby song of the northern Aranda, is unaccommodated man-woman; the percussion is the continuum within which tribal togetherness exists; the cellos humanely (and divinely?) sing as only cellos can, in their role as sublimated and extended male-female voices. Interestingly, this first version of a work to which the composer is peculiarly partial was made for an ABC documentary film and was intended to form a climax to the *Sun Music* series. It turned out to be the beginning of something new—the newness lying in the piece's melodically affirmatory character, as distinct from the *Sun Music's* reliance on timbre and architectural proportions.

The aboriginal words of Tailitnama's song are a hymn to the dawning day, apostrophizing both the earthbound (because dead) ancestors and the volatilely ephemeral birds of the air. Preludially, the soprano chants a wordless vocalize, off-beat, undulating between tones, aspiring through fifths and fourths, while the cellos, momentarily nonhuman, make dawn noises by way of over-the-bridge harmonics and pizzicato thrumming. Improvised percussion (water gong, guiro, wood blocks, and wood chimes) combines with shivery pizzicato strings to emulate, with startling verisimilitude, the dawn chorus. The first extended melody evolves from the ritual tune, the mode— A, B flat, C, D flat, F, G, and A—remaining unchanged throughout the polymetrical dance. That one doesn't know whether the tune is authentically aboriginal or Sculthorpe-invented makes a point, in view of the music's new-old status. It serves as an eternal present that anneals if it does not comfort and merges into a coda that, being over a now regular eighth-note pulse, sounds consummatory. Above it, the soprano solo floats a wordless incantation flowering from the preludial music. The root of the mode, having shifted between A and C, is now hoisted to E, and to that degree the harmonically static but rhythmically agile dance may be said to progress. Dawn is a new day; Australia's vernality is here "auralized" with primal simplicity.

The *Requiem* for cello, being for a solo string instrument, relates back to the first essential Sculthorpe piece, *Irkanda I.* Written in 1979, it is another work about death and a further tribute to the composer's father. As one might expect, it consciously fuses the Australian with the European. Its sections follow the sequence of the Roman Catholic plainchant liturgy, drawing on authentic plainsong themes; at the same time the music demonstrates that there is no necessary division between ritual mourning in the Roman Catholic church and in an aboriginal group. Death is undivisive, and the *Requiem,* starting with quotations from the Roman rite, evolves into aboriginal incantation—undulating by step, aspiring through godly fourths and fifths—and implicitly into ritual mourning for any person, any time, any place. The "Kyrie" rocks between false-related thirds; "Qui Mariam" is a funeral lament played arco, self-accompanied by pizzicato chords, wherein we may detect a distant reminiscence of Bloch, purged by the desert's emptiness. "Lacrymosa" stays closer to the plainsong source, while "Libera me" enacts the words by intervallic and metrical fragmentation. A partial recapitulation of the "Kyrie" leads into the coda, which glimpses "Lux aeterna." Although the plainsong is at first calmly enunciated, it is gradually stretched into tortuous arioso; the often augmented or diminished intervals, widely spaced, reinforce the earlier recollection of Bloch, now stranded and disembodied in the Outback.

In the same year as this *Requiem* (1979), which fuses Australia and Europe and an individual and a collective destiny, Sculthorpe created an orchestral work that has claims to being a masterpiece. Its title is *Mangrove,* but Sculthorpe tells us that the music is descriptive neither of mangroves nor of watery swamps. It is rather a *recherche du temps perdu:* "'memories of time spent among mangroves; thoughts of Sidney Nolan's rain-forest paintings, in which Eliza Frazer and the convict Bracewell become one through love, birds and butterflies and aboriginal graffiti; even recollections of a beach, mangrove-free, at Ise, in Japan; and thoughts of a New Guinea tribe that believes man and women to be descended from mangroves'"[3]—a word that, for Sculthorpe, "'in some way means man-woman.'"[4] This prescription embraces every aspect of the Sculthorpe experience, which is that of Australia.

Woodwinds and harp were omitted from the *Mangrove* orchestra, lest they might have tempted the composer to overobvious water noises. The scoring he adopted conforms to his habitual instrumental symbolism, in which strings are human, brass tends to be nonhuman—emulating the wilder forces of nature—while woodwinds may be flexibly avian, bestial, or human. We are not allowed to forget, however, that human and inhuman forces overlap, and percussion links them all, again acting as a continuum in which to live. The first section is an alarming auralization of creature-speak in which trombones, trumpets, and horns grunt, growl, gibber, and bark in polymetric chaos, driven to orgiastic ardor by percussion. The climax is echoed by sighs, *con tenerezza*, on muted strings, as though nature's hurly-burly was too much for us. Yet the sighs turn into a string chant that aspires to human identity, growing from the familiar stepwise undulation, with intermittent leaps of thirds, fourths, and fifths. This chant, first enunciated by cellos, fulfills the same function as the plainsong quotations in the cello *Requiem*, only this time it is based on a Japanese *saibura* court melody, "Isé-no-Umi." It no more imparts a flavor of exoticism than the Christian incantation renders the *Requiem* European. These rudimentary themes are ab-original in springing from the acoustical bases of song, which makes Sculthorpe a global village composer at the deepest possible level. This is allegorized in that the chant sung by one group of cellos is echoed by another, playing the same pitches in independent rhythm, *fuori di passo* (literally, "out of step"). This ghost of the tune is its and our rebirth, which inspires a paean of praise from created nature, evoked by *sul ponticello* and vibrato devices on the "human" strings, but over the bridge, *come veduta a volo d'uccello*. This duet of humanity and nature leads to a return of the "savage" brass music in snarling fragmentation, hounded by percussive ostinatos. At the climax the strings wail their original broken sighs, no longer muted, but *largamente, con desidero d'amore*. This may be Sculthorpe's most powerful statement of the spiritual as well as ecological interdependence of humans and the world they inhabit.

From the high plateau of *Mangrove* Sculthorpe could survey new horizons. He planned a larger work for full orchestra that he thought of as "Mangrove II"—the second member of another series comparable with the *Irkandas* and the *Sun Musics*. He abandoned this because he decided it wasn't what he most urgently needed, "'for whenever I have returned from abroad in recent years, this country has seemed to me to be one of the last places on earth where one could honestly write quick and joyous music, I decided therefore to write such a piece.'"[5] This makes sense as a resolution of the opposites effected in *Mangrove*, but we can also accept Sculthorpe's further reflection that "'it would be dishonest of me to write music that is altogether quick and joyous. The lack of a common cause and the self-interest of many have drained us [Australians] of much of our energy. . . . Most of the jubilation, I came to feel, awaits us in the future. Perhaps we now need to attune ourselves to this continent, to listen to the cry of the earth, as the Aborigines have done for many thousands of years.'"[6]

The next piece, finished in 1986, was in fact called *Earth Cry* and testifies to its crucial position in Sculthorpe's work in that it incorporates another version of the germinal piece of 1974, *The Song of Tailitnama*. That work was a ritual song of dawn; *Earth Cry* begins with slow gestures of supplication—melody emerging from word and body, as in the cello *Requiem* and in *Mangrove*, but flowering into a full statement of the chant, at first on strings, then joined by trumpets and horns. The unchanging mode is the same as that of *Tailitnama*, but several permutations of the tune occur simultaneously, building to so wild a degree of ecstasy that jubilation seems an inadequate word to describe it. Sculthorpe seems to be saying with T. S. Eliot in "Ash Wednesday," "Consequently I rejoice, having to construct something / Upon which to rejoice." This being so, it is not surprising that such jubilation should involve anguish, and even fury. In the long, slow coda, however, the preludial incantation sings in potentially universal grandeur, and in subsequent large-scale orchestral works power and praise often transcend lament.

Kakadu (1988) was engendered by human love, for it was commissioned by an American admirer of Sculthorpe's music, Dr. Emanuel Papper, as a birthday present for his wife. The title (which in German means parrot) here refers instead to the vast Kakadu National Park in northern Australia, once the traditional home of the Gagadju. After more than forty thousand years, the Gagadju are virtually extinct, leaving the landscape, from tidal coast to mountain plateau, almost devoid of human population. The opening section of the work, however, summons ghosts, reanimating ancient rituals in fast motor rhythms and percussive harmonies, the tune naggingly persisting in irregular stepwise movement. "Chant" incrementally gathers momentum as the corybantically syncopated rhythms attain climax in a coda that cannot decide whether its tonal root is F or C. That there is desperation within the joyousness testifies to the fact that for the aborigines power can only be retrospective, a point given another twist in a middle section based on an undulating melody for cor anglais—which represents, according to the composer, the voice of Dr. Papper himself, a human creature within nature's cosmos. His theme, beginning with an upward-aspiring sixth, is as poignantly expressive as the string phrases in the *Irkanda* series, though in *Kakadu* humanity is more vulnerable since the human song is disrupted—even assaulted—by the undisputed denizens of the wilderness: a babel of insects, reptiles, birds, and beasts naturalistically imitated not merely on freak string techniques, but by the whole orchestra. Again Sculthorpe demonstrates that he has no need of electronic assistance.

The positive qualities of this work are manifest in that these nonhuman chirrings and chitterings become a trigger to human fulfillment. Whatever the fate of the aborigines, humans learn from nature as they, in the person of Dr. Papper, are purged by the birds; as a wise wit put it, for Sculthorpe, even more than for Messiaen, the paraclete is a parakeet. When Dr. Papper's solo melody recurs, still on cor anglais, it serves as a bridge to a section wherein modern humanity, redeemed, proleptically enters the aboriginal Dream Time, for the strings sing a chant from Arnheim Land, known as Djilile or Whistling Duck—a stepwise-moving tune that literally *enchants* in its gentle flow, notated as a gentle 12/8. This tune seems to have become, for Sculthorpe, synonymous with the Dream Time; he has used it frequently, from *Port Essington* onward, and has made a beautiful, simple version for solo piano, possibly because he enjoys playing it himself. In *Kakadu* it murmurs faintly, as immemorially ancient backdrop to Dr. Papper's cor anglais tune, which is the hazardously hopeful present. And this time the accommodation between modern humans and their remote predecessors leads to a positive consummation, for when the fast, *ardente* ritual dance resumes, propelled by tom-toms and bongos, the human chant is transferred from poignant English horn to reverberating (and "natural") French horns, while simultaneously the birds, beasts, and insects chatter and chortle, buzz and burble, on improvising strings. There is even a tonal resolution, for the Whistling Duck tune, basically pentatonic over an E or A bass, now sings over a pedal C, which gradually dominates the final statements of the preludial incantation. The work ends with riotously uplifting fanfares, asserting C major as the C, D flat, F, G mode opens into purely pentatonic C, D natural, (F), G, C. Presumably this apotheosis must be, for the aborigines, wish fulfillment, for which we modern men and women, potentially regenerated, can only be grateful.

Kakadu synthesizes Sculthorpe's austere and fierce wilderness musics with his popular vein (embracing modern life), such as he explores in his film scores and in pieces like *Port Essington*. Compared with *Mangrove, Kakadu* might be called "easy" music; it goes down well in the typical orchestral repertory. That is not, however, to be deplored, for since Sculthorpe's music matters to our future, it is important that it should be readily communicable. An antipodal composer, in his ripe but still burgeoning sixties, he creates music that, admitting to humanity's solitude, senses that jubilation might yet be feasible. It cannot be fortuitous that the final celebratory music in *Kakadu* quotes directly—and according to the composer undeliberately—from the music of "relaxed sensuous pleasure" in the wind quintet *Tabuh-tabuhan* of 1968. Although that work was itself a minor achievement, it matters that its "relaxation" has become intrinsic to Sculthorpe's mature work. At this stage in the human story, Sculthorpe's fusion of West and East is as basic as his ecological fusion of Humanity and Nature. In both respects we may relate him to the California composer Lou Harrison, who, having in youth drawn on many, mostly early, European idioms, has evolved into an East-West composer who writes for a self-invented "American gamelan," appertaining at once to the (in more than one sense) Pacific Balinese and to industrialized Americans, especially those young in years or in heart.

In assessing Sculthorpe's stature it is helpful to think of him in relation to two North American composers whose influence he has acknowledged. One of them, Varèse, we have already mentioned as an artist who bypassed "civilized" traditions in order to begin again, creating during the twenties a few aboriginal works of which the vitality is undimmed. The parallel between Varèse and Sculthorpe is not, however, exact, for Varèse was an outsider who, having delivered his frontal assault, relapsed into silence, whereas Sculthorpe has *gone on,* integrating his aboriginality into modern life, where it might affect our everyday discourse. In this respect there is a closer parallel between Sculthorpe's position today and that occupied a generation back by Copland—especially if we recall the affinity previously discussed between Copland's neodiatonic pattern-making and the hard, linear desert music of the "abstract" piano music of Chávez. Copland was neither Mexican nor Australian, but a child of Brooklyn, New York, at the turn of the twentieth century, who asked in his first mature works a biblical question—Shall these bones live? In the African blue notes, the declamatory wails of the Jewish synagogue, the harsh metallic textures, and the rigidly geometric serialism of the Piano Variations of 1930 Copland gave a painfully affirmative answer, from the heart of industrial New York, and he went on to evolve an American vernacular in which the pioneer values of toughness, audacity, and courage find place also for hope, homespun humor, serendipity, even tenderness and grace.

Today, Peter Sculthorpe offers a comparable testament for *our* time. He has always lived in cities, but his affirmation has been wrung not from a mechanized society but from recognition of our powerlessness in the face of the Australian emptiness. In its day, Copland's Americanism spoke on behalf of the entire industrialized world. In our day, Sculthorpe's musicking of ecological issues brings home the acuteness of our in-human predicament and encourages us to reflect on our lost condition. This means that the "relaxation" we noticed in his later music is not so much an escape as a technique for survival. It is significant that one of his recent works returns to his recurrent death obsession and is in fact entitled *Memento Mori.* Scored for full orchestra, the work was inspired by the extraordinary monoliths on Easter Island, for so long an inexplicable mystery to archaeologists, but now believed to be hugely *super*human, propitiatory images dedicated to gods and goddesses whom people had offended by denying and destroying the earth they lived on. The population declined, perhaps partly because of some "natural" disaster but also because agrarian folk maltreated their land. In years of scarcity, human beings fought desperately for subsistence, ultimately resorting to cannibalism. But if human life was obliterated from the islands, the cycle of nonhuman creation was renewed: a process that Sculthorpe's single-movement work traces, in music so immediate that we realize that humankind today is reenacting the Easter Islanders' suicidal demise on a vaster scale. We must hope that, in a Christian context, the link between death and Easter may still have meaning; we may take comfort in that works by Sculthorpe such as *Kakadu* hint, in a non-Christian context, at Easter's promise.

NOTES

1. Robert Creeley, "The Dishonest Mailmen," *The Collected Poems of Robert Creeley, 1945–1975* (Berkeley: University of California Press, 1982), 123.

2. John Cage, "Lecture on Something," *Silence: Lectures and Writings by John Cage* (Middletown, Conn.: Wesleyan University Press, 1961), 143.

3. Peter Sculthorpe quoted in liner notes to *Peter Sculthorpe: Earth Cry, Kakadu, Mangrove,* Sydney Symphony Orchestra, Stuart Challender, liner notes by Graeme Skinner, ABC Classics CD 426481.

4. Ibid.

5. Ibid.

6. Ibid.

PART FIVE

Into an Old New World

12

Duke Ellington as Black Urban Folk Musician, Art Composer, and Showbiz Man

ALL THE COMPOSERS discussed in this book, apart from Villa-Lobos and Chávez, have belonged to post-Renaissance "Western" civilizations variously industrialized since about 1900. They have recognized that the concepts of wilderness and civilization are, in the words of the seventeenth-century theologian, writer, and putative scientist Sir Thomas Browne, "diverse, sheer opposites, antipodes": so that they created "works" of art that sought to establish personal identity by way of melodic shapes, harmonic textures, developing tonalities, and fluctuating rhythms. "Western" works of art project identity and awareness of power over other people and things into self-made artifacts, momentarily defying time to which people, being mortal, are subject.

Yet despite this Western heritage, these composers were also trying to reject it, since they were aware of, and sometimes lived in, wildernesses, and people so living are generally bothered not so much about identity as about identification. Surrounded by the unknown and perhaps unknowable, "wilderness" people seek "togetherness" rather than individualized differentiation. Far from defining what distinguishes them from their fellow creatures (including the birds, beasts, insects, and reptiles with which they cohabit), they attempt to establish, in terms of ritualized song and dance, a continuum to live in. The point about a continuum is that it continues, "for ever and ever," as in the fairy tale or, in theological terms, "as it was in the beginning, is now, and ever shall be." The musical techniques conducive to such a notion tend to be incantatory, a "paradise of archetypes and repetition" wherein brief melodic cells are reiterated as though endlessly, in linear and metrical rather than in melodic and harmonic terms. "Wilderness" humans want, as far as is possible, to annihilate time, whereas "civilized" humans, though they try to "freeze" time in their artifacts, are driven by the awareness that they must grow, change, and die, for better and for worse. Their art records their volatilities, whereas wilderness humans' art asserts their hopeful permanence.

We have traced through this book many veerings and tackings between civilization and wilderness and have noted moments of coincidence between them. But we have not as yet directly confronted the phenomenon of jazz, which occupies a crucial position in our century's evolution. This is not the place for a comprehensive survey of jazz history but, given the book's theme, we can hardly evade consideration of the points at which jazz as an urban black folk art came to terms both with Western art musics and with commercialized aspects of industrial technocracy.[1] In the previous sections of the book we have discussed composers who, starting from civilization, have embraced wilderness; in this final part we deal with two composers, one of whom, Duke Ellington, was black and the other of whom, George Gershwin, was a white New York Jew reared in Tin Pan Alley, whose work climaxed not merely in a commercial musical, but in a grand opera on the subject of African American life in the Deep South. Since the origin of our species is almost certainly in Africa the significance of this reversal is obvious. Given the catastrophes "civilization" has entailed, it is hardly surprising that something in the human race wants to *begin again*. If the composers discussed in this book reveal this at varying levels of complexity, so—if at barely articulate levels—do the musics of young people commonly designated as pop, whether they function in heavily mechanized perversions of ritual or in more nostalgic industrializations of what had once been country music.

Jazz began as a kind of country music transplanted into a new world in which black Africans, enslaved, used the musical techniques they had been reared on. These techniques were broadly those of the "wilderness" musics referred to above, depending on brief incantatory motives endlessly reiterated and on a rhythmic momentum that affirmed solidarity. For these uprooted new Americans saw themselves as members of an African people, their immemorially ancient "tumbling strains" being modified only by the language they sang in.

But this African music was to suffer a sea-change more radical than this, for inevitably it came into contact, and then conflict, with the musical manifestations of the New World, especially the American march and hymn. The march provided the four-square beat of military discipline; the hymn offered a cohesive substratum of tonic, dominant, and subdominant harmony; and when blacks took up the guitar—a plucked string instrument relatable to many African instruments—the usually monodic black field holler and the communal togetherness of dance were Christianized by the impact of gospel musics. March and hymn became almost literally a *prison* against which black singers and guitarists *beat*—sometimes desperately yet seldom in vain, since from tension was generated resilience. Against the military thump of the beat the flexible rhythms of African musics pranced and danced, the rigidity of the meter itself inducing an inner vitality as black and white rhythms interlocked; similarly black melody and white harmony interact in a pain that at once disturbs and heals. The phenomenon of "blue" notes epitomizes this, for the vocally natural flat sevenths of modal melodies clash with the sharp sevenths of *leading* notes demanded by Western *dominant*-tonic harmony. It will be observed that the technical terms carry a psychological and perhaps sociological import; and it is worth noting that blue notes reenact a process that had happened early in European history, when "false relations" occurred between the vocal flat sevenths of medieval monody and the sharpened intervals called for by post-Renaissance harmony. Blue notes in jazz are exactly comparable and point to the significance of jazz in the shaping of the modern world. It may even be that the shift entailed will prove no less crucial than that between the medieval and the modern world.

Although country blues was the root and heart of jazz, it did not directly affect mainstream music until considerably later, when it also played its part in the evolution of pop musics, many of whose protagonists, including Mick Jagger, used blues singers as role models. But around the time of World War I other forms of jazz, associated with the jazz band rather than with solo singers, became a decisive force that, in art musics both European and American, clearly expressed the disintegration of old values. The reasons for the jazz band's artistic potency are not far to seek, for the bands began in the cosmopolitan city of New Orleans, which fused a vast slave population with Spanish, French, Italian, Portuguese, and to a lesser degree German and English cultural groups. Black African blues and dance were rife, but so were not only the white march and hymn but also sundry types of European "light" music in the forms of waltzes, polkas, and quadrilles, to the performance of which African Americans, freed from slavery, increasingly contributed. Pianos, substituting for guitars and offering more harmonic potential, gravitated from drawing rooms to brothels and honky-tonks; military instruments marooned from the Civil War found ready devotees among the blacks. The great achievements of early jazz—the small bands of Louis Armstrong and Sidney Bechet—sprang from a creative tension between folk blues and gospel music on the one hand and on the other hand the European dance forms and operatic conventions of white society. Inevitably, this fusion encouraged a trend toward composition, alongside improvised polyphony. This is evident in Armstrong's masterpieces of the twenties, such as "West End Blues" and "Tight Like This," and in the pieces devised by Jelly Roll Morton—whose light skin poised him between Art and Show Business—for his Red Hot Peppers. These masterly pieces, dating from around 1926, allow scope for "red-hot" improvisation within binary and ternary forms derived from the European military two-step.

Since jazz is both a collision and a collusion between wilderness and civilization it inevitably had social and economic implications. Insofar as black musicians, stemming from Africa and slavery, had to find a *modus vivendi* within their white American home-away-from-home, they had little choice but to seek a rapprochement between their urbanized black folk music and the white world of commerce. In the formative years of jazz—from the beginning of the twentieth century until the late twenties, and again during the evolution of the "new jazz" during the forties and fifties—the music dealt in alienation, rebellion, and endurance, however much humor and animal high spirits contributed to the ability to survive. During the intervening thirties and early forties, however, compromise was the essence of jazz, and had to be, if the music was to prosper. Jazz was played by more powerful, certainly much larger, groups culminating in the Big Band, which called for artful Western-style arrangement and composition to balance the immediacy of an urban, improvised polyphony. The Big Band was an aural synonym for corporately driven Western society into which Africans must fit or perish. To fit in does not necessarily entail passivity; a jazz composer may be the arbiter of the band's and thus the social group's destiny, as is the case with Duke Ellington, who was the first, and remains the finest, representative of the transition from the small to the big band.

It is not surprising that Ellington shared with Mozart an intuitive awareness of the right time and place to be born. The time was the last year of the nineteenth century, the beginning of the end of "Europe"; the place was Washington, D.C., which fostered one of the largest black populations in urban America. Ellington's family was reasonably well-to-do, his father acting as butler to a great house of the ruling class, so Edward Kennedy Ellington enjoyed a childhood free of the poverty and violence that a Bessie Smith or a Louis Armstrong had to contend with. Edward earned the sobriquet of Duke as a boy because of the dignity of his bearing, his handsome, well-groomed appearance, and his courteous demeanor that was never *self-demeaning*. Having exhibited early talents as a visual artist (for which he naturally and prophetically sought outlet in commercial fields) he decided to concentrate on his musical abilities, playing piano at fairly polite, often white-sponsored, junkets. He founded a band of his own in Washington but moved, in his early twenties, not to Chicago in the footsteps of the great Louis Armstrong, but to New York. Ellington discovered, as genius is apt to, just what he needed in the metropolis, for there flourished jazz pianists such as his hero James P. Johnson, whose pianism fused the improvised stridency of barrelhouse blues with the formalized elegance of ragtime, the conventions of which derived from white dance music and operetta as well as from march and hymn. Johnson had also dabbled in notated orchestral music in Western style.

Back in Washington, Ellington's first engagements had been as a party pianist working with "legitimate" musicians geared to social dancing and theater shows. This experience was useful when, in New York, he began to explore his creativity; even in his earliest recordings we note that although the music stems from the improvised polyphony for soloists typical of Armstrong in the early twenties, it is moving toward formal discipline, with a beginning, middle, and end. Indeed, in his early work Ellington seems to have contributed the art, while the folk ingredient of blues improvisation came from his trumpeting colleague Bubber Miley. The collaboration wouldn't have worked had not blue passion been latent in Ellington, waiting to be sparked off; but it seems valid to say that "East St. Louis Toodle-Oo," which made Ellington famous in 1926, was a joint creation of Miley as an improvising "wilderness" man and of Ellington as a "civilized" artist.

The simple tune was the creation of Miley—a charismatic young man who never learned to read music or needed to, and whose part in Ellington's story was potent but ephemeral, since he died at the age of twenty-nine. Miley invented not only the tune but also the improvised "bubberings" that, by way of a variety of mutes, make his trumpet "speak" like a man or woman talking, laughing, giggling, gibbering, or bubbering in glee or distress or like some bird or beast of the jungle—with which jazz became identified in the imagination of a white public that simultaneously relished and reviled it. What in this piece made savagery amenable was the ostinato of moaning saxophones and tuba in which bandmaster Ellington enveloped Miley's bubberings; the technique is implicitly theatrical, and most of Ellington's early pieces were triggered by things that happened "out there." In this case a billboard advertisement may have tickled the Duke's fancy, along with the sight of an old black man shuffling down the dusty street. There's a fairly sophisticated romanticism in this notion; the ostinato is everyday destiny, from which the improvised solos cry yearningly. Such romanticism entails an element of self-consciousness, reflected in the alternations of the tune with the ostinato, in rondo style. Miley's thirty-two-bar tune and resolutory coda have greater musical substance than the sixteen measures each of San Nanton's trombone and of Barney Bigard's clarinet, but all "speak" meaningfully, and the rondo structure hints at possibilities for development. Improvisation was becoming composition, more so than in Armstrong's works, if not quite as much as in Jelly Roll Morton's pieces for his Red Hot Peppers. It is interesting that the improvisations, in later versions of Ellington's pieces, change only slightly, even when performed by different players. The parts are not fully notated since the manner of performance must seem spontaneous; when once established, however, the music appropriate to the context remains constant.

At first, Ellington had been a functional musician directed toward dancers rather than listeners. Gradually, his art began to impart a slight permanence to volatile activity, the more so as dance music merged into popular entertainment recorded, for future repetition, on discs. This mechanical fact meant that the pieces had to be restricted to around the three minutes then covered by a record: a limitation that proved an asset rather than a liability, for if improvisation remained the heart of the Duke's art, the conditions of recording ensured that improvisation had to be disciplined. Like Jelly Roll Morton, Ellington achieved his one-man control through a telepathic faculty and sheer force of character. Human empathy and intelligence helped him to find the collaborators he needed, and to keep them with him. Bubber Miley, Arthur Whetsol, and Cootie Williams on trumpets, Barney Bigard on clarinet, Johnny Hodges on alto sax, and Harry Carney on baritone sax formed, with Ellington as pianist-director, Sonny Greer on supportive drums, and Wellman Braud on functional bass, the nucleus of the band of the late twenties through which Ellington wrote not merely for specific forces and a given function but for a particular group of human beings. In Ellington's view, knowing the band members was as important as knowing the music they would play; this is why Ellington's preoccupation with new sounds was an extension of jazz's traditional preoccupation with melody as sublimated human speech. The more respect the band shows for the individuals that comprise it, the better it will be, so long as the cohesive force of the composer-arranger operates. Ellington seldom wrote out a score in advance, but never appeared at a rehearsal unprepared; he handed out scraps of paper with notations to each player. These personally directed notations served as a basis for re-creation in the per-form-ance the rehearsal was. Presumably Ellington remained the final arbiter in this technique, which compromised between the "primitive" *identification* with the "tribe" (or band) and the *identity* cherished by individual artists, while at the same time another dimension of "togetherness" was introduced by way of mechanical reproduction. These creations, made in the moment by a performing band controlled by an individual composer, would be endlessly multiplied and distributed to an ever-increasing public.

Duke Ellington seems to be prophetic of a new kind of composer transitional between the Old World and the New. Yet even as an "art" composer he didn't restrict himself to a single identity, for in 1939 an alter ego for the Duke appeared in the person of Billy Strayhorn, a composer-arranger who enjoyed, until his premature death in 1967, an almost filial relationship with the master, so much so that it isn't always easy to know who wrote what. The Duke's career as an incipient art composer had begun about ten years previously when, employed by New York's prestigious Cotton Club, his band worked in floor shows rather than as functional accompaniment for dancers. The social ambiguities in his position complemented his artistic ambivalence, for the Cotton Club hired black artists to entertain a white clientele. When criticized, as inevitably happened, for submitting to Jim Crowish demeanment, Ellington protested that all his music was Protest, simply in being what it was. Many years later, when the internationally famous Duke traveled the globe as the crony of presidents elect, one can say that Ellington, against the odds, had won acceptance for himself *and* the cause. For the time being, however, Ellington's Cotton Club music tempered its black folk elements with more consciously artistic techniques usual in theater and show business. It was during these years that Ellington earned celebrity as a composer of hit numbers in the vein not of the twelve-bar blues, but of the thirty-two-bar pop standard. This was an essential evolution if he was to take over the white music world; and although the style of performance in a number like "Black Beauty" may be folkily blue, the fetching tune itself is closer to Gershwin's work than to the blues. Similarly, Ellington's slow numbers, like "Solitude," have prototypes in the "lonesome" numbers of Broadway, though the close chromatic harmonies and clinging instrumental colors wouldn't be so haunting were the tunes themselves not distinctive. During these years when Ellington produced his richest crop of hit tunes Arthur Whetsol had taken over from Bubber Miley as lead trumpet. Whereas Miley was a wildman folk-blues player, Whetsol's sweeter tone and cantabile phrasing had some affinity with Bix Beiderbecke's performing style and vicariously with the music theater of Gershwin.

This greater concern with art in the melodic aspects of Ellington's numbers was complemented by a rhythmic evolution. "Rockin' in Rhythm" depends, as the title indicates, on the stimulation of a metrical pulse, but the riffs differ from those in New Orleans or Chicago jazz in being melodic— closely related to the tune, which is memorable enough to recall the captivating "Black Beauty." In "Hot and Bothered," a busily exhibitionistic rehash of the old Tiger Rag, orgiastic excitement submits to architectural discipline. The tragic fervor often latent in Armstrong's music is thus replaced by a quality almost comical, as was perhaps inevitable if wilderness blues was to become civilized. The primitive terrors beneath the surface of our lives are here admitted to, yet at the same time "placed," even laughed at, though not laughed away. The tiger's growl has to be a joke, if we are to confront it, whereas the wild cats in Jelly Roll Morton's "Wild Man," as played by Armstrong, are more scary than funny. One can face the tiger in New Orleans or even Chicago, but hardly in New York's Cotton Club. Ellington's genius lay in his creating a music for blacks and whites alike, balancing on a tightrope between reality and illusion.

The alternative to treating the unknown as comic is to romanticize it. We've pointed to a strain of romanticism in Ellington's first successful composition, "East St Louis Toodle-Oo"; many of his finest pieces exploit Allen Ginsberg's "mythology he cannot inherit," evoking mood and atmosphere by way of harmonic texture and scoring. Like white Bix Beiderbecke, black Duke Ellington explored impressionistic harmony not because it was "modern" (by the end of the twenties it wasn't), but because he instinctively realized that it was the only harmony apposite to blues-derived jazz since it was at once sensuous and nondeveloping. In this there was both profit and loss: static sevenths, ninths, elevenths, and even thirteenths could enrich a single moment, but would inevitably enfeeble the momentum of line and rhythm. This was admissable because jazz always had been, and was becoming ever more insidiously, ambivalent between the experience of here-and-now and whatever might be, by and by. What mattered was that the equilibrium between reality and dream be preserved, as it usually was by Ellington, whether his Debussyan, Ravellian, and Delian harmonies came to him vicariously from Tin Pan Alley or directly. In later years, after he'd become more musically sophisticated, the Duke paid verbal tribute to works like Debussy's *La Mer*, Ravel's *Daphnis et Chloé*, and Delius's *In a Summer Garden*, but this testified merely to a consanguinity of mind and a shared nostalgia. Ellington's artfulness remains empirical, and there is no comparison between, for instance, the ways in which he and Delius exploit their chromatics. Though Delius's music moves in no particular direction, it is all movement; the only thing that matters, he proclaimed, is the "sense of flow," which is why he needed time and space to move in. For Ellington, the mood and moment are all. His harmonic textures are close-knit, the chromatic lines wriggling around one another, while the forms are brief, unflowing. When, later, he seemed to tackle larger structures, they really tend to be suites—collocations of fairly short pieces.

While Ellington's creation of mood and atmosphere link him with the harmony and instrumentation of late romantic music and the polite pop musics that borrowed from it, it is also by way of harmony and instrumentation that his personal sensibility is most obvious. He makes the dream not a cliché, but a touching apprehension of urban humanity's nostalgia for Ginsberg's "beauty of his wild forebears." A key piece is "The Mooche" which, even in its earliest (1928) version, is not escapist music, since the moochers are simultaneously sleazy loafers in a New York bar and fierce felines in a jungle. The Duke's ripply piano prelude settles us comfortably in the city cocktail lounge, enveloped in an alcoholic haze. Yet when the tune emerges it is potently blue in feeling, its passionately plunging chromatics being intensified by the mutes and plungers through which Bubber Miley's trumpet and Tricky Sam Nanton's trombone gibber and growl. In the Duke's band, as in commercial dance music of the era, the oilily emotive saxophones begin to engulf the sharper clarinets, smoothing with their sensuous colors the blues' hard reality. There's a tricky relationship between the romantic pretend jungle evoked in the club and the harsh asphalt jungle outside; although the orchestral colors are dreamily romantic, the total effect is sinister, perhaps because the padding, catlike beat is exacerbated by the screwed-up cross rhythms of Lennie Johnson's guitar. The wordless scat-singing of Baby Cox (a vaudeville artist rather than a jazz singer) is even more ambivalent, for it sounds merry, yet also mad, and therefore dangerous. So neither the comedy nor the romanticism of the piece evades deep undercurrents, though they modify our attitude, since the sophistication implies a degree of conscious awareness. The symmetry of form, with a clear recapitulation, disciplines elements that might be inimical, just as wit tames the snarl of the tiger. That this is what "form" does in classical music offers further evidence as to Ellington's status as an artful jazzman or jazzy artist.

One of the finest among these vintage pieces is the "Black and Tan Fantasy," which the Duke himself was partial to, judging by the number of times he recorded it. A comparison of the 1928 and 1938 versions is revealing. In the earlier version the dream is contained in the background of liquid creole clarinet, sax, and muted brass, through which Bubber Miley's twelve-bar blues utters the heart's truth. The fantasy is an elegy on the lost world the

African American "cannot inherit": but insofar as that lost world is Eden, the valediction speaks for us all. This is why the quotation in the coda of the funeral march from Chopin's second piano sonata makes so pungent a point. In the 1928 version it is played in a manner simultaneously comic and pathetic, with a tinge of parody, as in authentic New Orleans funeral music. In the 1938 version the coda has become loud, wild, rather grand. The march came from Europe, but is now a funerary chant for the New as well as the Old World. This means that Ellington's lament becomes also ours—not merely a world we are invited to enter vicariously, if with delight.

In "Misty Mornin,'" another number from the same period, the old New Orleans scoring for trumpet, low clarinet, and trombone is used to very different effect. Arthur Whetsol's trumpet, in distinction from Bubber Miley's earthiness, meanders through a texture of chromatic inner parts that mistily touch on whole-tone and atonal progressions. The introversion is deepened by the oozy part-writing for saxes, and especially by Ellington's partiality for the baritone sax, which often has unresolved sevenths in the bass. Again, Ellington is an ear composer who, even or especially when "wrong" because ungrammatical, is aurally "right." Perhaps it is not fortuitous that Harry Carney stayed with Ellington for well over thirty years; he more than anything conditioned what Billy Strayhorn called "the Ellington sound"—an aural incarnation of his and our nostalgia. This piece's brooding sultriness is quintessentially romantic; yet again sensuousness is countered by lucid structure, which is not misty at all.

In the late thirties Ellington made several new versions of his triumphs of the late twenties, using them as springboards for another series of masterpieces created in the early forties. Bubber Miley was a decade dead, Whetsol died in 1940, and the revised, bigger band centered around Cootie Williams and Rex Stewart on trumpet and cornet, Tricky Sam Nanton on trombone, now supported by Juan Tizol, and by Ben Webster and Harry Carney on saxes. Sonny Greer's percussion and Fred Guy's guitar still combined with the Duke as rhythm section, which was however transformed by the sprightly string bass of Jimmy Blanton, a rare true innovator who, although dying of tuberculosis at the age of twenty-one, survived long enough to effect a revolution in jazz rhythm. The difference between traditional jazz and the Ellington band of the forties lies in that the new solos tend to have longer, more complex melodies that nonetheless *fit into* the composition. This is possible because the old notion of a regular earth beat against which the melodies pull and prance is superseded as the linear impulse of Blanton's bounding bass "lets in the light." Rhythm becomes an integral part of polyphony, and Ben

Webster's exuberantly lyrical tenor sax and Juan Tizol's singing valve trombone are basic to the modified idiom. If the picturesque jungle flavor is less obvious, the asphalt jungle is more dominant. In "Main Stem" the riffs have melodic appeal and structural purpose, and the music seems, in its fusion of energy with intelligence, almost to be laughing at itself—a further growth in "consciousness."

In "The Flaming Sword" the Latin American cross-rhythms, prompted by Juan Tizol's trombone, induce a simultaneous excitement and detachment, while the frenzy generated by Webster's vibrant tenor sax in "Cottontail" comparably explodes in rhythmic contradiction, only to be deflated in a comic coda. Irony—T. S. Eliot's "recognition of other modes of experience that may be possible"—is a common ingredient of big city sophistication, though in the most famous piece of these middle years, "Ko-Ko," it is present only in the sense that the music's blistering climax of rhythmic momentum is generated from an almost unrecognizable, corny old Tin Pan Alley standard. The music is too angry to hint at emotional deflation; elements of formal control prevent the music from going totally around the bend, despite the unremittent pounding, the whirligig screeches from clarinet, the barks from the brass tutti, and the minatory venom of the Duke's piano solo. This is a tragic piece worthy of comparison with the greatest moments in Louis Armstrong's playing; in the next generation Charlie Parker will make a no less harrowing version of it. As one might expect, Ellington's version is the most consummately realized in "artistic" terms.

In slow pieces made during these vintage early forties, such as "Sepia Panorama," Ellington explored mood pictures of Harlem by way of contradictory motives, dense harmonies, and tense riffs yoked together not by violence but by art. The variety of mood reflects the multifariousness of the Harlem scene, no longer by way of red-hot participation between players and listeners who were often also dancers, but in a Wordsworthian sense of "emotion recollected in tranquillity." The piece, if not entirely convincing, effectively mates wilderness with civilization, especially in the savage brass interjections into the Duke's forlornly wandering piano. This is not only Harlem music but also urban American music relatable to Copland's *Quiet City,* which has as its subject a New York jazz trumpeter, nocturnally lonesome. The alienations of African American and Jew prove to be complementary.

This miniature tone poem provides a transition to the concert music that Ellington increasingly cultivated in later years. His first experiment in extended form, the "Creole Rhapsody" of 1931, casually strung together a number of episodes; it wasn't until the late thirties, with "Reminiscin' in Tempo" and "Diminuendo and Crescendo in Blue," that he learned how to control the rise and fall of motion and emotion through an expanded series of riffs, sometimes in irregular phrase lengths. Even so, the attempt at extended form was in a sense paradoxical, since the African roots of Ellington's art, creating a continuum to live in, had no need of—were in a sense opposed to—the "growth through conflict" that has been Europe's musical *modus vivendi*. Ellington's compromise between worlds inevitably entailed compromise between concepts of art and function. The most powerful music of Ellington's late years is still in small forms, for which it has no need to apologize.

We'll take as impressive examples some movements from the suite *Such Sweet Thunder*, written for the Stratford Festival of Canada in 1957. By this time many of the old Ellingtonians had died or moved on. Harry Carney was still imperturbably present, and Johnny Hodges had returned to the alto sax desk, rejuvenated by absence. The lyrical Terry Clark and the stratospheric Cat Anderson now dominated the trumpets; Paul Gonsalves was a songful tenor saxophonist of considerable flair and staying power, if without Webster's punch. The suite is not an attempt to emulate Shakespeare or to create music collateral to Shakespeare's characters; it is Ellington music, prompted by his reaction to Shakespeare. The Shakespearean quotation that is the suite's title is indeed an apt description of Ellington's wildly civilized music.

Unsurprisingly, there are two pieces about Othello. The title number depicts the marvel-narrating warrior who casts his spell over Desdemona. A swaggering ostinato on trombone suggests his glamoursome adventurousness, but Ray Nance's solo trumpet has a fallible wobble in its nobility (can Othello's tall tales be true?). This prepares us for the other Othello piece, "Sonnet in Search of a Moor," a wistful little number in which there are no heroics, but much of the hero's alienated lonesomeness. The tune reminds us of Gershwin's crippled Porgy, which makes Othello a pathetic hero, a black man in a big white city. If the aerated hissing of percussion and the vacillating clarinet filigree hint at mysteries, this only makes him seem the frailer; and the stalking pizzicato bass, a jazz cliché, rotates around itself, suggesting Othello's murderous steps through the silent night; it is himself, rather than Desdemona, whom Othello is "in search of." This Othello is in part Ellington, testifying to the effect Shakespeare may have on us. In this number there is also an evident influence from art music, for Ellington seems to have been listening to the Moorish episodes in Stravinsky's *Petrouchka*, a ballet about a puppet. Ellington's forlorn Moor sounds like a clown buffeted by, rather than in control of, circumstances; and this heroic-pathetic Othello is in tune with the pervasive irony of Ellington's later music.

"The Star-Crossed Lovers" calls on Paul Gonsalves's tenor and Johnny Hodges's alto sax to sing the fateful loves of Romeo and Juliet. The tune is beautiful, in the ballad style of Gershwin, yet unmistakably Ellingtonian. Being a pop song, it has an adolescent fervor appropriate to twentieth-century teenagers in a big city, though the music indicates that these Shakespearean adolescents know more about love, as well as sex, than do the lovers in Bernstein's brilliant *West Side Story.* The tune's sustained lyrical line, deeply sonorous scoring, and disturbing harmonic twists give it a hymnic, even tragic, quality totally without sentimentality. Johnny Hodges, through his long career, never soloed more heart-rendingly; and if the Duke's preludial cascades on piano evoke a cocktail lounge rather than an internecine feud, that may be the point; they admit that the youthful tragedy occurs in a context of social persiflage and illusion. This number, in its threefold fusion of art, jazz, and pop music, is of historical as well as intrinsic significance.

In this piece passion is at once as savage and as civilized as sixteenth-century Verona, and twentieth-century New York can only be honored by the comparison. "Madness in Great Ones" is more modern than Elizabethan; Ellington must have known that as a portrait of Hamlet it doesn't go far. Even so, that Hamlet, though mixed-up, was indubitably a "great one" allows him to stand archetypically for modern youth; and the piece is like us in exploiting sensation, violence, disruption, and surprise. The sudden breaks, in both the literal and the technical sense, the conflicting sonorities, the near-simultaneous sounding of opposites, are Iveslike, though it is unlikely that Ellington had heard much of Ives's music at that date. The mad exhibitionism of the number is wildly funny, Hamletlike in unpredictabililty but with no hint of the emotional resource latent in his soliloquies. Hamlet's typical irony is given a brittle edge that makes a hero of a mixed-up kid and at the same time satirically debunks him. Cat Anderson's stratospheric coda prevents our taking the mixed-upness too seriously, though it doesn't promote contempt for the screwy. There's a similar ambivalence in "Half the Fun," wherein the joke is more in the title than in the music, which is as serious as it ought to be, given that this languid Cleopatra can be staled neither by custom nor by commerce. Ostinato patterns on percussion make a backdrop to melismata that merge into Hodges's eloquent solo. These and other Asian influences were probably picked up by Ellington on his Far Eastern tours and became basic to quite a lot of superior travelog music. Here the music reminds us that jazz has as much in common with the linear techniques of Asiatic, as well as African, musics as it has with European stylizations.

The suite concludes with "Circle of Fourths," a brief coda that represents the artist's (Shakespeare's or Ellington's) control over his creation by scuttling pell-mell through a cycle of fourths, covering the complete chromatic range. It is a gimmick rather than an artifact, but knowingly so, since Ellington metamorphoses himself into a shaman-showman, ending with a terrific solo break wherein he, as composer and theater man, steps forward from his creation to take his bow. Ellington does not claim to be Shakespeare; he was a modest man. But he stands there, welcoming our applause, knowing that in bridging the gaps between momentary performance, a work of art, and popular entertainment he was shaping a future.

Ellington's status as a "between worlds" artist is most potently demonstrated when, at the height of his latest and "artiest" phase, he belatedly entered into collaboration with Louis Armstrong, supported by his All Stars (Barney Bigard on clarinet and Trummy Young on trombone, with Mort Herbert on string bass and Danny Barcelona on drums completing the rhythm section with the Duke). In their sixties, the two grand old men of jazz came together to play numbers covering over thirty years of Ellington's creative life. What Armstrong does to Ellington is to reveal afresh the wildness and strangeness beneath the surface; the artist is not destroyed, though in this renovated wilderness there is no compromise with the taming effect that pop music conventions often have. The superb new version of "Black and Tan Fantasy" preserves the mysterious flavor of Ellington's piece, into which Armstrong's trumpet solo injects sudden bursts of fury or ecstasy that are an apotheosis of the New Orleans–Chicago spirit; the Duke's faithful collaborator, Barney Bigard, is inspired to equal heights. The Ellington sound thus acquires a weird vehemence, and the Chopin funeral march quotation loses all suggestion of pathos or grotesquerie, seeming to epitomize the sorrow of the ages. The new version of "Mood Indigo" is similarly deepened in range. It was always a beautiful nocturne, with its solo trumpet murmuring above chalumeau-range clarinet; the close-moving chromatic harmony created an atmosphere curiously dense and tense, despite the tune's relaxed nostalgia. But in the new version Armstrong's fiercely symmetrical solo deep stains the indigo in the mood and then inspires Bigard's New Orleans–style clarinet and Louis's own scatting voice to jerks and wails of piercing plangency. Ellington's piano arabesques have a comparable incisiveness, creating extreme tension by way of rhythmic displacements in a very thin texture. If during most of his career the Duke was a band composer who played the piano, he here becomes a pianist in his own right. Inspired by Armstrong, he has learned something relevant to his piano style from the great Count Basie also, fusing Basiean metallic brittleness and elegance with Ellingtonian ripeness in tremolandos and false relations. Clearly, the heart of the matter survives in those who have the strength to apprehend it. The lures of "New York" have not destroyed the truths that Armstrong, as a young man, had blown for; nor are those truths denied by Ellington's necessary affiliation with a commercialized world. This theme will dominate our final chapter.

NOTES

1. For a short, relevant jazz history see part 2 of Wilfrid Mellers, *Music in a New Found Land: Themes and Developments in the History of American Music* (London: Faber and Faber, 1987).

13

Porgy and Bess as a Parable of Restitution

GEORGE GERSHWIN WAS NOT reared in regions where High Art was fostered or on the slagheaps from which some of the greatest jazz artists came. He did not have the benefit of attending a musical academy or university, but grew up on Broadway itself, where he pursued a glamorous if harried career in show business. Like many big names in this arena, he was a New York Jew of European—strictly speaking, Russian—extraction. His father was a busy small businessman, while his mother tended to be uncaring because she was incorrigibly narcissistic. George's brother, Ira, was the bright boy and the "good" one; George, born in 1898, was not conspicuously academic and did not apply himself. But he did have exceptional instinctive gifts as a pianist, on the basis of which he found himself working as an overtly "commercial" musician, playing potential hit numbers to a potential public in a music publishing house. His early heroes were jazz pianists like James P. Johnson and Lucky Roberts, in which his enthusiasms overlapped with those of Ellington. Being a young man of charisma, he consorted easily with the white entrepreneurs and theater people who came his way and was soon producing show music himself. Like most song pluggers on Broadway, he peddled wares dedicated to hedonism or nostalgia, courting the common heart and the commoner appetite.

Yet Gershwin, even more potently than his immediate predecessors like Jerome Kern and Irving Berlin, proved that hedonism and nostalgia need not deny human verities, though they might sometimes threaten them. In a song like "The Man I Love" cliché is reborn, and the girl's adolescent love dream proves truer than truth. This song was never included in the show for which it had been written, yet it has been performed innumerable times and arranged, rehashed, and improvised on in innumerable guises. As a showbiz man Gershwin was successful enough to lead the "fabulous" life of F. Scott Fitzgerald's Beautiful People; at the same time, aware of his genius, he yearned to make the grade in the world of art music performable at venues like Carnegie Hall. He brought it off in that concert works like *Rhapsody in Blue*, the Piano Concerto in F, and the symphonic poem *An American in Paris* were not only performed in such places but are now an established part of the concert repertory. Although "serious" critics tended to dismiss them as strings of good show tunes tied together with Lisztian tinsel, they have worn remarkably well; even the tinsel seems reluctant to fray or tarnish. Although these works don't pretend to be "great," they have survived when hundreds of more pretentious pieces have gone with the wind. And Gershwin's ultimate vindication came when, in the last few years of his short life, he lighted on DuBose Heyward's novel *Porgy*, which deals somewhat artily with African American life in the tenements of South Carolina, around Charleston, where the Heyward family had long lived. Although George Gershwin was not an intellectual, or even much of a reader, he manifested his genius in recognizing—with an acuity comparable to Benjamin Britten's—that here was his essential theme. Given that recognition, Heyward and George Gershwin, with Ira Gershwin as their clever lyricist, could produce a fully fledged opera, exploiting an interplay of speech, recitative, arioso, and aria (often in pop standard forms), and exhibiting a musical-theatrical craft rivaling that of Puccini or even Verdi.

Heyward's novel is a parable about alienation, oppression, and the inviolability of a radical innocence of spirit, even in a corrupt world. George Gershwin was not, like Porgy, an African American, nor, in the material benefits of life, was he desperately deprived. He was, however, a poor boy who made good: an American Jew who knew all about spiritual isolation and, in Tin Pan Alley, had opportunity enough to learn about corruption. And although he was not, like Porgy, physically crippled, he was emotionally crippled, victimized, like so many of his generation, by maladjustments and the usual escapes from them in alcohol and promiscuity. So, in his Broadway musical comedy that perhaps unwittingly turned into a full-scale opera, he sang with honesty and strength of the spiritual malaise inherent in twentieth-century pop itself. His instinct for the nostalgia at the heart of the common experience rivals that of Stephen Foster; the difference lies in that Gershwin's art intuitively recognizes the nostalgia as such. His opera is about the impact of the world of commerce on those who once led, would like to have led, may still lead the "good life," based on a close relationship between human beings and nature.

This theme applies, obviously, to urban, industrialized humans; the plight of poor southern African Americans during this time merely offers one peculiarly pointed manifestation, because the contrast between Porgy's innocence and Gershwin's urban sophistication is acute. Gershwin sees the parable in terms of his own experience, which is why it is of no consequence that the book offers a synthetic picture of African American life. The theme is outlined in the verses with which Heyward prefaced his novel:

> Porgy, Maria, and Bess,
> Robbins, and Peter, and Crown;
> Life was a three-stringed harp
> Brought from the woods to town.
>
> Marvelous tunes you rang
> From passion, and death, and birth,
> You who had laughed and wept
> On the warm, brown lap of the earth.
>
> Now in your untried hands
> An instrument, terrible, new,
> Is thrust by a master who frowns,
> Demanding strange songs of you.
>
> God of the White and Black,
> Grant us great hearts on the way
> That we may understand
> Until you have learned to play.[1]

Broadway is indeed a long way from the "warm, brown lap of the earth," and most of the songs it sings may inculcate evasion rather than understanding. Nonetheless, even on Broadway Gershwin sounds the "three-stringed harp" of passion, and death, and birth with unequivocal power. He accepts his world as it is, never loading the scales; we should honor him for his "great heart."

Porgy and Bess is a wilderness opera in that the central characters live on Catfish Row in Charleston, South Carolina. The tenement the African Americans inhabit had once been a colonial palace, a double irony referring simultaneously to "the glory that was Greece" and to the fact that in Heyward's and Gershwin's view blacks ought to, but won't, inherit the earth. Governors and "ambassadors of kings" have vanished from this squalid environment, but "civilization," compared to the "wilderness," is a negative force. The black folks' natural language is song, whereas the whites who intrude, usually in an authoritarian capacity, are restricted to clipped speech that—unlike the spoken dialogue in conventional musicals—fits into the opera's musical universe only because it is usually metrically organized and often percussively accompanied. Distinctions of color are not what really matters, for as the action unfolds the theme of the opera proves to be the search for an equilibrium between the "black" jungle and the "white" town that exist, whatever the color of our skin, within us all. The orchestral prelude evokes Eden: a state of happiness in the present moment, incarnate in rapid pentatonic figuration, nondeveloping ostinatos, and minimal harmony, pervaded by oscillating fourths. Even so, the persistent cross-accents induce a jazzy agitation beneath the merriment, and the fourths of the ostinato garner higher chromatic discords until the curtain rises on Jazzbo Brown, a sophisticated Jelly Roll Morton figure playing boogie piano on stage. While the chorus chants pentatonic da-doo-das, Jazzbo appends the tawdry glamor of Tin Pan Alley chromatics; already the two worlds of the folk community and "New York" are juxtaposed.

This evocation of background merges into a musical-dramatic statement of the contrasting poles of experience. Clara, nursing her baby, sings the "Summertime" lullaby. The mother-child relationship is the basic human positive, and the song, being human, involves more than the vacuous happiness of the prelude. Thus the words are a dream of Eden, when it is always summertime, when "the livin' is easy, fish are jumpin', an' the cotton is high"; when "yo' daddy's *rich* an' yo' ma is *good-lookin'.*" But though the line is still basically pentatonic, it is now not merely a merry doodling, but a pliant, expressive tune, the innocence of which is modified by the blue notes, the ellipses of the rhythms, and the nostalgia of the chromatic harmony, at once sweet and sensuously yearning. Though within the convention of the pop standard, the lullaby, like many of Gershwin's tunes, has the authentic spirit of the blues, which may be why true jazz musicians have admired him and have frequently used his tunes as a basis for improvisation or recomposition. (Louis Armstrong made a canned jazz version of *Porgy* with Ella Fitzgerald, while Miles Davis and Gil Evans created from it a potently evocative Big Band suite.) Moreover, the blue melancholy points to the deeper roots of this haunting number, for the sadness admits that the Eden dream cannot be squared with the facts of experience. The baby *will* cry and must one day "spread [its] wings." The desire for security ("nothin' can harm you with Daddy an' Mammy standin' by") is in all of us; yet we have to pass beyond attachment to the mother, let alone regression to the womb. This equivoca-

tion is suggested by the rocking chords combined with the ambiguous tonality, which oscillates between Dorian B minor and diatonic D major with
whole-tone implications. This tonal fluidity is the more expressive since it
follows the nearly static E major innocence of the prelude—E major being
habitually Schubert's Eden key.

The lyricism of the mother-child relationship is brusquely swept away by
the violence of the crap game music, which is at once hedonistically brilliant,
and therefore exciting, and grittily tough, as a life ruled by chance is bound
to be. The significantly named Sportin' Life—a high tenor with very light skin
who represents the world of commerce and New York—acts as the master of
ceremonies, making the appropriate comment when, invoking the dice, he
says, "It may be in the summertime an' may be in the fall, but you got to *leave*
yo' *baby* an' yo' *home* an' all." All the basic human positives inherent in the
lullaby have to be sacrificed to a world of exploitation. If one cannot have a
stable relationship with family and community, one has to admit that life is a
gamble; and most of the characters, "good" or "bad," are gamblers whose
fecklessnes is a consequence of their awareness that they don't belong. The
only people who disapprove of the gambling are religious fanatics, like Serena;
and she is far from serene, admitting in conversation with her husband,
Robbins, that worship of the Lawd can be as much of an escape as the worship of chance or the body. Jake's crap game song, which excuses his gaming
as a relief from toil, evokes more sympathy from the onlookers and us than
does Serena's liturgical—and rigid—incantation, since his rapid changes of
meter and unstable mediant modulations follow the heart's waywardness.

Soon the two modes—the humanity of the mother-child relationship and
the feckless inconsequence of gambling—are counterpointed against one another, as Clara croons the lullaby while the crap game continues. It looks as
if the fecklessness is destroying the humanity, for Clara's man Jake complains
because she can't get the baby to sleep, but he says that he'll soon "fix it." So
the lullaby's ostinato turns quick and agitated in 3/8 and leads into a jazzy
number in boogie rhythm in which he aggressively shouts that "A woman is
a sometime thing." The key, G minor, is the complement to the opera's key
of simple happiness, G major, and there's a hint of frenzy in the rhythmic
drive and in the chorus's ejaculations of the refrain to falling minor thirds.
Yet even though the song is antiwoman and antimother, we see in retrospect
that it is a positive statement also. The child's relationship to its mother is not
enough. We have to grow up; and the opera is about the difficulty of doing
so in a world dominated by Sportin' Life and commerce. However uncon-
sciously, Gershwin was here motivated by personal experience.

Jake's brusqueness is no more effective with the baby than its mother's tenderness. It continues to wail; and the men jokingly remark that Jake is better at crapshooting than at nursing. Another world is introduced by the appearance of Peter, the old honey man, who croons a pentatonic honey call in (of course) G major over a drone ostinato and a beelike buzzing of sixteenth notes, with flat sevenths and sharp (Lydian) fourths. The honey man seems to come from a distant, pristine world where humans and nature live in harmony. Significantly, he heralds, with a return to the initial pentatonic Eden music, the approach of Porgy in his goat cart. The opening paragraph of the novel runs thus: "Porgy lived in the Golden Age. Not the Golden Age of a remote and legendary past; nor yet the chimerical era treasured by every man past middle life, that never existed except in the heart of youth; but an age when men, not yet old, were boys in an ancient, beautiful city that time had forgotten before it destroyed."[2] A little later we find this: "No one knew Porgy's age. . . . A woman who had married twenty years before remembered him because he had been seated on the church steps, and had given her a turn when she went in. Once a child saw Porgy, and said suddenly, 'What is he waiting for?' That expressed him better than anything else. He was waiting, waiting with the concentrated intensity of a burning-glass."[3] His essence may be latent in his musical theme, in heavenly E major, which is dominated by falling fifths of a primal simplicity but succeeded by blue minor thirds approached by crippled "crush notes," while the accompanying parallel triads begin in diatonic stability but grow chromatically disturbed, "waiting" for fulfillment. In parlando recitative the men tease Porgy about being "soft" on Crown's Bess, whom Maria (representative of the old communal values) and the religious Serena both dismiss as unfit "for Gawd-fearin' ladies to 'sociate with." Porgy denies any acquaintance with or interest in Bess and introduces the theme of alienation when, in pentatonic arioso, he tells us, "When Gawd make cripple, he mean him to be lonely. Night time, day time, he got to travel that lonesome road": a remark that applies to a Jewish or Gentile "cripple" hardly less than to Porgy. Thus is the opera's central theme related to Gershwin—and to us all.

With a violent hubbub that "frightens children who run past the gate in the street yelling," Crown enters, with Bess, to a ferocious syncopated rhythm that will be associated with him throughout the opera. Later on, we'll realize that Bess's two lovers, Crown and Porgy, are not to be thought of as villain and hero; they are not so much opposed as complementary, but divided, parts of a human whole that ought to be indivisible. Porgy is prelapsarian, innocent and good, but broken and unfulfilled; Crown is fallen, yet a Lucifer impressive in pride, brute strength, and self-reliance. Both are immensely strong physically, though Porgy's strength is compromised because he is unaware of it. Both are bass-baritones, and the same singer was suggested to Gershwin as being suitable for either role. Both, in the crap game, invoke fortune or the dice, Crown with a snarled curse, Porgy with a quasi-liturgical appeal to his "little stars." The simplicity of this sounds the more moving and the more vulnerable because the crap game is mostly spoken rather than sung, as though the players were momentarily adopting the market values of the whites in the opera. The sharp sonority of xylophone imitates the clatter of the dice, and the "Woman is a sometime thing" tune is cynically threaded into the gaming music.

The scene culminates in a fight, prompted by the drunken Crown, that animates the crap game music with his sadistic syncopations. During a wild "ensemble of perplexity," tense in energy and savagely scored, Crown carelessly murders Robbins with a cottonhook—doubly symbolic in being the instrument whereby the blacks are ground down into servitude, while also being evidence of Crown's uncontrollable sexual libido. Everyone disperses before the arrival of the police. Crown, with Bess's encouragement and financial help, goes off to hide in the wilderness of Kittiwah Island, so Bess is left to fend for herself. Momentarily, she is alone with Sportin' Life, who is the indirect cause of the catastrophe, since he had been plying Crown with rot-gut whiskey and dope. In sleazy blue notes and slithery chromatics he croons to Bess: "I's the only frien' you got left," and she accepts a touch of happy dust to steady her nerves and shaking limbs. That Sportin' Life peddles dope is inseparable from his involvement in commerce, prostitution, and "New York"; he offers forgetfulness in the same way as does Tin Pan Alley. And although or because he is a snake in the grass, he has the serpent's insidious attractiveness, for Eve in Eden, for Bess in Catfish Row, for Gershwin in New York, and for us all. In any case he is a fact; like Tin Pan Alley or today's media, he is what life is like, since the Fall, and it doesn't help to pretend he is not there. But Bess, though she cannot resist the happy dust, spurns his invitation to accompany him to New York, and it seems that, with Crown gone, she has no one to turn to. Maria—representing the "Old World" of the folk community—rejects her, calling her "a liquor guzzling slut," and it is then that Porgy invites her into his hut. The scene ends with a theme swelling from pentatonic simplicity, a lyrical extension of Porgy's arioso of lonesomeness. It will recur in a very different context.

This incipient love theme in pastoral F major remains, in its sequential thirds, more primitive, less adult, than the later song of love fulfilled. It's at this point that we begin to identify ourselves with Porgy, as Gershwin did, for we usually think of ourselves as good if broken. There may be an Oedipal undercurrent too, insofar as Bess is, for Porgy, not only passion but also an Eternal Beloved. In the novel, Maria refers to her as "Porgy's she-Gawd": not only a lover but also a mother who will give the babe rest. In this context Crown is the father figure, dreadful in his potency, against whom Porgy has to assert himself to conquer an infantile fear of impotence. Crown repeatedly taunts Porgy because he is crippled: "Ain' dere no whole ones left?" Something of this survives in the postlude to the scene, for the chromatics of the wailing arioso imbue the simple, pentatonic tune with an oddly febrile quality.

After the violence of this scene the second scene of act 1 is static. It begins with a lament for murdered Robbins, in which solo voices declaim in pentatonic ululations, based on Gershwin's experience of genuine gospel "shouts." The chorus intones the word *gone* in a descending whole-tone progression, harmonized in unrelated concords. Each chord sounds like a thudding of earth clods, while the harmonies' lack of relationship suggests the opening of an abyss. Though the harmony may have little relation with real gospel music, it is equally remote from Tin Pan Alley. The key, G minor, seems in the opera to be a key of tragic reality, as it is in works by composers such as Mozart, but here the tragedy is epic and communal rather than personal. Porgy and Bess come in to make their contributions to Robbins's "saucer burial." Serena refuses the money until she's told that it comes from Porgy, not Crown. Everybody sings a spirtual, "Fill Up the Saucer Till It Overflow," in which, while descending chromatics wail against life, the "overflow" phrase, rising up diatonically, literally overflows.

The frenzied chanting is broken by the appearance of a white detective investigating the murder. The emotional letdown occasioned by his speaking part makes the white world he represents villainous in the context of the black reverence for the dead, so we're not surprised when the old honey man, Peter, is carted away as a witness, pending the arrest of Crown. Porgy points out, in a musing arioso, that it isn't fortuitous that starry-eyed Peter should be made a scapegoat; though just as he reflects on the injustice of life, chromatic weaving in the orchestra hints remotely at his adult song of love fulfilled. The arioso also leads into Serena's song of loss, "My Man's Gone Now," wherein the tragic note is sounded for the first time in the opera. The pentatonically simple tune is compromised by the fierceness of the false relations created by the blue minor thirds, while the energy of the Creole rhythm is undermined by rapid, often semitonic, modulations and by the chromatic refrain in which the chorus—we the people—participate. So, from the apprehension of loss comes an affirmation of the will to go on living. In context, we probably associate the dead Robbins with the imprisoned honey man, and the loss of innocence is our loss too: just as Crown's crime and banishment are ours because we are all fallen creatures, and not many of us are as courageous as Crown. The immediate effect of Serena's song is to induce compassion in the undertaker, who agrees to save Robbins from the teaching hospital even though the saucer hasn't attracted sufficient money. Everyone joins in chanting a spiritual of gratitude, in which rhythmic and harmonic ostinatos become a train piece. African Americans, and modern humanity in general, are heading for the Promised Land because they have no earthly home. The delirious pace of the choo-choo suggests that the promise is a long way off.

As an epic figure Porgy belongs, like Peter, to the Golden Age. Unlike Peter, however, he has to learn to deal with the world as it is, including the flesh and the devil, for in Catfish Row as well as in New York the gold is tarnished. The second act concerns Porgy's attempt to grow from child to man; and although it begins in the morning, in apparent relaxation, we for the first time become conscious of the unconscious, which is the sea—the ultimate wilderness. Fishermen are repairing nets and singing a rowing song that begins pentatonicaly in blessed G major but winds its way to the "reality" of G minor for the refrain, "It takes a long pull to get there." It does indeed, even though the verses pretend to be easy about the vast sea and its unknown mysteries: "If I meet Mister Hurricane an' Hurricane tell me no, I'll take ole Mister Hurricane by the pants an' I'll throw him in de jailhouse do.'" But of course we know that although you can lock innocent Peter in a jail, you can't do that to a hurricane; and in the refrain everyone admits that in going over the unknown sea they are committing themselves to a pilgrimage that may or may not lead to the Promised Land.

Against this awareness of the wilderness of the eternal sea is poised the human solidarity of the island picnic at which, carefree, we seek in togetherness a refuge from the unknowable. Porgy's banjo song, "I Got Plenty O' Nuttin'," complements this in personal terms. Significantly growing from his invocation to the dice, it is a prepurgatorial expression of the happiness of not having; it is basically pentatonic, and in G major, sung over a rudimentary oom-pah accompaniment. He sings against commercial exploitation and material possessions:

Oh, I got plenty o' nuttin'
An' nuttin's plenty fo' me.
I got no car, got no mule,
I got no misery.
De folks wid plenty o' plenty
Got a lock on dey door,
'Fraid somebody's a goin' to rob 'em
While dey's out a-makin' more.
What for?

There is no cynicism but a melancholy irony in that the hero of the playboy who amassed millions should croon these words; Porgy is to learn, as Gershwin himself learned, that "misery" is not so easily discountable. Perhaps he suspects this in his heart, even while he sings, for the G major tonality and the childish rhythm are disturbed by tentative modulations to E and C sharp, which are abruptly, perhaps shamefacedly, yanked back to G, as though he dare not follow the waywardness of his heart.

Pointedly, this happy song is succeeded by two (parlando) incidents that attempt, superficially and inconclusively, to banish evil. First, Maria as spokeswoman of the Old World gives a dressing-down to Sportin' Life, while the orchestra weaves a web of his serpentine tritonal triplets. She says someone has to carve him up and "set these niggers free," and it might as well be her. But although she threatens to scatter his remains to the buzzards and the rattlesnakes, it is he, musically, who survives, for the devilish tritones and triplets will turn into his anti-creed song, "It Ain't Necessarily So." The comedy in Maria's berating of Sportin' Life is thus double-edged; and the same is true of the next episode, wherein Frazier, a black lawyer, attempts to sell Bess a divorce from Crown. The blacks in this opera cannot entirely eschew white corruption, and there is a "complication" about Bess's divorce in that she has never been married. While the parlando dialogue and the chorus's interjections are funny, there's an element of unease also, for the episode brings the theme of commercial exploitation into Porgy's own experience. He pays up, though Bess, less credulous, tries to persuade him not to. His "childishness" is part of his tragedy, for in personal terms his credulity parallels Jake's simplemindedness in taking his boat out to the Blackfish Banks at the time of the September storms. Jake's answer to his wife's fear is that if he doesn't make *money* he won't be able to give their son a college education. The two worlds are incompatible.

The Frazier incident is concluded with the appearance of the white man Archdale, who cautions Frazier about his divorce racket, but lets him off "this time." Archdale informs Porgy that he has stood bail for Peter. Despite general cries of gratitude, a buzzard appears in the sky immediately after the revelation of this apparently disinterested action, and the cries of joy turn into yells of superstitious horror. Porgy's "Buzzard Song" is the turning point of the opera, since it forces him to face up to reality and suffering. The anguished appoggiaturas, the strained, gawky leaps, and the flapping-winged chromatics are more sinister than any music we've heard previously, since the anguish is now that of personal experience and is not, like the dirges, communal lamentation. The buzzard marks Porgy's realization of the significance of his love; and although conflict informs the rondo structure, the song turns into a victory for love and life over death. "Ain' nobody dead dis mornin'," says Porgy; "livin's jus' begun. Two is strong where one is feeble; man and woman," together, may share grief as they share laughter, and because there are "two folks livin' in dis shelter" there "ain' no such thing as loneliness." Here even the pop music cliché of a climacteric eleventh chord is given fresh meaning in "pointing" the apex of the tune; so the buzzard flops off, and the chromaticized A minor tonality resolves in A major, that key of youth and hope—ending with a luminous added sixth at that.

Immediately afterward Sportin' Life, whom Maria had dubbed a buzzard as well as a rattlesnake, tempts Bess with his happy dust. The slimy chromatics and sequences of his song, "Picnics Is Alright for These Small Town Niggers," reject the Old World's solidarity in favor of New York and the "big money": a use of pop music cliché for satirical purposes that are again insidiously attractive. Bess contemptuously rejects his advances and Porgy overpowers him with the strength of his *hand:* "Gawd, what a grip for a piece of a man!" Sportin' Life, cursed by Porgy as rat, louse, and buzzard, sneaks off, but not before he has reminded Bess, in a craftily chromatic recitative ending on a high A, that though her men may come and go, "ole Sportin' Life an' the happy dus' here all along."

Since both the buzzard and Sportin' Life are temporarily routed, however, the public merriment of the picnic may proceed, and Porgy can grow into his song of adult love, "Bess, Yo' Is My Woman Now." This marvelous number insists first on an awareness of personal identity ("yo' is, yo' is"), then on their togetherness ("two instead of one"): a compromise between "civilized" identity and "jungle" identification. That they belong to one another, if to nothing else, is contained in the sweep of the line, in the strain that has gone to create "Two-ness" in the leaps of sixth and ninth, in the blue notes and crushed notes that are cries of pain, and in the mediant modulations that urge the music upward and onward. Urgency is stilled in the falling fifths and rising fourths of the "mornin' time an' evenin' time" refrain, which is the fulfillment of Porgy's "night time, day time" arioso of lonesomeness in act 1. The first ensemble number in the opera occurs when they sing the "I is, yo' is" chorus in duo, a third higher in D major. Bess vows to be Porgy's woman "for ever and ever" while he sings, to wistfully declining chromatics, "O my Bess, we's happy now."

The extraordinary emotional weight this song bears in context is achieved within a convention still recognizably that of a popular ballad, though Tin Pan Alley would have frowned on the wide vocal range, the difficult leaps, and the unconventional modulations. The dramatic placing of the song is masterly, for immediately after this liberation of personal feeling the crowd surges in on its way to the picnic, singing a vacuous pentatonic tune related to Porgy's banjo song, but brashly exuberant, in the same G major tonality. The community, the hoi polloi, cannot follow Porgy through his purgatory toward adulthood. Moreover, although Bess has promised that she will stay with Porgy for the fairy tale's ever and ever, she submits to public opinion when Maria, now on the side of social conformity rather than of piety, says she'll spoil the fun if she doesn't go to the picnic; and Porgy abets her. Triviality and conformity may be allies of evil, for the duo had told us that the personal love relationship is the only truth in a shifting world; to relinquish it in favor of communal sociability could be fatal. This is the second turning point in Porgy's tragedy, which must be why Bess's good-byes in rising thirds and sixths have a poignancy in excess of their ostensible relation to the situation. When she has gone Porgy returns to his banjo song, but in E flat major, flat submediant to the original G. Trivial though the incident may seem, it may not extravagantly be termed tragic irony.

This is underlined by the picnic music that opens scene 2. There is something scary, as well as exuberant, about the pounding tom-toms, the pentatonic ha-da-has, and the barbarous three-plus-two ostinato, for they deny the complexity of the love relationship as expressed in the duet. The words explicitly refer to a preconscious state, without awareness of guilt: since "I ain't got no shame," I can do what I like. At this point Sportin' Life, in his anti-creed song, "It Ain't Necessarily So," betrays the link between this unthinking and ultimately unfeeling animality and modern corruption. Having no shame, though potentially a virtue, may become a vice—the "easy livin'" of urban sophistication. Yet Sportin' Life's vice remains attractive. Gershwin's directive that he should sing his song "happily, with humor" is not ironic, and in a sense what he says is true: life *is* like this and, for most of us who cannot live through the Porgy-Bess experience, it *ain't* necessarily so.

The verbal wit of Sportin' Life's inverted gospel sermon makes us laugh at "religious" simplicity, which we have seen to be inadequate; and his serpentine triplets and tritones become blandly humorous now that they have grown into so captivating a tune. The savage da-dos that return as a ritornello seem in context ludicrous, and it is appropriate that their key should be E flat, that of Bess's good-byes, of the last version of Porgy's banjo song, and indeed of the stock Tin Pan Alley ballad, as contrasted with Sportin' Life's honestly dishonest G minor.

Certainly when Serena answers Sportin' Life with quasi-liturgical incantation, accompanied by the savage drumbeats of the picnic, we recognize that her response is no answer at all. The Tin Pan Alley sevenths and ninths of Sportin' Life's number, cumulatively reinforcing the swing of the tune, have more vitality than her pentatonicism, and one reason why the opera is so movingly relevant to us today is that it admits that there is no answer to Sportin' Life's anti-creed except the struggle toward personal fulfillment and togetherness that Porgy and Bess seek. The religious certitudes of the Old World of Maria have gone, withered by Sportin' Life's New World of commerce and the market; wishful thinking won't bring them back. So it is at the picnic, on the island, after the junkets, that Bess remeets Crown, a Lucifer fallen but still wearing his crown, devastating in courage and potency. The interview, mainly spoken against his cruelly jagged rhythm, is superb theater. She tries to speak on behalf of Porgy, who needs her, but her frenzied song, "What Yo Want Wid Bess?" is, in its thrusting triplet syncopations, as much sexy as desperate. Enharmonic modulations grow wild as Crown joins her in the opera's second ensemble number, and the contact with his *hands*— potent throughout the piece in both a positive and a negative sense—is too much for her. She moans a ululation about them, as she submits to the violence that, being within us all, has to be admitted to. The episode is often called a rape scene, which it both is and is not: for Bess is deliriously acquiescent, and Crown's triumph music is a raucously scored version of the Bess-Crown duo, violently syncopated yet unmistakably related—in its falling fifths and stabbing sixths, which are Porgy's thirds inverted—to *Porgy's* theme. The thematic relationship makes its effect, though we don't as yet realize how Porgy and Crown are complementary, even in a sense identical.

After this tremendous climax the third scene of act 2 returns to Catfish Row at dawn. Quietude is expressed by way of chiming bells built from superimposed fourths—the static chord of the first act's prelude; but sliding chromatic sequences suggest unease beneath the calm. The gently rocking sea, in a 12/8 larghetto, is pricked by false relations, as the fishermen set out to the rowing song, reminding us that they will anchor in "the Promised Land." The deceptive tranquility is broken by cries from Bess, offstage in Porgy's room. After being three days away with Crown she has returned delirious, in a fever; she screams of hands and rattlesnakes on Kittiwah Island, her yells accompanied by oscillating tritones. Devils of lust, rape, and wilderness erupt in her sickness, at the height of which Peter the honey man, in ultimate dramatic irony, returns from prison. He sings an exquisite G major aria of acceptance ("De white folks put me in, an' de white folks take me out, an' I ain' know yet what I done"), which gives a hymnic resolution to Porgy's falling fifths. Perhaps it even suggests a fusion of the black spiritual with the white hymn. Certainly its radiance is no longer a mere return to primal innocence, for it pours balm on Bess's (Lydian) agitation; induces Porgy to croon to her a lullaby related to Peter's tune, but with blue ambiguities since he is a sufferer in this world, not a vision from a mythical Golden Age; and leads Serena to pray for her, with declamatory encouragement from Peter. With the release of Peter, the religious sanctions of the Old World become momentarily reoperative; so Serena's pentatonic incantation summons the street criers: honey man, strawberry woman, and even devil crab man. The effect of these calls, recreated from folk sources, is literally magical. Time stops; there is no harmonic movement, only a drone with added sixth; and this return to Eden, complete with crab (apples) that are sold for money ("I's talkin' about yo' pocket book") releases Bess from her madness. While the clock chimes its fourths she comes out to greet Porgy on the step. The love song sounds distantly, while he whispers, "Thank Gawd."

Outside time, this lovely passage looks forward to a day when spiritual innocence and the material world of buying and selling will be compatible. It is a vision, not a realizable fact, as is indicated in the pathos of the ensuing dialogue. Bess says she has been lonesome in there by herself; and they whisper in haltingly tender arioso of Porgy's intuitive knowledge that she has been with Crown, of her fear of Crown's inescapability, and of their need for one another, while fragments of the love song sound fraily forlorn. But the adult love song cannot reestablish itself. Bessie's aria, "I Wants to Stay Here, but I Ain't Worthy," regresses to the embryonic love theme that had concluded act 1, scene 1, in the same key of F major. The broken arch of melody, rising through pentatonic thirds, pausing at the top, then falling, conveys the vacillation within her—a wave that cannot reach the shore. The orchestra's false relations add to the ambiguity; only in the middle section, when she sings of Crown's return—of how he'll *handle* her and hold her and it will be "like dyin'"—does the movement press forward, reinforced by chromatically rising ninths. Porgy promises to protect her, so they sing the "I Want to Stay Here" song da capo, in duo, and faster, more urgently. Bess's broken waves, stretching from low B flat to a high A, sound more desperate, if less forlorn, than when she sang alone.

Out of the strange pathos and ultimate desperation of this scene comes the hurricane, expressed musically through sliding chromatics related to the buzzard's skirls, merged into Sportin' Life's tritonal triplets and Crown's syncopations. This outburst of elemental fury is the ultimate manifestation of wilderness, which is this time a negation; and in the next scene the African Americans are huddled in Serena's room praying in multifarious, near-chaotic pentatonics over a G minor drone, while the storm howls outside. Among those appealing to God to spare his *children*, Sportin' Life alone remains himself, and by no means unsympathetically cynical. "We had storm befo', I ain' so sure this is Judgement Day." While Porgy and Bess murmur in a corner, he confident of her, she thinking of wild Crown on wild Kittiwah Island, the others break into a spiritual, "Oh, de Sun Goin' to Rise in de Wes'," and Clara, singing the "Summertime" lullaby to her baby, counterpoises the security of the womb against the chaos that has been loosed within the mind and without. At the height of the hurricane comes a terrifying banging on the door. The crowd screams that it must be Death and lurch into a hysterical chanting of "O dere's somebody knockin' at the do'." When, in a magnificently theatrical climax, the door is scrunched in, the visitor proves to be not death but Crown, as large as *life* or larger, come to claim his Bess. Against his violent rhythm he taunts Bess and Porgy: "You ain' done much for yo'self while I been gone . . . does you call dat a man?" As Bess screeches that Crown should keep his hands off her, Crown comes Lucifer-like into his own. Shouting a fierce, high chant, he defies Porgy, the crowd, and God: "If Gawd want to kill me, He had plenty of chance 'tween here an' Kittiwah Island. . . . There ain' nothin' He likes better than a scrap wid a man. Gawd an' me is frien'." Horrified by this blasphemy, the crowd roars a spiritual about the sky tumbling. But Crown shouts them down: "Don' you hear Gawd a'mighty laughin' at you? Dat's right, Gawd laugh, an' Crown laugh back." His rhythm takes over and he swings into a triumph song about his sexual charisma—a crudely irresistible barrelhouse tune about the red-headed woman who, though she may make a choo-choo (to the Promised Land?) jump its tracks, will never make a goddam fool of Crown. Everybody yells, "Lawd save us, don't listen to dat Crown." But listen they do, and Crown's supreme moment is still to come. Clara, at the window, suddenly screams, for she has spotted her husband's boat, wrecked. Handing the baby to Bess, she hurls herself into the hurricane. Bess says someone must go to help her, and Crown, after further jibes at Porgy ("Yeah, where is a man?") goes unafraid to the rescue. As the door opens, contrary motion chromatics enact the storm's putting out of the lights. The scene ends, in every sense, in darkness, as the crowd returns to its pentatonic howling over a G minor drone and a dolorous thudding of timpani. While the crowd prays to be released into those "golden meadows," Crown stands alone, breasting the storm.

But Crown fails, no less than Porgy. Though he survives, for a time, he does not save Jake and Clara; and act 3 opens with the chorus trying to reestablish their innocence, singing to dead Clara and Jake to follow Jesus and be *safe*. The hypnotic falling fourths of the chant, the D flat tonality with flat sevenths, induce a state of trance at the furthest possible pole from Crown's music, for paradoxically it is Crown, the wild man, who here stands for identity rather than identification. Again Sportin' Life's cynicism acts as a mean between life and death: "I ain't see no sense in makin' such a fuss over a man when he's dead." When Maria reprimands him he gloats about his power over Bess who, in having two men, has none, for the "good" and the "bad" forces will destroy one another, if they have not already done so. At this point we realize that Porgy and Crown are, or ought to be, one man. Porgy's simple nobility and Crown's courageous passion should be complementary, since both are necessary for growing up. What prevents their working in harmony is the nonvalues of commerce, prostitution, and the sportin' life, whereby savagery becomes callous, and innocence savage. Porgy and Crown are both gamblers, and both lose. What they lose is Bess, as mother, lover, and Eternal Beloved.

So the nemesis that follows is the unfolding of what has already happened, which is suggested musically when the second murder takes place to a modified recapitulation of the music for the first one. Bess is singing the "Summertime" lullaby to Clara's baby, which is now vicariously hers, while Crown approaches stealthily through the night to a dry, sinister repetition of the crap game music. Attempting to enter Bess's window, he is stabbed and then strangled by Porgy's strong *hands*. The son-against-father motif becomes explicit here. Porgy has to acquire Crown's sexual violence to assert his relationship with Bess, so the scene ends with his hysterical guffaws of triumph ("Bess, you got a *man* now") accompanied by Crown's rhythm rounded off by a permutation of Porgy's falling fifth tune, which emphasizes its relationship to Crown's theme. The fifth is God's interval and here, like Lucifer, it falls. Porgy *becomes* Crown, instead of being fused with, reconciled to, him. This is the tragedy, the disharmony for which Sportin' Life is responsible.

The second scene opens with a necessary relaxation of tension. The pentatonic figures suggest the bustle of everyday life—now centered on F sharp minor, rather than on an E major Eden. The inquiries of the white detective and coroner are counterpointed against the innocence of the blacks; but this time the situation is inverted, because the innocence is really craft. The comedy of the trio of women who "ain't seen nuttin'" relates back to the Frazier episode of act 1: the difference being that whereas in the first act Porgy faced up to the buzzard, defeated Sportin' Life, and sang his chant of adult love, this time his credulity undoes him. Asked to go to identify Crown's body, he trembles with superstitious dread, which Sportin' Life exploits by insinuating that Crown's wounds will bleed as soon as his murderer looks on him. At this point Sportin' Life parodies Porgy's pentatonics. After Porgy has been carried off, fortified by Bess who says that he can keep his eyes tight shut and needn't see what he doesn't want to see, Sportin' Life teases her also. He convinces her that Porgy's guilt is already known, and he'll be lucky if he's locked up for life, rather than executed. He exploits both Porgy's simplicity and Bess's weariness. He knows that life has taught her that things usually go wrong and offers her a way out: the happy dust that will scare away those lonesome blues. She may not have a man, or her own baby, but she can have a Good Time and a release from fear.

So he croons to her his marvelously seductive song, "There's a boat dat's leavin' soon for New York, come wid me," with its serpentine chromatic bass. Yet although he invites her to a world with no roots and no "shame," in a music that starts from the tawdriest clichés of Tin Pan Alley, the song has a remarkably positive jauntiness. The upward thrust of the tune, the Lombard syncopations, the blue false relation on the word *come,* fascinate, while the rumba rhythms and the increasingly chromatic harmonization of the rising arpeggio create a cumulative energy that becomes irresistible. When he sings, prancing up through a B flat arpeggio to a G flat (a pungent twelfth superimposed on a dominant ninth), and then up to high B flat to clinch the assertion that "Dat's where we *belong,*" we have to admit that he is right, if one can talk about belonging in so feckless a world. Perhaps it is not an accident that the key, B flat, is that of Porgy's love song, and that the middle section in which he tempts Bess with silks and satins is in G minor, B flat's relative. However morally dubious, *that* dream at least could come true. Porgy is destroyed because part of him cannot grow up and accept Crown's darkness. Crown is destroyed because his passion cannot rediscover Porgy's innocence. Bess, losing them both when she needs them both, is left with the eternal serpent. Though she rejects his invitation with fury, while the orchestra screeches devil tritones, Sportin' Life leaves the happy dust on the doorstep as he slinks out, while the orchestra plays a triumphant version of his New York song, a tone higher. We, and Bess, have no choice but to accept Sportin' Life and New York. Having done so, it is up to us to find there new life, rather than death: to make the happy dust dream come true or to substitute a better dream for it.

Certainly the last scene is in part a rejection of the old life. It opens with a ballet of work and play, which includes a children's Eden song in E major, mainly in prepentatonic falling fourths, identical with those of the trance song over the dead Clara and Jake; "You boun' to go to Heaven . . . if yo' good to yo' mammy an' yo' pappy," the words tell us. Into this apparent paradise Porgy returns, released after a period of imprisonmnet for contempt of court, since he had refused to look at Crown's body: the half of himself that *he* had slain. The music recapitulates the original preludial music and the *first* version of Porgy's tune. Returned from his purgatorial state, he is full of pride at having defied the white rules and is laden with presents, which he ritualistically distributes. He is a god offering largesse, the biggest presents being reserved for Bess. He returns, with unconscious irony, to the G major banjo song: but fragments of the love song wander through mediant modulations as he gradually realizes that something is wrong. It is Maria who tells him, with some satisfaction, that Bess has gone, with Sportin' Life and the happy dust, to New York, leaving the baby with Serena. There is a hint of G minor as his theme sounds in its original form and in augmented inversion in the bass; but Porgy brushes aside Maria's denunciatory morality as the music swings back to E major. He sings his great final aria, "O Bess, O Where's My Bess," wherein the love song is metamorphosed into a triple-rhythmed song of yearning for the state of togetherness as opposed to lonesomeness; but Bess is now the Eternal Beloved rather than a flesh-and-blood woman, and the song's upward octave leap and strained chromaticism are counteracted by the painful dissonance of the blue flat third. The intense longing for Eden that now springs *from* the pain of consciousness is strikingly similar to the "O Past, O Happy Life" epilogue to Delius's *Sea Drift*, in the same key of E major.

After Porgy has sung his aria alone, Maria and Serena join in trio, singing different music as they try to convince him that Bess, being worthless, deserved nothing better than Sportin' Life. The modulations in this almost Mozartian ensemble grow increasingly unstable as he appeals to them: "Won't somebody tell me where's my Bess." But he returns to E major when he stops addressing the women, maybe recognizing that an Eternal Beloved cannot be temporal. He asks God to give him the strength and show him the way. Flat sevenths on "where? tell me the truth" fight up to the sharp seventh, and then to resolution on the tonic. This appeal to God is not an escape but a plea for fortitude. Perhaps, now that Crown is dead, he can reconcile Crown's virtues with his own; perhaps there is a point in that he sets out, in his goat cart, for *New York,* though it is at the ends of the earth or even "in a heavenly land." Of course there is no hint in the final spiritual, "O Lawd I'm on My Way," with its rising arpeggio theme and its potent rumba lilt, of a conventional happy ending. He will not find Bess or New York; and she is more likely to succumb to the happy dust than to discover new life in a new world. But he is making a symbolic gesture in going, even in his goat cart, crippled as he is, toward New York and Bess; and there is a sense in which the Promised Land *is* New York, where the new life can grow only when he and Bess can meet, accept the city as home, and see Sportin' Life no longer as buzzard and serpent. This apotheosis cannot, of course, come yet. The final chord of the final chorus is not the unsullied E major of the Promised Land but a triad of E with both the major and the "false," or blue, minor third, encapsulating the *technical* ambiguity of the whole opera.

This ambivalence had, as we've seen, personal implications for Gershwin insofar as he hoped that the elements within him that were Porgy might one day come to terms within the more obvious aspects of him that were Sportin' Life. Certainly the cathartic effect of the opera depends on its achievement of "restitution," in psychological terms. Porgy's credulous nobility, Crown's ruthless courage, Bess's divided passion are all human characteristics, alike in their strengths and limitations. Porgy and Crown are forgiven for their murders, Bess for her defection; even Sportin' Life, the cause of their nonfulfillment, is forgiven for being what he has to be. The act of forgiveness is Gershwin's forgiveness of himself, and of us, insofar as he stands for a lost, alienated people. If restitution seems even less likely to occur in the New York (or London or wherever) of today than it was in Gershwin's city of the thirties, that makes Gershwin's opera more, not less, crucial.

The end of the opera is, in this respect, significantly different from the end of the novel, which leaves Porgy crippled in every sense, an old man alone "in an irony of morning sunlight."[4] So negative a conclusion would not have been theatrically effective, but that Gershwin can bring off his more positive consummation is a tribute not only to his theatrical instinct but also to the much deeper human implications his opera raises. The sentiment is never sentimental, because the opera never takes sides and can afford to do so because it springs so deeply from Gershwin's own experience. What would have happened had he not died at the age of thirty-nine, in 1937, so soon after *Porgy* had been launched? Was this intuitive self-knowledge the beginning of his career as an art composer or had he, in making his testament—which stood for an epoch—said all that he needed to say?

That may not be the right question, for we're beginning to understand, as the potency of Gershwin's opera increases rather than diminishes with the years, that he was a new kind of "between worlds" composer analogous to Duke Ellington. Initially, *Porgy and Bess* was considered fraudulent—by some African Americans who thought it condescending and, more predictably, by the mean white Daniel Mason, whose rabid anti-Semitism sounded almost unhinged, and even by the brilliant Virgil Thomson whose surprising (and devastating) attack was the severest blow to Gershwin as an art composer. How sad that political correctness, on whatever side, could then as now deafen ears and numb sensibility. At this date the authenticity of Gershwin's parable cannot be gainsaid, nor can his technical probity, for within his sophisticated harmonic and orchestral textures—like Ellington's, they recall the powerful nostalgia of Delius and Ravel, and occasionally the expressionist intensity of Alban Berg—Gershwin found scope for elements stemming from black folk traditions: the magical street calls, the funeral wakes, the festive junkets, all of which Gershwin had relished at first hand. Above all, he embraced the black blues, which he understood more deeply and intuitively than any art composer, thereby tingeing with veracity the memorability of the tunes.

If the "wilderness" aspects of Gershwin's opera had this integrity, so did its "civilized" aspects, for although he had no institutionalized education in music, he worked industriously on Joseph Schillinger's "do-it-yourself" system, had formal instruction in harmony and counterpoint from musicians in show business music, and had a few lessons from composers like Wallingford Riegger and Henry Cowell; on orchestration and theatrical techniques he welcomed hints from colleagues in the world of show business. Mostly, however, he worked by ear and sharp wits and probably wasn't all that disappointed when Ravel turned him down as a composition pupil on the grounds that he already had all the technique necessary to his imaginative ends. Conservative musicians interpreted that as meaning that Gershwin was congenitally incapable of learning his craft, whereas for his rabid admirers it meant that he was endowed with everything a Mozart needed. But Ravel surely meant precisely what he said; and we, like Ravel, can only marvel at the subtlety and ingenuity of Gershwin's musical-dramatic structures—the interrelation of leitmotives and themes and the complex (basically traditional) symbolism of keys and of rhythmic patterns. Still more remarkable is that in his disposition of speech, recitative, arioso, aria, dance, and chorus he broke through conventional norms to explore techniques appropriate to film, and ultimately to television. In any competent performance of *Porgy*—and many are now much more than competent—we no longer recall that some of the orchestral textures used to be considered overblown and some of the transitional passages perfunctory. With clear ears and a decent respect we now recognize that *Porgy and Bess* is not merely a good opera but is a great one on any count, situated somewhere between the ongoing per-form-ance of folk music and jazz and the fully notated forms of art. How moving it is that this great music maker should have created, in the tragic denouement of his masterpiece, music that makes us want to live more abundantly, however desperate the odds.

There is a good reason for Gershwin's "between worlds" status, for the psychological theme of his opera is precisely the equivocation between art and commerce that is its technical *modus vivendi*. "Civilization" and "Wilderness" are slippery terms. Although in *Porgy* the black people are the central protagonists and the white civilization is, especially in its highly industrialized forms, the enemy, the black hero, heroine, and villain are all part of a single consciousness, since the theme is the fusion of spontaneity with consciousness that is necessary if we are to grow to adulthood, as Porgy couldn't. Gershwin may not have been aware of the psychological burden of his opera while he was making it, but he went through many years of psychological "treatment," painted (as did Schoenberg) revealingly expressionist self-portraits, and knew about "restitution" first hand. Between worlds, he was, like his Porgy, "waiting"—in the words of Lawrence Ferlinghetti—"for the lost music to sound again / in the Lost Continent / in a new rebirth of wonder."[5] From the heart of technocratic New York he could have said, with Henry Thoreau at Walden Pond, that he longed for "wildness, a nature which I cannot put my foot through, woods where the wood thrush forever sings, where the hours are early morning ones, and there is dew on the grass, . . . a New Hampshire everlasting and unfallen."[6] At the start of a new millennium, there is a point in that Gershwin's *Porgy and Bess* is a complement by inversion to Janáček's *Cunning Little Vixen,* for Gershwin's characters in an industrial environment play the role of the love-drunk foxes in Janáček's agrarian environment. We wait, in fear and trembling, to see if this fable could ever come true, bringing salvation, as well as restitution.

NOTES

1. DuBose Heyward, *Porgy* (New York: George H. Doran, 1925), 7.

2. Ibid., 11.

3. Ibid., 13.

4. Ibid., 196.

5. Lawrence Ferlinghetti, "I Am Waiting," *These Are My Rivers, New and Selected Poems, 1955–1993* (New York: New Directions, 1993), 103.

6. Henry David Thoreau, *The Writings of Henry David Thoreau*, ed. Bradford Torrey (Boston: Houghton Mifflin, 1906), 5:293.

Epilogue

THE TWO FINAL CHAPTERS of this book were about the music of a black folk musician who became an internationally acclaimed composer and a white New York Jew who, reared in the world of commerce, dramatized operatically a black myth. Given everyone's ancestry in Africa's forests and deserts, it seems that Africa may be a legendary Eden whose strong gods may be reinvoked. It therefore seems appropriate to add a postscript about an African composer-pianist who lives peripatetically between "old" Africa and "New" York, while intermittently traveling the globe as a touring musician whose performances are as much rituals as recitals. He is Abdullah Ibrahim, born in 1934 as Adolki Johannes Brand. He initially adopted the soubriquet Dollar Brand, thereby fusing in potent ambivalence an African burning brand with the almighty dollar.

His father was a Basuto and his mother's family was of Bushman stock. On his mother's side the family was Christian, and both his grandparents played piano by ear at church and at social gatherings. Abdullah had music lessons from his mother and from a local teacher and could fluently read European music by the time he was seven. But music wasn't, for him, something to be learned from teachers or books, but was

> everything I soaked up from the world I lived in. The kids I went around with played any instruments they could lay their hands on—all kinds of bottles, pots and pans, flutes, saxes, drums, guitars, banjos, violins, pianos and harmoniums; and the music we played was partly traditionally African, partly white missionary, mixed up with Cape Malay music (originally introduced by Malasian slaves), with snatches of European folk musics and of Afrikaans music—which was only a little Dutch and about 80 percent traditionally Bushman. The Bushmen that

my mother came from were the oldest inhabitants of southern Africa; but there was a big Muslim population too, and we heard a lot of music. Then of course on radio and records we heard much American and European pop music too. We never thought about where the different aspects of our music came from; we just picked them up from the air around us. As a kid I played the flute and sax and drums and piano and harmonium, mostly in bands for dancing to. There were lots of pianos around in Cape Town—about one to every home. There were many piano players too, some of them good. We played real African music, as well as missionary music and ragtime, on the pianos; and we played African music on harmoniums too, holding down drone-notes, usually in fourths, with match-sticks. The street bands were called *marabi* bands, and what we played was a mixture of traditional African music and hymns, ragtime, pasodobles, quadrilles, lancers, square dances, anything that kept us moving.[1]

This musical diet was not very different from that on which Louis Armstrong had been reared in New Orleans, except for the important fact that the African elements were immediately at hand. Looking back to the year 1964, when Ibrahim earned international fame with his first disc, *Anatomy of a South African Village*, one can trace three strands in his music that coexist. The first relates to the African township musics within which he was nurtured in his Cape Town adolescence. The second strand springs from his work in the United States, to which he was invited by the great Duke Ellington to play at the Newport Jazz Festival in 1964. Working with Ellington and with Thelonious Monk, he lived for some years in New York's famous-infamous Chelsea Hotel, accepted as a leading member of the Modern Jazz movement and as part of the New York scene. The third strand in his work is that in which he becomes an African jazz composer, aided perhaps by his "classical" studies with Hall Overton,[2] but owing most to a process of self-discovery that was also an apprehension of "Africa" in relation to the United States and Europe. Indeed, the story incarnate in Ibrahim's music is the story of Africa's transition from an indigenous agrarian culture to a global village. The township phase is childhood, a blissful escape into euphoria; the American phase jazzily confronts tension and anguish, personal, social, and political: in New York he teetered on the brink of nervous collapse. This was healed as he moved into his African phase that, in reintegrating the contradictory facets of his experience, became an act of (Muslim) religious affirmation. The three phases of his music function in roughly chronological order, since his adolescent music was naturally in township style, his most American music was created during his New York years, and his most African music has been created since his partial return to Africa and his achievement of status as a "global" musician. This evolution complements the profound sociological and psychological changes in African "consciousness" during the Nelson Mandela years.

Even so, Abdullah Ibrahim still creates in all these manners: the strands overlap; and his creation, like all urban African musics, is *collage* at heart. Both within the sequence of numbers that make a set and within each number itself Ibrahim juxtaposes surprising contrasts of material, on structural principles that are circular rather than linear. Despite his start as a township musician, Ibrahim's genius is that of a composing-improvising pianist who writes little or nothing down, but imaginatively *remembers*. His piano style owes a little to his early training as a "straight" pianist, but far more to the American barrelhouse stompers of the twenties, especially Jimmie Yancey and Meade Lux Lewis; there's also a relationship between the nervosity of his finger technique and that of Thelonious Monk and between the deep-bedded sensuousness of his chordal sequences and those of Ellington as pianist. Interestingly enough, Ibrahim's most "positive" pieces during his early years tend to be those that most brusquely juxtapose opposites: snatches of African tunes and of British missionary hymns, pounding African rhythms and harmonic clichés from Western hymnody and even from Tin Pan Alley. *Tintinyana* is a superb example that Ibrahim still frequently plays: African ostinatos interact with British mission–style hymnic progressions, flowering into American jazz variation. Even when he plays American numbers, such as the Duke's signature tune, "Take the A Train," Ibrahim hands the music back to Africa. The surge of sound reverberates, in the rumbling bass, like an African drum choir or, in the tintinnabulating treble, like a marimba band. The American train carries this black man to his African home, and when he's there, it's nowhere. The train, entering mythological rather than chronological time, clatters in a round dance, an eternal circle. Modern humanity has been dedicated to material ends; yet at the point they have reached the only possible "progress" is to be end*less*. Railway line and musical line must be hooped once more into a circle.

While most of this comes across forcefully from recordings, to hear Ibrahim playing live is a different, more wonderful, experience. In the corybantically African sections his whole body vibrates as, rolling out his chordal tremolandos, he builds up massive waves of sound to engulf us; or, while playing, he dances one rhythm with his right hand, another with his left hand, a third with his shoulders, a fourth with his head, becoming almost a community in himself. Yet this community is no longer closed, being without barriers, part "necessity" in the African sense, part "art" in European terms, and on both counts global. North American, South American, European, Indian, Asian, Malaysian, Chinese, Afrikaans, and white British idioms coalesce with basic black Africanism; and the mish-mash jells, through Ibrahim's improvising art.

Today, Abdullah Ibrahim is carrying his art's self-reliance to an ultimate point, for he's become a one-man band playing piano, bamboo flute, cello, and sax in alternation or simultaneously on prerecorded tape, as well as playing in combos with other musicians who, like those in Ellington's band, become alter egos for himself. The longest recorded version of *Sathima*, dedicated to Ibrahim's (sweet-singing) wife, is representative. It opens with a slow prelude for bamboo flute with voice blowing into it, the weirdly magical sonority being thereby veiled in the fuzz-buzz effect beloved of many African musics, evoking the immemorially ancient continent. Clanging bells on piano try to banish the land but really renew it, since Christian hymn is alchemized into pastoral pentatonics, which Ibrahim calls "rural lament." The tune is hesitant, lifting up through a tone, over a drone, unchangingly static. Gradually rhythm solidifies, until flute and piano arabesques swirl into rippling waters of life. The climax comes in a piano cadenza, no longer a dream, but complex in polymetrical rhythm and in (Ellingtonian) harmony. When the pastoral melody returns it is lyrically resolved, fading into thin air, from which the original bambo flute tune reemerges, heard with new ears because both the old Africa of rural lament and the new Africa of the big city seem to be contained within it. The Edenic dream exists, while the old Africa persists, in a fusion of African circular form with European (and American) linearity, enacting the ongoing process of African history.

As I type these words President Clinton is on safari through several African nations, offering a new start to the continent from which humankind putatively sprang. Though the reasons for this are more political and mercantile than cultural, and although much of Africa is dominated (as is "liberated" Russia) by corruption, we have to hope, if not think, that the ragbag of consciousnesses that makes a global village just possibly might, one day, embrace the ultimate disparities of line and circle, forging new life from an act of praise. One doesn't need to be Muslim to understand what Abdullah Ibrahim means when he says that his tragicomic music is, both intrinsically and in the context of history, "a gift of God." In going back to Africa jazz was intuitively trying to rediscover its religious heart, a quest in which we anxiously join, not in painfully emergent new Africa, but in the Old World, "distracted from distraction by distraction," in which we ourselves, balanced on a razor's edge between hazard and hope, precariously live. As Abdullah

Ibrahim has put it, "We have to be *vigilant,* the same mode of thinking as the samurai. But when I talk of my piano as a sword, I'm not really thinking politically. My interest in Zen, in herbalism, in homeopathic medicine, is a force identical with my music. Ultimately it's a human question—the struggle of humanity against inhumanity, anywhere and everywhere. And that's what music has always been about."

NOTES

1. All the quotations from Abdullah Ibrahim derive from a letter he sent me when, in the seventies, I was first writing about him. In a modified form, they have been previously published as an appendix to an essay on jazz piano I contributed to *The Book of the Piano,* ed. Gill Dominic (Oxford: Phaidon, 1981).

2. When Abdullah Ibrahim worked in the sixties with Hall Overton, Overton—having studied composition at the Juilliard School and later with Wallingford Riegger and Milhaud—was in the front line of twentieth-century American composers; he also developed formidable skills in jazz improvisation, working with jazz musicians of the caliber of Stan Getz and making brilliant arrangements for the Thelonius Monk Orchestra. In tune with our theme, he made an opera based on Mark Twain's legendary American boy in the woods, Huckleberry Finn, produced in 1971. Overton died in the next year, at the age of fifty-two. He is briefly discussed in Wilfrid Mellers, *Music in a New Found Land: Themes and Developments in the History of American Music* (London: Faber and Faber, 1987).

Index

WILFRID MELLERS has taught at Cambridge University, the University of Birmingham, the University of Pittsburgh, and the University of York. For forty years Mellers was a prolific composer, specializing in music with literary and theatrical associations. He is the author of eighteen books and is currently at work on a study of Benjamin Britten's *War Requiem* and a book on religious masterpieces of European music.

Typeset in 10.5/13 Minion
with Minion display
Designed by Dennis Roberts
Composed by Barbara Evans
at the University of Illinois Press
Manufactured by Thomson-Shore, Inc.

University of Illinois Press
1325 South Oak Street
Champaign, IL 61820-6903
www.press.uillinois.edu